Heroes, Gods and the Role of
Epiphany in English Epic Poetry

ALSO BY E.L. RISDEN

Sir Gawain *and the Classical Tradition:*
Essays on the Ancient Antecedents (McFarland, 2006)

Heroes, Gods and the Role of Epiphany in English Epic Poetry

E.L. Risden

McFarland & Company, Inc., Publishers
Jefferson, North Carolina, and London

LIBRARY OF CONGRESS CATALOGUING-IN-PUBLICATION DATA

Risden, Edward L., 1957–
    Heroes, gods and the role of epiphany in English epic poetry / E.L. Risden.
        p.   cm.
    Includes bibliographical references and index.

    ISBN 978-0-7864-3541-8
    softcover : 50# alkaline paper

    1. Epic poetry, English — History and criticism. 2. Heroes in literature. 3. Gods in literature. 4. Epiphany in literature.
I. Title.
PR509.E7R57   2008
821'.03209—dc22   2008020055

British Library cataloguing data are available

©2008 E.L. Risden. All rights reserved

No part of this book may be reproduced or transmitted in any form or by any means, electronic or mechanical, including photocopying or recording, or by any information storage and retrieval system, without permission in writing from the publisher.

On the cover: William Blake, *Adam and Eve Sleeping* (illustration to Milton's *Paradise Lost*), pen and watercolor on paper 19⅜" × 15¼", 1808

Manufactured in the United States of America

McFarland & Company, Inc., Publishers
   Box 611, Jefferson, North Carolina 28640
      www.mcfarlandpub.com

Table of Contents

Preface   1

1. *Epiphany* and the Western Epic Tradition   9
2. The "Duty" Theme in the Epic Tradition   37
3. Epic Individualism   49
4. *Beowulf* and Sub-liminal Epic Epiphany   64
5. Epiphany and the Rhetoric of (Dis)Enchantment in Spenser's *Faerie Queene*   75
6. *Paradise Lost* and the Resimplification of Epic Epiphany   93
7. William Blake and the Personal Epic Fantastic   109
8. Wordsworth's Spots of Time: Romantic Epiphany and Nature Spectacular   118
9. *Aurora Leigh*: Victorian Epic and Woman's Social Epiphany   142
10. Walcott's *Omeros*: Postmodern/Postcolonial Epic Epiphanies   157

A Postscript on Tolkien and the Epic Novel, and a Conclusion   165
Chapter Notes   181
Bibliography   195
Index   201

Preface

Epic poetry, despite its current absence on bestseller lists and its wane in college and university curricula,[1] remains perhaps the most important genre to the literary historian. While professors who don't specialize in the early periods may consider epic poetry a literature of oppression, the form remains essential to the cultures that have produced epics of their own and to our ability to attempt cultural criticism. While epic has often derived from and served "patriarchal" forces, it need do neither, and its ideas and purposes far exceed such limitations. Epic, both as poetry and in the quest it narrates, stretches a culture to the extreme of what it dare achieve. It locates what a culture struggles most to find, and it encapsulates the values of that culture for future generations to practice and future societies to study and understand, often to appreciate and occasionally to incorporate, though seldom to emulate.

Bakhtin asserts that three particular features characterize the epic as genre: a "national epic past," a "national tradition" (rather than personal experience) and an "absolute epic distance" from the present; he finds there a world of "beginnings" and "peak times" and "bests" told from the "reverent point of view of a descendent."[2] Notions of peaks and bests have always implied heroism, but heroism need not mean glory in martial conflict: it does in the early poems — though we must read deeper than the literal levels — but the preoccupation with the glory of warfare fades over time. Heroism has always balanced duty and individuality, and the heroic act often tends to take the actors outside themselves. Further, the forum for heroic action gradually attaches itself, through history, more specifically to the social goals toward which we can see the society working.

Preface

Even now our societies build not from nothing, but from their predecessors; as Northrop Frye observed, "Anagogically ... poetry unites total ritual, or unlimited social action, with total dream, or unlimited individual thought. Its universe is infinite and boundless hypothesis."[3] While Frye refers not specifically to epic, the point applies, I think, especially there. Epic crystallizes tradition so that the next individual may honor the past by stepping beyond it. Bakhtin and Frye don't here contradict; one deals with the foundations that allow us to hypothesize boundaries and the other with the means to reach and surpass those boundaries. Erich Auerbach finds in the "Homeric style" a need "to leave nothing which it mentions half in darkness and unexternalized"; he doesn't mean thoughts and feelings, but narrative detail, because of where narrative leads: to the boundaries epic teaches us to cross.[4] Epic as ritual teaches us the narrative steps to recapitulate the journey to epiphanal boundaries.

While our earliest extant literature fashions mythic, epic, and heroic tales, and the Western model for epic derives obviously from Homer, English literary history has a particularly rich epic tradition, aware of its antecedents but ever evolving to address its own cultural, intellectual, and artistic frontiers — not only heroic ones, but also social and personal ones. As Geoffrey of Monmouth and the *Gawain*-poet show us, the English hoped to ground their heritage in what they must have perceived as the two greatest cities of the ancient world, Troy and Rome. Vergil guides the English questing spirit no less than he does Dante's, and England's epic poets dialogue with him (if not, as does Derek Walcott, with Homer) — Spenser and Milton directly and obviously and probably even the *Beowulf*-poet, if less overtly: as he did, they sought the essence of a people's character, of its heroism.

Aristotle in his *Poetics* names tragedy the monarch of literary genres. As a response to Plato's worries about poets in the *Republic*, that they arouse unhealthy and undesirable emotions that erode our most important quality, rationality, Aristotle explains that literature at its best promotes mental health by eliciting the cleansing of excessive or undesirable emotions. Tragedy, because of its brevity, concentration, and intensity, best serves that end, he asserts, purging pity and fear, emotions that may otherwise stultify reasonable decision making and subsequent action. He notes that epic poetry has many of the same traits and effects as tragedy, but that its length and diffuseness inhibit its ability to act as powerfully on an audience: for him, focus works better than *copia*. But epic poetry, too, as many scholars have argued, has a claim not only to its own particular literary frontiers, but also perhaps to emotional and thematic primacy among genres. Epic has, as W.P. Ker asserts,

> an immediate association with all that a people know about themselves, with all their customs, all that part of their experience which no one can account for or refer to any particular source. A poem like *Beowulf* can play directly on a thousand chords of association ... [and the hero] has all the life of his people to strengthen him.[5]

Borrowing from Victor Turner the idea of the special significance to our experience of boundary phenomena — what happens to us at the edge or doorway between one state of nature and another[6] — Dean A. Miller argues that "the hero and the shaman are liminal specialists"[7]: the hero represents his (or her) culture at a boundary that has proven too difficult to cross. Gilgamesh and Enkidu enter the great Cedar Forest despite the fearsomeness of its guardian, who scares all others away. Gilgamesh, with the help of the boatman Urshanabi, crosses the waters of Death to visit Utnapishtim the Faraway to find a remedy for his friend's (and his own) mortality. Achilles accepts an early death for the glory of defeating Hektor and for the privilege of an immortal name: he takes valor in battle to an extreme no one else can or will, as Odysseus takes cunning and persistence beyond previous human limitations to bring about the end of the war and to return to Ithaka so that he might retake his home and his family. Aeneas leaves a burning city, the greatest city of its time, to fulfill the duty the gods have given him and found the colony that will enlarge itself to what Vergil would consider the greatest city/empire of all time: Vergil used epic as a tool to legitimize Rome, a vaster and yet prouder phoenix arising from Troy's ashes.

Elaborating on the mythic hero, and following the thought of Erich Neumann, Miller adds that

> the details that construct the myth of the hero follow the sequence of hard-fought victories over powerful and destructive forces that allow the conscious ego to coalesce and form itself, or to be formed.... [T]he hero's mythic biography replicates and dramatizes the processes by which full human individuation is reached.[8]

Pushing boundaries, both those of human experience and endurance and those natural barriers and frontiers that challenge our ingenuity, brings about the gradual creation of the self, which both derives from and filters back into the evolution of the culture. Boundary phenomena represent our movement into another order of being, whether as topographical challenges (climbing Mount Everest), athletic ones (running the four-minute mile or ten-second hundred yards/meters), or even planetary ones (putting the first human on the moon); we seek answers to our limitations, stays against mortality, and assurances that through achievement we may draw ourselves beyond the mundane and nearer the divine. The culture determines what it must do, and the hero, especially the epic hero, represents those needs at the Great Threshold, to whatever force or fear or god he — or occasionally she — may meet there. Miller finds that where heroes achieve the boundary, the theme of most epics is heroic opposition not to forces outside the human frame, but, ideally, to *other* superhuman images and forces, forces defined as heroic in their interior nature.... The hero's opponent may wear or declare some *differentia* identified with the Other, or even of evil, but usually he is simply the hero's mirror image.[9]

But I'd like to suggest that, while the hero does often find at the liminality a reflection of himself, the essential point of epic requires a willingness to meet a force, evil or not, that has greater power than his self and that comes from a position that seems sufficiently foreign as to threaten personal and social demise — in a sense, an apocalypse. The hero faces, as Miller asserts, mortality, but not the common mortality: a mortality that leads to immortality of whatever sort the culture offers. The hero must locate or acquire there something that the culture needs or values. The epic deals necessarily in esoterica, which comprises both its immortality and, as a genre, its potential downfall, and depending on the culture from which it comes, the hero may find self or selflessness.[10]

In *Heroic Poetry* C.M. Bowra observes,

> The decline of heroic poetry is no doubt to be explained by social causes which belong to some wide historical processes. Foreign conquests or religious movements or cultural influences from abroad may in a short span of years undo what has endured for centuries.... But commoner perhaps than any of these collapses is the imperceptible process by which a society

changes its tastes and advances from the simple to the elaborate or from the communal to the personal ... a need for something more original or varied.[11]

The rise of the novel and the lyric poem as "popular" genres has in recent times limited public attention to the great, long heroic poems so significant to our past. But who (with the possible exception of Michelangelo) more than Dante and Milton has influenced the Christian imagination, and who more than Homer and Vergil has taught us the ups and downs of martial heroism? I would argue that they continue to do so, even though we don't necessarily remain aware of their constant presence in our subconscious understanding of who and what we are. Heroic poetry in epic form (at least in the English tradition) hasn't died: it remains alive and on a recognizable, even predictable, trajectory. The next incarnation may need only time to show itself: the next great epic will appear, Arthurlike, when we need it most.

Epics schematize our hard, heroic work. They occasionally exploit tragic results or feelings, but they need not, and typically they take the hero and the audience to the idea that, whether in success (and they often do succeed) or failure, the heroes have faced a challenge or concern that takes their culture forward, that has merited the effort regardless of the result. Who can say that Lear, or Macbeth, or Othello has lived and behaved well (though in *Oedipus at Kolonos* we may say that of that most powerfully suffering Greek protagonist)? Some critics have argued Beowulf guilty of pride or greed, but as J.R.R. Tolkien writes in "*Beowulf*: The Monsters and the Critics" (where the critics sometimes are the monsters, as opposed to John Gardner's *Grendel*, where the monster is the critic), how would we rather have the hero die than in the dragon battle, facing the greatest foe his world can create for him? Who would want Beowulf to die quietly in bed? Certainly not he. *The Odyssey*, were it a drama, would fall from Aristotle's point of view into *the* realm of *comedy*— it has a happy ending, at least from Odysseus' and Penelope's perspectives — and *The Aeneid* shows Aeneas achieving, through the piety and duty central to Roman notions of virtue, and with the help of the gods, the groundwork of Rome's empire-building. Elizabeth Barrett Browning shows both in her title character and in her epic action a woman achieving the feat men said she could (and should) not even attempt, opening territory for more than half that population who had until her time and accomplishment been denied it. Blake finds Romantic epiphany in the forge of his own creativity: both epic and culture turn their interests, as Freud would a century later, inward. As we move from the great epics of the old world, those in which as Bowra argues community comes first, to those of the modern world, in which the individual gradually emerges both for her culture and for her own sake, heroes continue to reach boundaries, cross them, and find some boon that allows cultural evolution to take a liberating course. Epic poetry turns to the personal as its culture does so: it directs our attention to whatever boundary or liminality its culture needs to cross, as long as its people survive and show the will to get there. No wonder a strong vector of epic influence turned, in the great age of the novel, to science fiction and fantasy, realms both external (time and space travel) and internal (long-lost, imaginary, or cybernetic worlds).

This book begins with a chapter on ancient (international) epic, on what the great poems of antiquity teach us about how the heroes meet their gods and what they learn there. Following that introduction to the tradition comes a chapter on the idea that movement toward the boundary has traditionally required a focus on the sense of duty: whether or not that theme emerges as central to epic, it nearly always contributes to its motive factors. Chapter 3 counters, or extends, that argument with its corollary: as a pressure for the assertion of individual rights and the primacy of individual experience gains power culturally, so it does in epic, and epic themes turn to the joys and pressures of personal inspiration. Subsequent chapters will then take up the main subject of this book, the evolution of English epic poetry, rich and varied as we find it, and speaking ever at the forefront of the concerns of its time. We'll trace the epiphanies — how the heroes meet their gods — from the anonymous Old English *Beowulf*, to Edmund Spenser's *The Faerie Queene*, to John Milton's *Paradise Lost*, to William Blake's *Milton*, to William Wordsworth's *The Prelude*, to Elizabeth Barrett Browning's *Aurora Leigh*, to Derek Walcott's *Omeros*. While I have left out a number of poems and have in some cases selected what may not seem an obvious choice, each chapter will argue for the importance of that particular epic at that particular time. Each will aim to show that we have always used great poems not just for entertainment, and not to inflict prevailing modes of oppression on an unwilling populace, but rather to find ways to liberate ourselves from those human constraints from which liberation is possible.[12] While the English literary tradition has produced other epic poets and other epics, those I have chosen for this book have emerged as most important to their times, attracting the greatest fascination and the most study. Though *Omeros* arrives freshly on the scene, and from abroad, I don't think I'm taking too great a chance in calling it the most important English epic of our time, not because of English colonialism, but because Walcott claims the traditions, both Mediterranean and English, as equally his own and creates a new epic literary "space" that allows for the next logical step in epiphany and the great epic questions.

Each epic proves in itself, both through its poetry and in its ideas, a fascinating study, and together they schematize the evolution of a society, through its continual struggle to find itself and its relation to the divine.[13] The poems endlessly reward reading and rereading, and I believe they retain the capability of moving a modern reader because they dare to ask the great questions — not in spite of that fact.

I'll be working throughout with a fairly traditional definition of *epic*: a long, narrative, heroic poem with supernatural elements that addresses a quest or question central to a culture's understanding of itself.[14] I find particularly helpful Robert Hamner's thought on epic as genre, which I have simply condensed a bit: "The classic prescription calls for an objective, extended, elevated narrative poem commemorating a superhuman leader whose exploits are of interest to the gods and a race or nation"; he adds, significantly not only for his study of Derek Walcott but also for mine of epic more generally, "Whatever the motivation, even in our decidedly iconoclastic century, writers persist in undertaking works with epic aspirations."[15] I hope and believe his point will remain true.

One textual note before we begin: while scholars have established "standard texts" for most major works (sometimes one edition, sometimes a couple between which we argue over the one we consider more authoritative), gaining permission to quote from those texts can be problematic.

So in some chapters I have chosen to quote from sources that I consider trustworthy, that agree with standard editions or at least deal with questionable passages reasonably, but that public domain laws have made available for general use. In most editions of the great works the vast majority of lines agree exactly from one text to another; where any concerns have arisen, I have sought originals or compared texts to find the reading that I think represents the most trustworthy (I do believe authorial intention and have tried to keep that in mind, to the degree that I believe I can discern it). Given the extent of this undertaking, I would like to express my particular gratitude to The Noonday Press, Farrar, Straus and Giroux, for their generous permission to quote from Derek Walcott's *Omeros* (New York, 1990), a poem that deserves a vastly greater readership than it has yet acquired.

In the case of translations, where I have used others than my own, I have chosen the one I think best renders the work in English or that students will find most useful and readily available. In no instance would my argument in this book have changed based on the use of another (standard or otherwise) text.

Chapter 1

Epiphany and the Western Epic Tradition

Beowulf scholar Charles Donahue writes that Homer's epics embody "what it meant to be Greek,"[1] and he implies similarly of *Beowulf*, that it defines the character of the Anglo-Saxon. One may say about all of the great epic poems that to some degree they define their culture, or at least some of their cultures' most definitive characters, most importantly backgrounds, milieux, and central concerns. They present models for how to deal with cultural problems "heroically" (or sometimes how one should *not* deal with them). As W.J. Johnson observes of the *Bhagavad Gita*—while not Western in the modern sense, it is Indo-European—to Hindus it incarnates both "the word of God" and the "values inherent in Hindu culture," while the whole epic that surrounds it, the *Mahabharata*, displays "the poetical history of mankind."[2] For Arjuna and for its audience, Krishna's revelations in the *Gita* define epic heroism no less than do Homer's for the Greeks and Vergil's for the Romans. The *Gita* embodies the traditional notion of what being Indian means and, beyond the *Gita*'s local context and social implications, what it means for any human being to accept adult responsibility for daily life and yet retain spirituality, ultimately the central, defining facet of human existence. Homer showed that while soldiers may not always behave laudably, their heroic deeds on the

Heroes, Gods and the Role of Epiphany

battlefield may at best win fame and glory; Vergil showed that, for the Roman, fame and glory meant not nearly so much as doing one's duty, the greatest of Roman virtues; Beowulf, while distant in time from Homer, sits not so far from him in epic tradition: the Germanic hero must win *lof* and *dom* (praise and glory)—and even that may not be enough to fulfill cultural needs or longings. Epics tend to approach both ancient and modern notions of prophecy: they diagnose the problems of the present while hinting at concerns to come.

In this chapter I propose to range through epic history without absolute restriction to national boundaries. I would like to suggest that, like the *Iliad* and the *Odyssey*, like the *Mahabharata*, of which the *Bhagavad Gita* forms the centerpiece, and like *Beowulf*, each significant epic poem also unfolds or addresses some question or quest that the culture from which the poem arises believes it must answer or undertake. Each epic also defines the heroic nature or aspects or ideals of the culture that produced it. To understand the epic means to enter and to understand the Heroic World; to understand the nature of heroism even in later cultures places us centrally amid their *ethos* as surely as following swift-footed Achilles leads us to appreciate Homer's Greece or journeying with dutiful Aeneas embodies Vergil's Rome. Arjuna seeks the bridge between the mystical search for Brahman and a required devotion to class and family. Beowulf must with steadfast courage resist the monsters of chaos while perhaps falling short of the Christian salvation to which his culture gives him no access. Dante must descend into hell before he can understand purgatory, and he must transcend purgatory to prepare to glimpse heaven. To understand heroism in any age we must unearth the quest or question that epic heroism develops and, further, consider how the heroes meet the gods who either abet or impede their heroic quests or questions. By exploring the progression of epic questions and epic *epiphanies*, that is, how the epic heroes meet their gods in the process of their quests, we may understand the hard, gem-like flame of epic history as the center of gravity in literature, philosophy, and culture, the fountain from which subsequent facets of culture flow. The history of the evolving genre of epic poetry spotlights the individual poems' continuing, pivotal place in world literature and the course of thought internationally. Epic, as the product of the *vates*, the poet-prophet, inspired speaker of culture, as the eminent source and

1. Epiphany *and the Western Epic Tradition*

spectrum for definitions of quests and heroism, gives us a remarkable field of experience upon which to cast comparisons and draw connections from age to age, culture to culture.[3] Whether or not we accept the notion of the inspired speaker, the epic as product of its time and of its privileged voices, partly because of its magnitude, partly because of what Matthew Arnold would call its "high seriousness," speaks with an authority few other genres claim.

Before we examine the most significant epics in the English tradition, let's consider the historical matrix of epic poems from which they emerge. England didn't create the epic tradition, but because of a healthy obsession with scholarship in Classical and Oriental models — and quite possibly because of an inherent desire for empire-building — English poets constantly built on the grandest models they could find. Out of its love of pre–Christian models, the lingering appeal of its Dark-Age Germanic heritage, and an ongoing effort to remake Mediterranean Christianity as its own, England grafted epic in the center of its garden. While we think of Shakespeare as essentially English, he is more quintessentially human, his drama an amazing historical aberration. Spenser, Milton, Wordsworth, Barrett Browning: they teach the struggles of English culture to define its character — and no surprise that Seamus Heaney would colonize *Beowulf,* Iricise it, turn out the language of the firmest root of English literature as English politics has often tried to do with Irish. For contemporary American audiences, however distant we may feel from it, English epic remains, because of our derivation from English culture, an inescapable part of our intellectual and spiritual heritage as well. Milton's meshing of the moral and sensual imagination resonates within our own struggles with religious nationalism to this day; he sought in his epic to transcend history by pre-dating it even as he aimed to transform the history to which he contributed.

Epic begins, as far as we know or may ever know, with *Gilgamesh,* the heroic Mesopotamian tale of that hyperactive king who proves for himself and all time that human beings must all, finally, suffer mortality. When Enkidu, sent by the gods to keep Gilgamesh busy and to give him some notion of human empathy so that he will stop deflowering all of Uruk's virgins and wasting all of its youth in war, dies of illness, Gilgamesh grieves horribly until he determines his true quest: to travel to the land of Utnapishtim "the Faraway" to learn the secret of immortality so that he might restore his friend to life and prevent his own death. Gilgamesh fails Utnapishtim's tests and must return to Uruk with the answer that no human (not even those who like him descend partly from the gods) is immortal, that the best we can do in this life is to live well, care for our families and our peoples, and enjoy our particular lot of happiness.

Epiphanies arise commonly and easily in *Gilgamesh*, but never without consequences. When the people of Uruk need help dealing with their hero-king, they pray to the gods for help, and the gods send Enkidu. Enkidu, human but heaven-sent, terrifies a young herder, so the herder seeks guidance from his father, who sends him to Gilgamesh, who affirms the father's solution that Enkidu must be civilized by means of the sexual touch of a "temple girl." Knowing nothing of his origin, they yet know how to domesticate him, to humanize this strange "epiphany," Enkidu himself, the gift of the gods to the people. Enkidu succeeds in the task for which the gods sent him, becoming Gilgamesh's friend and companion, and together they subdue Humbaba, the giant of the cedar wood, who represents the evil of the darkness that makes the wood inaccessible to humans. Subsequently they destroy the "Bull of Heaven," sent by the goddess Ishtar as a plague upon humans because Gilgamesh refuses to accept her as a lover. To punish the heroes for killing the bull, the gods infect Enkidu with a mortal illness, and Gilgamesh, grieving for his dead friend, seeks Utnapishtim, the Noah-like survivor of the great flood, to find the key to immortality. Along the way Gilgamesh meets Siduri, the divine wine-bearer, who prophesies Gilgamesh's failure in his quest, urging him instead to return home and enjoy his life, his family, his kingship: those things allotted him by life and fate. Gilgamesh, angered at the suggestion of his limitations, presses on to his goal across the waters of death with the help of the divinely appointed ferryman, Urshanabi, and finds whom (but not *what*) he seeks. Untnapishtim says that Gilgamesh must merely remain awake for six days and seven nights, but Gilgamesh immediately falls asleep. Seeking redemption for his failure, Gilgamesh asks for a second opportunity, and Utnpishtim describes a flower that Gilgamesh may find beneath the waters, a flower which, tasted, grants renewed youth. Gilgamesh finds the flower, but before he can return home, a serpent rises from the waters, consumes the flower, sheds its skin, and disappears back into the deep. The hero-king returns

1. Epiphany *and the Western Epic Tradition*

with this boon only: he writes down his story for all to read in ages to come, so that we may accept our own mortality and seek our own happiness within the limits of our talents and our fate.

Gilgamesh, replete with epiphanies that occur as simply as one might cross a city street (perhaps with the added difficulty of rush hour), eases us with the balm of story into our mortality and the pleasures — or at least compensations — granted us in this life by the gods.

Having established the answer to that first and foremost of human questions (and a baseline for epiphany), we must move on to the next human problem: since my body cannot live forever, and since I remain uncertain of an afterlife, what can I do to preserve my fame on earth? The answer: I can be a hero and perform deeds by which my fame will live after me, and people will remember me with honor, or, in today's vernacular, I can "live fast, die young, and leave a good-looking corpse." That is the question Homer takes up, not because he knew *Gilgamesh*, but because humanity had already integrated its answer. Homer asks, what is heroism, and what can it do for me or my tribe? And, despite my mortality, how can I best behave heroically so that I will gain honor and glory that will live after me?

The *Iliad* begins with:

> Sing, goddess, the anger of Peleus' son Achilles
> and its devastation, which put pains thousandfold upon the Achaians,
> hurled in their multitudes to the house of Hades strong souls
> of heroes, but gave their bodies to be the delicate feasting
> of dogs, of all birds, and the will of Zeus was accomplished
> since that time when first there stood in division of conflict
> Atreus's son the lord of men and brilliant Achilles [lines 1–7].[4]

Achilles, though he has the reputation (and because of his semi-divine parentage, the power) of the world's greatest hero, behaves, because of his wrath, childishly, and he puts himself in danger not only of losing praise, but also of receiving the ridicule of history. His wrath causes many more deaths than those fated by the Trojan War alone, and even his heroic vengeance proves intolerable as he not only kills Hector, but also drags his dead body about the field, refusing to give it up for proper burial, offending against the heroic code and the gods who have protected him (should he persist).

Heroes, Gods and the Role of Epiphany

Achilles' anger begins with Agamemnon's slight: since Achilles counsels the Greeks to return Agamemnon's "prize," the beautiful young Chriseis, to her father to end the current curse upon their venture, Agamemnon insists that since he must give up his prize, and he is their chief, Achilles must turn over *his* prize, the equally beautiful Briseis, to the man appointed by age and grandeur his superior — one sacrifice calls for another, and the chief among men, Agamemnon argues, must not give up more than lesser men do. Achilles, viewing himself as lesser than no man, gives up Briseis, but returns to his tent to sulk and cry and lament his blotted honor, leaving the Greeks without the labors of their best hero. Though the other Greeks perhaps achieve greater heroism on the field of battle even without Achilles, the gods do not permit them victory, and the Trojans advance as far as the Greek ships, preparing to burn them and annihilate their attackers. Soon Achilles has an even greater reason, though a different target, for his anger: his friend Patroklos borrows Achilles' armor and joins the fray to turn the tide of battle, but he is killed by Hektor, who strips the body for its spoils. Achilles, mourning his friend, forgives Agamemnon and the other Greeks and turns his vendetta upon Hektor, with the help of Athena killing his mark, achieving vengeance and the nominal heroism deriving from the quality of the foe he kills, Hektor, greatest of the Trojans.

Achilles finally achieves true heroism, though not in battle, but in answering the great question of his age: when Priam's tears move him to remember his own father and show compassion, giving up his enemy's body and accepting that wrath must give way to honor, Achilles, purposefully or not, shows that glory comes finally only through honorable, not merely bloody, deeds. Having learned with Gilgamesh that we are mortal, we learn from Achilles that, being mortal, we achieve lasting fame through heroic (and martial) deeds *tempered* thereafter by compassion.

Achilles dwells not so far from Gilgamesh's youthful unawareness of his own mortality, and only Priam's white hair brings the Greek hero face to face with it. Achilles' own death lingers in the shadows, but when his fated time comes, he will die with the reputation of a warrior great and pious, a friend loyal and wise, and an enemy deadly but just: a symbol for Greece upon which it could build a culture. Odysseus through his many adventures and unyielding perseverance refines and extends that image.

1. Epiphany *and the Western Epic Tradition*

When one has fought and conquered in a distant land, won glory and renown, avenged and restored what was lost, what quest remains for the hero? Odysseus must simply *get home*, a task complicated by the ill-will of gods offended by the razing of Troy and the lovesickness of sorceresses enticed and enticing.[5] *The Odyssey* begins:

> Tell me, Muse, of the man of many ways, who was driven
> far journeys, after he had sacked Troy's sacred citadel.
> Many were they whose cities he saw, whose minds he learned of,
> many the pains he suffered in his spirit on the wide sea,
> struggling for his own life and the homecoming of his companions
>   [lines 1–5].[6]

He cannot save them, for they have foolishly eaten the oxen of Helios, and though nearly all the gods by that time pity at least Odysseus, Poseidon will not stem his wrath for the injury done by the hero to his son, Polyphemos the Cyclops. Years of adventuring strip Odysseus of his companions and all the spoils of a war, but they do not diminish his resourcefulness or his desire to return home.

And what a series of adventures! From the sack of the Cicours' city to the land of the Lotus-eaters, to the land of the Cyclops, where Odysseus gains Poseidon's unrelenting enmity for blinding his son, Polyphemos, to Aeolia and the god's gift of the winds later loosed—within sight of Ithaca—by his untrusting companions, to the land of the half-man, half-giant cannibalistic Laestrigonians, to the isle of enchanting Circe, to the land of the Cimmerians to summon Teiresias for advice, through the magical music of the Sirens and the deadly channel between Scylla and Charybdis, to the fateful island of Hyperion and his men's theft of the god's cattle, to the island of sexy Calypso, and finally home—Odysseus' tale would seem a boy's fantasy rather than the ground of culturally central thought.[7] Odysseus' many adventures demonstrate his resourcefulness (the epithet Homer gives him), quick wits, willingness to test boundaries, and commitment to his home and family, and the fame he wins enlarges him as epic hero beyond the limited bounds of Ithaca into heroic history and our collective consciousness.

Odysseus' fame precedes him wherever he wanders—as a hero he need win no more than that—but the probing Greek mind asked the obvious question: after Achilles, what comes next? Have we nothing to hope for but victory and blood and death? Odysseus teaches the next lesson; his persistence and resourcefulness match Penelope's patience, and he does return home only to find his house besieged by suitors and would-be usurpers — though one may assert that after nineteen years they could rightly have presumed their king dead.

Odysseus' bloody resumption of kingship represents more than completion of the soldier's task: it accomplishes a "return to normalcy." It also suggests, long before we knew about post-traumatic stress syndrome, that the soldier may have become so inured to violence that he will overreact to any sign of challenge and bring the horrors of war home with him. And considering the legend of Odysseus' resuming his wanderings after becoming bored with home life, we might further guess that the author of the *Odyssey* believed, along with Thomas Wolfe, that one can't come home again. Home has changed, and so has the hero, and both are ironically stuck with trying to deal with each other. The poem answers the question, "What do I do after heroic deeds?" with the suggestion that, while the need for heroism remains, one might temper violence with reconciliation and wanderlust with familial duty and love — though one must know danger and not stint from removing it. The answer to the question, "What comes next after heroism?" seems to be, "Get home to resume your life, your place in the world, and take care of your family into the next generation."

And Odysseus adds a twist to epiphany as established in the *Iliad*: one can so "no," even to gods. He leaves Circe and Calypso, outwits Polyphemos, depends upon Athena and yields to Zeus, but must defy Poseidon if he intends ever to reach Itaca. The *Odyssey*, in some ways an adventure story for boys, points toward a personal and cultural coming of age in one's acquiring the ability to weigh decisions, even spiritual ones, and make choices, even bad ones, as long as one ultimately faces responsibility.

Vergil picks up where the *Odyssey* left off, though Aeneas lacks some of Odysseus' spunk. "Pious Aeneas" (he doesn't challenge the gods as Odysseus does) must put *duty* first, duty to the gods and duty to his people, since, for the Roman, that duty is both what produces heroism and what constitutes it. Whatever love Aeneas has for his drowned friend or for pining Queen Dido, the gods require that he put foremost his fate to found what will become Rome. The irony that at the end of the poem our

1. Epiphany *and the Western Epic Tradition*

sympathies may pass at least in part from Aeneas to Turnus doesn't change Vergil's focus on the primacy of legendary Roman duty. Vergil answers the question, having achieved fame and a concern for others, should anything higher than personal development direct my actions and feelings? Vergil's answer lies in Aeneas's epithets.

Vergil's proto–Romans hearken back to the *Iliad* in terms of how they meet their gods, at least if they wish to live rightly. They cannot resist the gods as Odysseus can, but then we would not expect them to in an epic about duty and piety. Like Achilles, Aeneas can fight enemies such as Turnus with all necessary commitment, even brutality, but like the post–Hector Achilles he can understand human frailty: he willingly leaves behind those followers not up to completing the task (yet does not feel obligated to strip them of honor) and will pardon and mingle with the wayward Latins. Like Odysseus he can sail the world, from burning Troy to Buthrotum, then to Sicily, where his father dies, to Carthage, where he falls in love with Dido (though he readily leaves her when duty calls him), to Sicily again with its games and where the women, tired of traveling, attempt to burn the Trojan ships, and to Cumae, where the Sibyl leads him to the Underworld and Anchises unveils for him the future of Rome. Finally has journey takes him to Latium and the recruitment of King Evander (by which we see Aeneas as accepted among Italian peoples), and then into battle with the Latins. The adventures provide the backdrop for the theme: Aeneas's pious commitment to the duty the gods require of him and to the empire that will derive from his legacy.

Aeneas's epiphanies have more in common with Achilles' than Odysseus', but they serve a different purpose. When, amid burning Troy, Aeneas stops to expend his wrath upon Helen, Venus interrupts and sends him after his family, to save them from the conflagration: he sees Ilium falling about him and obeys with no further thought to Helen. When the hero would linger at Carthage, Mercury appears to him with the gods' message that he must press on to his destiny. Aeneas leaps from sleep and without hesitation sets sail. Like the epiphanies of Homer, those in Vergil direct meetings with gods and direct response; though Odysseus may seek to evade, he may not ignore, and Aeneas seeks only to respond quickly and dutifully.

From Vergil, after a long age, we move to that first great Germanic vernacular primary epic, *Beowulf*, where we may see a stage much closer to Homer than to what we shall see ahead from the great Italian epics to James Joyce, but as with Joyce, also a poem without any actual "meeting with a god" who can legitimize the epic question.

Beowulf asks and answers a number of significant questions: How does a good king act? What traits make a good thane? Can a king also be a hero? Do acquisitiveness and pride help a king or destroy him? But perhaps most important, *Beowulf* returns to an immediately post–Homeric and post–Vergilian concern with *how* one, having achieved heroism, maintains it. Thus *Beowulf* adds a refinement to the questions Homer and Vergil raised. The poet's answer crystallizes the epic's theme: steadfast courage. Beowulf must ultimately fail, as king or hero, since he must finally, one way or another, die, leaving the people he has defended to defend themselves. He chooses to fight Grendel to gain *lof* and *dom*, praise and glory, the words from which come our modern *love* and *doom*; he finds himself in a position in which he may hardly refuse to fight Grendel's mother; he *must* make sure that the dragon can no longer ravage Geatland. In the fight with Grendel, Beowulf wins partly by strength, but mostly by superior courage; in Grendel's mother he finds a more courageous (or committed) adversary, but he maintains courage and prevails by keeping his wits and by the intrusion of fate and a bit of luck—finding the magic sword near at hand—for only the courageous could benefit from such luck. "Fate oft preserves the undoomed one, if his courage holds," Beowulf observes with taciturnity (ll. 572–573).

The first question one asks upon confronting the nature of epiphany in *Beowulf* involves whether or not the poem even has epiphanies, since no gods appear. The word *god* appears, used by both the narrator and Hroðgar, but does the reference imply the Christian God or the Germanic Oðin?

Scholars have argued at length about whether the poem is Christian or pagan, some asserting a pagan poem with a Christian coloring, some a Christian poem with a pagan coloring. Fred Robinson in *Beowulf and the Appositive Style* draws the distinction between a Christian poet and pagan subject matter. Other recent scholars such as Mary Parker have drawn the conclusion that the poem interlaces pagan and Christian worlds comfortably. The poet may have left religious reference intentionally ambiguous

1. Epiphany *and the Western Epic Tradition*

so that the poem would work with both Christian and Germanic reference. The poem exhibits, in Albert Rothenberg's term, a *janusian* quality,[8] looking at once into Christian and pagan Germanic worlds. But despite even these ambiguous references, no character has a meeting with God or a Germanic god or has a vision of heaven or hell (though scholars have long compared Grendel's tarn to medieval visions of hell, especially that which appears in the *Visio Sancti Pauli*, hell appears only by descriptive comparison, not as hell itself).

Beowulf does have, though, meetings between characters of different orders of being: Beowulf's fights with the monsters, creatures of nature but with special powers of destruction that can toss both culture and individual spirit into chaos. These meetings of men and monsters provide the epiphanies appropriate to the poem's purpose and show us the kind of epiphanies that concerned the branch of the Anglo-Saxon culture that produced *Beowulf*, one still caught in heroic fatalism and not fully converted to Christianity, when sin, redemption and salvation will become epic's consuming passion. From the Classical and medieval epics to nineteenth and twentieth-century incarnations of the genre, epics explore the history of heroism, heroic activity and heroic quest, and the results of heroism, but they also reflect cultural notions of piety. As Joseph Campbell argues in *The Hero with a Thousand Faces*, a *monomyth* underlies much of heroic literature; that monomyth involves various steps in the life and career of the hero, such as a miraculous birth, the undergoing of a quest, a meeting with a divine being, and a return with a boon for the culture. Nearly all of our epic heroes follow that monomyth, and the boon they seek answers the epic question.[9]

Beowulf does not conclude the search for epic questions; depending on when we date it and what we consider its origin, *Beowulf* has a nearest cousin perhaps in the *Chanson de Roland*. Beowulf scholars often come near to fistfights over dating the poem; a later date, around the tenth century (the sole manuscript is early eleventh century) seems most likely to me based on the presence of cultural conditions congenial to such a tale. And French scholars date the *Chanson* around the end of the eleventh century — it may have served, if one may use the word, to encourage knights to take up the first Crusade. More important for the current study, like *Beowulf* it has no actual epiphanies (though unlike *Beowulf* it does have clearly Christian prayers and a fighting archbishop). It runs a bit longer than *Beowulf* (just over 4000 lines), lacks also some of the Classical machinery of epic, such as an invocation of the Muse, and often falls under the category of "heroic poem" instead. But it fulfills what I have defined here as epic, and doubtless the French have seen it as formative in their sense of themselves as a nation and people. It does not pursue a specific quest, but it does ask a question of enormous importance typical of late– and post–Classical epic: what does it mean to do one's duty? Roland defends the rearguard of Charlemagne's army with the utmost courage, but a terminal sense of honor: he won't blow his war horn to call for aid until his soldiers have been slaughtered to a man. As Oliver laments, Roland has acted honorably and heroically, but unwisely; the poem questions the nature of heroism much as does Beowulf in the hero's closing battle with the dragon. A paradigm shift takes place between the medieval epics and those of the Renaissance, where a great hero who wins a place among the "Nine Worthies," Godfrey de Bouillon, succeeds by measured leadership and faith rather than by foolhardy personal acts of personal martial prowess. We must await the Renaissance to trace such new wrinkles in epic history.

Dante's *Commedia* embodies Everyone's quest to move from despair at the suffering of this world and exile from the provinces of people or God through a full understanding of what rejecting God means, to proper penance, to free acceptance of blessed Grace and a final vision of God: Dante reminds us of the Final Cause of Christian life, asking "Given that bad things happen to good people, how do I direct my life and talent to God?" Dante the exile becomes Dante narrator, who becomes Dante the epic poet. Torquato Tasso's *Gerusalemman Liberata* asks if steadfast courage is enough. Answer: no — one must direct it toward the holiest of quests, which for Tasso consists of liberating the Holy Land. We see this impulse in the steady movement of Arthuriana toward the Grail Quest, which by the time of Malory becomes the centerpiece of the stories of Camelot as the *Gita* takes center stage in *Mahabharata*. Edmund Spenser adds to Dante's answer that the Christian gentleman, born into a world of greater complexity than the Middle Ages, must direct his talents and virtues not only to the Holy Quest, but also to his social duties. Toward that end, though Holiness will serve as his chief virtue, as it does in the

1. Epiphany *and the Western Epic Tradition*

first book of the *Faerie Queene*, with the Redcrosse knight's quest to defeat the "dragon" and free Una (the One True Faith) and her family from Infernal domination, the ideal knight must acquire other virtues to deal with the infinite number of challenges in daily life that threaten person, Church, and State. Thus Spenser adds a new question: What range of virtues do I need for daily living, and how do I acquire them? As the Renaissance abuts against the Age of Reason, John Milton simplifies Spenser and even Dante. How do I follow God's will? he asks; Adam finally clarifies and utters the answer he has known all along: "Henceforth I learn that to obey is best." The Christian's first, basic task, obedience to God, sets all else on the right course.

In *Paradise Lost* (*PL*) Milton refines Spenser's "Christian virtue" project with that simple (but not simplistic) conclusion: Adam and Eve's error comes from disobedience, the premise Milton sets up from the incipient passage:

> Of Man's first disobedience, and the fruit
> Of that forbidden tree, whose mortal taste
> Brought death into the world, and all our woe,
> With loss of Eden, till one greater Man
> Restore us, and regain the blissful seat,
> Sing Heavenly Muse [1.1–6].

Adam and Eve's first "disobedience" is *Dis-obedience*: they obey Hell rather than God. The *fruit* refers multiply to the fruit they eat, the sin they commit, all the events that result from the Fall, and the Fruit that shall hang upon the tree to redeem them: Christ. The "mortal taste" makes them mortal and literally, in Milton's mythology, brings Death, the child of his incest with Sin, into the world to devour all living things. The "greater man," Jesus, restores the "epiphany lost" when Adam and Eve sin; the "seat" they regain is the new Eden or "New Jerusalem" of the post–Apocalyptic world. Before the Fall epiphany is easy for Adam and Eve: they meet God in the Garden and talk with Him, and they welcome Raphael to dinner. After the Fall they find epiphany intolerable: they hide from God and fear Michael's approach as he brings them postlapsarian instruction about the course of their fallen world. Even the invocation of the Muse represents an epiphany, a Classical motif Christianized, necessary from Milton's view to the proper completion of his Christian epic.

Heroes, Gods and the Role of Epiphany

Paradise Regained, then, provides the postscript to *PL*: since Adam and Eve fall by disobedience, Milton chooses not the crucifixion for his subject, but the temptation of Jesus in the wilderness. Satan tests Jesus as he tested Adam and Eve, but with different results: Jesus will give in to neither sensual lures nor to the desire for earthly power nor to Satan's urge that Jesus tempt God: "I to thy father's house have brought thee.... Now show thy progeny; if not to stand,/ Cast thyself down; safely in Son of God" (Fourth Book, lines 552–555). Jesus stands upon the pinnacle of the temple, and Satan in consternation falls: "Tempt not the Lord thy God, he said and stood" (4.561). Only then do the angels appear to buoy the Son to earth. The "Second Adam" passes the test that the first failed, he *obeys* by not himself tempting the Father to exhibit his power as if it were magic, since Jesus, full in his faith, suffers no danger at Satan's hands. *Paradise Regained* (*PR*) does more than re-establish an eventual paradise for fallen humanity: it restores epiphany, "justifies" God and humanity by bringing us together in the person of the incarnate Son. *Paradise Lost* shows the loss of epiphany, the loss of paradise in the loss of direct, comfortable converse with God; for Milton *PR* "regains the blissful seat" by restoring the possibility of obedience and its fruitful yield: salvation, granted if sought. The poet, too, experiences the restoration of epiphany in the answer of the Muse (the Holy Spirit) to the petitioner, the poet: the epic poem itself, inspired and whole, its theme — obedience to God alone — doctrinal and exemplary to a nation (England, Christendom, humankind).

That answer may seem to oversimplify an immense, learned, gorgeous baroque epic, but it typifies the best epics and the best epic questions in its directness and clarity and summarizes all that comes before. Can I live forever? No. What do I do then? Live heroically. How? Martial virtuosity tempered by compassion. Is that enough? No: duty and piety. How do I get and keep those virtues? Steadfast courage. Once I have it, how do I direct that courage? To save your people. Consider the people only? No: you must also seek God. How do I best do that? You must be courageous, but you must use all your talents to the very end of your life and apply your virtue to social as well as religious problems. That sounds complicated; can I simplify it somehow? Yes: obey God.

One might comfortably guess that epic ends at that point in literary

1. Epiphany and the Western Epic Tradition

history, and some scholars would agree, at least technically: the Age of Reason no longer believes in Old World Muses and epiphany but turns to scientific models of history — and more pragmatically, cruel leaders — rather than imaginative, heroic figures of the past. With the Renaissance the world had already changed, Humanism became at least for some not damnable, and epic questions took up new, more personal turns. William Blake, as he shows in his prophetic book *Milton*, saw himself as Milton's heir in the poet-prophet tradition and who, rejecting what to him seemed Milton's infernal, stultifying obedience, found a central question of his own to add to the mix. While the prophetic books in general weave a phantasmagoria of broken and reconstituted epiphanies as Blake plots an often cacophonous course toward personal, social, and universal spiritual health, *Milton* particularly shows Blake having accepted the epic torch from his dangerous and looming forebear.

Blake, if we may take *Milton* as an avatar of Blake's belief, thought Milton, for all his poetic greatness, had mistaken the proper course for humanity in Adam's final declaration in *Paradise Lost*: "Henceforth I learn that to obey is best,/ And love with fear the only God" [12.561–62]. Blake, in the midst of the emergence of Romanticism, saw God in individual inspiration. "I must create my own system, or be enslaved by another man's," says Los, the voice of the poetic imagination in the fallen world, and Blake saw himself as taking up the epic torch that Milton's demise had left lightless. Recalling Paul and the way from Tarsus to Damascus, Blake, in the beginning of *Milton*, has Milton's star, shooting down from the heavens, strike the character (also narrator and prophet) Blake in the *tarsus*, entering his spirit to counsel the "new" poet that obedience doesn't lead to the mystical or quotidian fulfillment of God's will: imaginative creation true to one's own inspiration does. Blake's prophetic books comprise, *in toto*, at least for their creator, epiphanies, inspired, sustained utterances of the creative power that God invests in people and which those inspired have an obligation to share with others through acts of creativity. Blake eschews orthodoxy for the primacy of personal imagination: without anyone particularly noticing, he had achieved his quest and changed the world.

William Wordsworth takes the more conservative Romantic approach, finding epiphanies in the "spots of time" he describes in *The Prelude*, those moments in which the power of nature touches the depths of one's being and raises the consciousness of the soul to sublimity. Wordsworth follows Milton rather than Blake and takes the Romantic alternative that one might argue began the environmental movement that lives today: where do inspiration and power come from? From the spirit of God through Nature. He pursues, not as Keats might say an *egotistical sublime* so much as a *natural sublime*: if nature really never did betray the heart that loved her (see *Tintern Abbey*), and we actually do enter the world trailing clouds of glory (see the *Immortality Ode*), then Nature bears for each of us the potential to mediate a mental, physical, and spiritual movement toward God better than can any book or word. *The Prelude* serves as an account of the growth of one creative person's mind — not an instruction manual for the growth of others' — so that we may find like solace and inspiration in Nature should we choose to do so.

Elizabeth Barrett Browning teaches us in *Aurora Leigh* equal-opportunity inspiration. Her question: can a woman undergo the quest, and how does she do it? Her answer: yes, women have the same poetic power as men, and if they have the courage to use it, they can and will produce classics that will, despite the grip and grimace of prevailing stereotypes and oppression, persist and inspire generations. Men of her time asserted that a woman couldn't write epic poetry, that they hadn't the strength, the will, the soul for it. Only a century and a quarter later, finally, *Aurora Leigh* began to receive its due. Barrett Browning, through her protagonist's ability to join sacrifice, friendship and generosity, love and goodness, talent and accomplishment, democratized the epic, the quest, and the Great Question: women and men can fully become themselves and benefit their culture by following their inspiration.

The Romantics and Victorians turned epic theme and quest inward, yet the boon remained the imaginative gift to society: find our individual quests, whoever we are, whatever they may be, pursue them, and therein we find peace, fulfillment, joy. We all participate in the Myth if we listen to the voice of inspiration.

Returning to Joseph Campbell, we may remember that he borrowed the term *monomyth* from James Joyce. He might as well have borrowed a second term that I have been using here, *epiphany* — the meeting with a being of a different order — since the hero traditionally meets a god

1. Epiphany *and the Western Epic Tradition*

or some sort of miraculous creature on the quest. The history of the epic genre is, I would argue, the history of heroism and of our epiphanies: how we live well and how we meet our gods. Joyce, of course, puts an entirely different and thoroughly twentieth-century spin on the old notion of epiphany, but in doing so he doesn't break, but rather continues a tradition that has been part of heroic literature and epic since its beginnings.

Paul Merchant defines epic as a long narrative poem that incorporates elements of the supernatural.[10] I would add to that definition that epic normally narrates the quest or adventures of a hero or heroine (or, as a former colleague used to like to say, *shero*) and that those adventures normally show the struggles of the hero to acquire something, an object, a quality, or the answer to some pressing question of significance to that time and culture. Steps to complete the quest or the ends of the quest itself require an *epiphany*, during which the hero moves beyond boundaries assumed by the poem's audience (and sometimes, previously, by the hero) to be natural limitations to meet creatures of a different "order of being" or to enter a different order of being himself or herself. The audience, following the heroic quest, participates also in the act of epiphany, sharing it with the hero, thus sharing the process of finding or receiving the boon, which gives an answer to a pervasive, troublesome question. Alternatively, the achieved epiphany or even the quest itself may offer a method by which the audience can deal with a contemporary problem or concern. Even though epics are often set in a historical or even mythical past, they pursue some notion of heroism or define an epiphany urgent to the writer's contemporary culture.

Joyce's epiphany takes a different spin (as do epiphanies in each major epic as we proceed age by age) than those of any previous epics. We cannot expect the results of his epiphanies to include a meeting with a god, standard fare in earlier epics, since the twentieth-century "waste land" landscape does not permit so ready an answer to its problems. The Joycian epiphany is a literary or verbal epiphany, a "shift in perception" based on the creative imagination's "blending of sight and sound" resulting in the "modern sublime."[11] The perceiver (author, character, reader) achieves an instantaneous recognition of the nature of an object, its "whatness," and this experience becomes "fraught with meaning beyond itself," precipitating a revelation that our century finds "quite as valid as the religious."[12]

Heroes, Gods and the Role of Epiphany

Robert Longbaum suggests that whereas Yeats and Pater used art "to bring us back to religion or mysticism," Joyce established art as a "rival to religion"[13] in its ability to evoke the epiphanal experience: the "pure but transient vision, the aesthetic or timeless moment ... of non-didactic revelation,"[14] the anagoge imminentized yet secularized, "all symbols being united in a single infinite eternal verbal symbol."[15] Epiphany has come to mean the epiphany of the symbol, then finally of the words creating the symbol. And Richard Ellman points out that while Joyces's epiphanies are sometimes "joyful" or "eucharistic," they are often "unpalatable" or even "splenetic": they may convey the experience of "things to be got rid of, examples of fatuity or imperceptiveness."[16]

This definition of *epiphany* comes particularly from *Stephen Hero*, Joyce's preliminary version of *A Portrait of the Artist as a Young Man*. Stephen is walking, grumbling to himself over what he sees as women's (his mother's and Emma's) blind acceptance of dogmatic, hierarchical religion when he hears a young woman and man engaging in playful love dialogue. He begins to think of creating a book of poems describing such instances, a "book of epiphanies":

> By an epiphany he meant a sudden spiritual manifestation, whether in the vulgarity of speech or of gesture or in a memorable phase of the mind itself. He believed that it was for the man of letters to record these epiphanies with extreme care, seeing that they themselves are the most delicate and evanescent of moments.[17]

The epiphany represents an instant of *claritas*:

> *Claritas* is *quidditas*.... This is the moment which I call epiphany. First we recognize that the object is *one* integral thing, then we recognise that it is an organised composite structure, a thing in fact: finally, when the relation of the parts is exquisite, when the parts are adjusted to the special point, we recognise that it is *that* thing which it is. Its soul, its whatness, leaps to us from the vestment of its appearance.... The object achieves its epiphany.[18]

Curiously, in *A Portrait of the Artist as a Young Man*, Joyce changes the context for this discussion and leaves out the word *epiphany*. Stephen is walking with his schoolmate Lynch and, in the process of defining beauty, turns (again) to Aquinas's three components of beauty: *integritas*, *consonontia*, and *claritas*, the last of which he translates as *radiance*, the quality that indicates the "whatness" of a thing:

1. Epiphany *and the Western Epic Tradition*

> This supreme quality is felt by the artist when the esthetic image is first conceived in his imagination. The mind in that mysterious instant Shelley likened to a fading coal. The instant wherein that supreme quality of beauty, the clear radiance of the esthetic image, is apprehended luminously by the mind which has been arrested by its wholeness and fascinated by its harmony is the luminous silent stasis of esthetic pleasure, a spiritual state very like to that cardiac condition which the Italian physiologist Luigi Galvani, using a phrase almost as beautiful as Shelley's, called the enchantment of the heart.[19]

The psychological orientation of the passages changes; we move from the object achieving its epiphany to the perceiver being enchanted by the perception. The experience is still sensory rather than spiritual, but it becomes more human and less mechanical.

The epiphany takes a different and more traditional, though still human rather than divine, turn in the garden scene toward the end of *Ulysses*, with the interpersonal epiphany that occurs among Stephen, Bloom, and Molly. Bloom, reflecting on the question of human perfectibility and social inequities and feeling dejected, leads Stephen into the "penumbra of the garden," leaving his lighted candle at the door, and the two stand beneath a "heaventree of stars."[20] Looking at the stars, Bloom meditates on the "infinitesimal brevity" of human life[21]; he proceeds to identify the constellations and observes that he sees "not a heaventree, not a heavenbeast, not a heavenman. That it was a Utopia ... an infinity."[22] As he begins to reflect on the "affinities ... between the moon and woman," Bloom and Stephen see in the second story of the house by the light of a lamp the outline of Molly. Bloom and Stephen then look at each other for a moment, then each in turn urinates in the garden while gazing at the "luminous and semi-luminous shadow" of Molly projected against the window blind. After accounting for the trajectories of their urine streams, Joyce turns again to a heavenly image: "A star precipitated with great apparent velocity across the firmament from Vega in the Lyre ... towards the zodiacal sign of Leo."[23]

The epiphany takes place not between a person and a god, but between two people, Stephen and Bloom, one might say under the auspices of Molly's presence. The star that flies between the constellations of the Lyre (Stephen, the poet) and Leo (Leopold Bloom) represents a human connection that defies words, sense of empathy or mutual humanity bound by the problems of the world but able at least to communicate, if only at odd moments, and to find a light in the darkness (beauty?) that catalyzes communication.

When *Portrait* ends, Stephen intends to leave Ireland "to forge in the smithy of my soul the uncreated conscience of my race,"[24] a cultural epiphany could he (or anyone) complete such a task. But in *Ulysses* we find Steven (and Joyce) returning first to an epiphany of word and finally to an epiphanic recognition of human mutuality in friendship, with its pleasures but also its limitations, a moment of compassion, of shared feeling and humanity, with another person standing beneath the stars. For that same epiphany the remainder of the twentieth century has been periodically striving: to move beyond our words to some sort of mutual understanding and appreciation, at least enough so that, though we may not understand let alone love one another, we may at least achieve peaceful coexistence.

Joyce shows what our twentieth-century epiphanies have become after a long journey beginning with *Gilgamesh*. That journey has proven not circuitous, but surprisingly and logically linear. After Joyce, what? Stephen Vincent Benét's *John Brown's Body*, a patriotic appreciation of freedom amid dubious violence, and William Carlos Williams' *Paterson*, an epic of the power of place and of the particular, the small detail: do they represent possible courses of future epics or dead ends? Only the future will tell, but as the Western epic impulse flags, diluted into science fiction, fantasy, and cinema, more and more scholars turn to other traditions to bring back the power of epic epiphany that we may have lost.

In the West we tend to think of epic as a Classical genre, but with some variations in form and convention, the epic impulse appears nearly worldwide. I'd like at this point to take a digression into further consideration of the *Bhagavad Gita*, not because of any particular influence on English epic, but because it provides a perfect example of epic in this broader, international context. I might as well have chosen *Kalevala* or *Kalevipoeg* as intentional epic reconstructions by authors who sought from traditional tales a unified model that spoke to them as in some way rooted in the most significant aspects of their cultural understanding. But they may have greater affinity to Tolkien's *Silmarillion* than to epic tradition: they attempt to fill the need for a "mythology" of their country more than

1. Epiphany *and the Western Epic Tradition*

to pursue a specific quest or question. The *Shah-Nameh* would, I think, work equally well, in part or as a whole, in its movements from mythical to legendary to historical kings and heroes and the mirror they hold up to magistrates of any age, but I have less familiarity with it. To me the *Nibelungenlied* reads more as proto–Romance than as epic; *Volsungasaga* fills a middle ground much like *Shah-Nameh*, bubbling up amid myth, legend, and refigured historical bits — any scholarly essay must suffer its own quirks.

In terms of its epic question and its epiphany, the *Gita*, in our "line of vision" about two hundred years before Vergil, exhibits remarkable parallels to the *Aeneid*, but it miraculously retains an even greater cultural centrality.[25]

As but one facet of the larger epic it inhabits, the *Gita* resolves a conundrum of Indian thought, connects two halves of an enormous narrative, and allows the chief characters of the *Mahabharata* to fulfill the lifelong spiritual quest that lies at the heart of Indian life. The *Mahabharata* derives from an oral tradition begun as early as the ninth century B.C., approximately contemporary with Homer, and it engages the universal themes of "what constitutes Dharma or Law (the ways things really are and therefore the way they should be), how men and women can acquire knowledge of the truth, and how they should act in relation to it."[26] The *Gita*, incorporated into the larger work around the third century B.C., condenses or "crystallizes" around the particular theme of the warrior class and its duty to fight — thrown into relief against the "renunciatory ideal of nonviolence."[27] Like Hamlet, Arjuna finds himself in a situation where he cannot act, between two sets of values."[28] Learning of the immortality of the soul, the insignificance of individual human worries, and the value of duty as part of the natural order, he takes up his rightful position at arms.

The *Mahabharata* as a whole relates, among a vast array of adventures, a long intrafamilial struggle for a kingdom, the intricate history of the "great" Bharatas. Particular complications arise as Pandu rules instead of his older brother, Dhritarashtra, because the elder was born blind. When Pandu dies, his five sons (the "Pandavas," actually the sons of gods rather than their human "father") expect to inherit the throne which Dhritarashtra has claimed, arousing the hopes of his own sons (the "Kauravas").

Heroes, Gods and the Role of Epiphany

Dhritarashtra equitably divides the kingdom between the two groups of cousins, but Duryodhana, eldest of the Kauravas, challenges Yudhishthira, eldest of the Pandavas, to a game of dice: winner take all. Duryodhana wins, and the Pandavas lose everything, including the wife they share, Draupadi, and they go into exile. When they return, the inevitable war results, and the *Gita* takes place between the lines as they two massed armies prepare for battle. There Arjuna's charioteer, Krishna, reveals himself as an incarnation of Brahman and stills the hero's doubts. Following the events of the *Gita*, the Pandavas, led by Arjuna, win the battle, and Yudhishthira gains his kingship. Later, in a couple of odd twists, Krishna dies in a hunting accident, and the Pandavas give up their hard-won kingdom to seek the spiritual mysteries of the Himalayas. Only Yudhishthira, the embodiment of spiritual growth, achieves the quest.[29]

Epiphany does not begin in *Mahabharata* with the *Gita*, though it reaches a fulfillment there.[30] Even in just those events that lead to the *Gita*, several occur. Amba, a princess of the previous generation, through spiritual austerities invokes encounters with Vishnu and Shiva, and she reincarnates as a man, becomes Arjuna's charioteer, and kills her old enemy Bhisma, who had wished to see her married to his brother rather than to the king she loved. The Pandavas have divine fathers. Krishna, who will only later reveal his identity to Arjuna, has been born as grandson to King Sura, appears a number of times in the story prior to the *Gita*. He gives his sister as a second wife to Arjuna, serves as political advisor to Yudhishthira, enlists Bhima and Arjuna to help him slay his enemy, the evil King Jarasamdha, and counsels the Pandavas to send a peace envoy to the Kauravas before the battle that follows the *Gita*.

Krisha's revelation to Arjuna, among the greatest epiphanies in all of literature because of its complexity, yet explicitness — combined with its literary power — develops slowly through the philosophical discussion that leads Arjuna to his realization of the epic theme of duty in renunciation.

As the *Gita* begins, Sanjaya, Dhritarashtra's minister, reports the events to his blind king, beginning in typical epic fashion: reciting a "catalogue" of the warriors assembled for battle. The great leaders blow upon their conch shells, and the sound thunders among the host, echoing between heaven and earth. Arjuna, greatest of the Pandava warriors, raises

1. Epiphany *and the Western Epic Tradition*

his bow and calls to Krishna, serving as his charioteer, "Achyuta, draw up my chariot between the two armies/ That I may look on these mean, at the ready, eager for battle, with whom I must engage in this great enterprise of war" (Chapter 1, verses 21–22).[31] Krishna drives the chariot into the middle of the field that lies between the combatants, and Arjuna casts his eyes about, spotting "fathers, grandfathers, teachers, maternal uncles, brothers, sons, grandsons, friends,/ Fathers-in-law, and companions in both armies " (1.26–27), and seeing them, Arjuna, "overcome by deep compassion" and "in despair" (1.28), tells Krishna, "My limbs grow heavy" and "I have no desire for victory ... or kingship, or pleasures" (1.29, 32). The hero has reached what seems to him an impossible dilemma: how can he fight, even in what he and his brothers see as a just cause, realizing not only that he has family and friends on both sides, but also that each of the men assembled has a full life, the matrix of which touches so many others in so many different ways. Each is someone's child, someone's husband, someone's brother, someone's friend, so should Arjuna slay even one, even the most distant from his own life and concerns, he brings sorrow and suffering without reparation to all those touched by that life. The significance of the tragedy of each stoke lights upon him. He loses all desire to fight, let alone kill, observing that "though they are killers themselves" and "even if ... their minds are overwhelmed by greed ... [h]ow can *we* be so ignorant as not to recoil from this wrong? The evil incurred by destroying one's own family is plain to see" (1.35, 38, 39), and he drops his weapons and sinks down into his chariot, unable any longer to stand (1.47). Krishna's advice becomes immediately apparent as the next chapter begins, though his argument unfolds through the remainder of the *Gita*. "Arjuna, where do you get this weakness from at a moment of crisis?... A noble should not experience this [hesitation]. It does not lead to heaven," Krishna adjures, but rather "it leads to disgrace. No impotence, Partha" (2.2–3). Already in the midst of the epiphany (Krishna's presence at Arjuna's side), we also have the question and the answer: What must I do? Your duty. "Instruct me!" Arjuna begs (2.7). However, as we all know, no significant answer settles into our hearts so simply — despite their setting in a heroic, supernaturally charged world, epics have a remarkable tendency to crystallize such simple psychological truths. The purpose of the *Gita*, like that of any epic, revolves around, as Sir Philip Sidney points out in his *Defense of Poesy*, spurring mental and spiritual as well as physical action. It does not amount simply to telling us the truth, but also moves us to do it: that is the secret of the power of literature and what separates it as a necessary extension of history and philosophy.

As Franklin Edgerton points out, "The *Gita* attempts no concrete definition of duty, but contents itself with saying that man should do his duty simply because it *is* his duty, and with perfect indifference to the results"[32]: that idea constitutes the doctrine of renunciation. And the *Gita* can counsel no particular duty, because Krishna's mode of action urges the individual to find his own *yoga*, the "disciplined activity" that in the *Gita* takes precedence over the quiet life of solitary, ascetic meditation.[33] That theme envelopes the *Gita* and the reason for its book-length epiphany; the rest of the episode follows the steps by which Arjuna and audience may be brought to a realization of that truth, and it prepares both Arjuna and audience for the full revelation of the Lord Krishna as Brahman, the center and source of the dance of the universe.

Arjuna experiences a desire not to destroy, not to cause suffering, but Krishna explains to him, "You utter wise *words*, yet you have been mourning those who should not be mourned; the truly wise do not grieve for the living or the dead./ There never was a time when I was not, or you, or these rulers of men. Nor will there ever be a time when we shall cease to be" (2.11–12). Pleasure and pain, all aspects of the passing moment, have no permanence, Krishna adds: "therefore fight, Bharata!" (2.18). *Renunciation* involves not renouncing action for inaction, but in detaching oneself from results and realizing one cannot change the course of the universe, which continues its eternal dance regardless of individual instants of glory or suffering: "this embodied self in the body of everyone is eternally unkillable. Therefore you must not grieve for any beings at all.... For there is nothing better for a warrior than a duty-bound war.... You will either be killed and attain heaven, or conquer and enjoy the earth" (2.30, 31, 37). The warrior must set a good example, fulfill his place according to the shape his life has taken, and learn his yoga: "evenness of mind" (2.48). Krishna does not seek to upset the social structure, but to show how one may live in it. As Johnson suggests, "For most Hindus the *Gita* is not simply part of the epic story but a religious teaching, transmitted to them personally by the guru–God Krishna"[34]; however, its

1. Epiphany *and the Western Epic Tradition*

"primary meaning may not be in its metaphysical or philosophical content at all, but in the story it tells, and in the relationship it dramatizes between God and human beings"[35]—the epiphany of the *Gita* embodies everyone's existence in the presence of Krishna/Brahman, and it clarifies everyone's right action, as he or she performs appointed duty without attachment. Johnson contextualizes the importance of this message historically, arguing that the *Gita* appeared at a time of social and religious "tensions, the most significant being between those ... who enjoined the fulfilment of one's prescribed social and religious duties as a member of the class into which one had been born, and those who advocated renouncing that ascribed status altogether in favour of a life of homelessness and spiritual discipline."[36]

"Liberation and bliss" come from "right action" undergirded by faith—with the revelation of faith comes the culmination of the epiphany of the *Gita*. While Krishna counsels proper meditation and the cessation of thought and the practice of discipline to still the desires, he concludes, "of all yogins it is the one possessing faith who shares in me, with his inner self given over to me, whom I consider to be the most disciplined" (6.47). "Practising yogic discipline," he adds, "you shall know me entirely and unreservedly" (7.1); as Krishna begins the process which will culminate in Arjuna's vision of Deity, he says explicitly, "I am the origin and dissolution of this whole universe.... I am the eternal seed of all creatures, I am the intelligence of the intelligence.... I am the strength of the mighty, freed from passion and desire" (7.6, 10, 11). This passage echoes in Chapter 10: "I am comprehensively the source of the gods and the great seers ... of speech I am the single syllable *Om*.... Of weapons I am the thunderbolt.... [O]f rivers I am the Ganges. Arjuna, I am the beginning, the middle, and the end of creations, the knowledge of supreme self among sciences" (10.2,25,28,31,32–33). One chapter later the vision reaches its climax.

Arjuna asks, "Lord, if you think I am capable of seeing it, then, great lord of yoga, show me your indissoluble self" (11.4). Krishna does so: "Partha, see my hundredfold and thousandfold forms—diverse divine, variegated, and manifold"(11.5); he cautions, then, "But you will not be able to see me with your natural eye, so I give you a divine eye—behold my lordly power!" (11.8) At that point even the reader must have an intermediary, for Krishna unveils to Arjuna what no one else has ever seen: Sanjaya re-emerges as Dhritarashtra's eyes to explain that Arjuna sees the universe both in its entirety and in its infinitely complex individualities all at once: mouths, eyes, weapons, robes, suns, brilliant, infinite in all directions; Arjuna, his hair bristling, bows, terrified, tries to explain to Krishna what he sees, pours forth praise and apology for failing to have recognized God in all his fullness.

At that point Krishna must simplify: "simply by acting for my sake you will attain success.... [R]estrain yourself and abandon the fruit of all your actions" (12.10–11). Krishna encourages Arjuna to abandon worry, abandon hate, abandon possessiveness and expectation, to have faith: "Having freed oneself from egoism, force, pride, desire, anger, and possessiveness, unselfish and serene, one is able to become Brahman" (18.53); "[f]ix your mind on me.... I promise you: you are dear to me" (18.65). What more can Arjuna hope for? "My delusion has been obliterated.... I shall do as you say" (81), he concludes, and thus returns to the Pandava battle line to lead them, detached, to victory.

Unlike Semele, burned to ashes by the vision of Zeus she unwisely begs, Arjuna finds, briefly, what he seeks. Beyond the *Gita*, as beyond any story, life goes on, and along with Arjuna we continue the struggle of our yoga, action with detachment, faith amidst the pleasure and suffering of the myriad forms that leap in the dance of the universe. Once again in the course of epic questing we, questioning with Arjuna, have renewed our faith and our place in the world, achieved our epiphany, found our boon, returned with hope of apotheosis. Like the other great epics, the *Gita* puts us in touch with the Divine by the means its contemporary culture finds most expedient, effective, and — here, if not in all epics — reverent. After the *Gita*, as after Milton in the West, as we have "modernized," our epic quests and questions turn from the cosmological to the quotidian — no less creatively, but perhaps with some forgetfulness.

The contribution of Dante's *Commedia* and Milton's *Paradise Lost* to the Western religious imagination (perhaps even greater than that of Michelangelo and Leonardo Da Vinci) parallels that of the *Gita* in India. The literary explication of epiphany serves as a basis for cultural understanding and also for the individual reader to see more clearly a means to live a good life. Though the good may in cases such as Arjuna's imply

1. Epiphany *and the Western Epic Tradition*

violence, in Dante's a horrifying journey through the Dark Night of the Soul if not literally through Hell and Purgatory (and to a not entirely unfrightening Bright Morning of the Soul thereafter), and in Milton's an unwonted and unwanted obedience, yet the audience gains an eminent (and immanent) perspective on what to seek and what to avoid. Through the history of epic the culminating moments have followed a course from theophany to hierophany to material epiphany to cultural epiphany — and today *epiphany* implies no more than an instant's realization of anything from the theme of a book to a good price on a new set of clothes. As true theophanies, and also as true epics, the *Gita*, the *Commedia*, and *PL* connect engaged readers to ideas of God in much the same way as do the Bible for Christians and Jews and the Koran for Muslims. Further, they connect us to essential cultural roots in the struggle for the right to personal religious expression and to attempt the ever-dangerous task of giving voice to a culture's greatest social concerns. They also speak thematically with a kind of clarity and applicability that makes as much sense now as it did twenty-three hundred years ago: they deal directly with the search for a "good life," and I don't know of much that has greater importance than that. To have faith and courage, to know and perform our duty, whatever it may be, to try to understand our relationship to God or the Transcendent: those desires, those needs, both in terms of the individual life and death and the human place in the cosmos, even as the universe evolves, never change.

The next chapter will elaborate on duty, and the third will detail its obverse of reward: the rising tide of individualism in epic. Always present historically, notions of individualism evolve just as epic questions do, and individualism in a sense *becomes* a duty, even the duty: one must achieve individually both as a model for others and as the culture's representative, but also because the self gains primacy over the community. In those chapters beyond we will examine individually the most persistently influential of the *English* epic poems. England has a particularly rich, varying epic tradition that pursues an eerily consistent pathway. The movement of the poems calls to mind a biological maxim: "ontogeny recapitulates phylogeny." That is, the growth of the individual mirrors the evolution of the species, or in this case the epics, in their questions and epiphanies, show especially clearly the evolving concerns of English society. Most significantly they show poets, far from mere dreamers, searching for answers beyond the common capacity: they, like Browning's Pippa, like this book, seek answers beyond their grasp — else what's a heaven for? But first we'll return to the heroes of old.

Chapter 2

The "Duty" Theme in the Epic Tradition

> Sing, goddess, the anger of Peleus' son Achilles
> and its devastation, which put pains thousandfold upon the Achaians,
> hurled in their multitudes to the house of Hades strong souls
> of heroes
>
> — the *Iliad*, lines 1–4[1]

Homer's *Iliad* begins by showing the devastation wrought by Achilles' failure to do his martial duty, illustrating without the necessity of explicit statement the definitive importance to Homer's age of attention to duty. Paralleling Donahue's point about the Homer which I quote at the beginning of Chapter 1, translator/editor Keith Bosley has suggested of the more modern, nineteenth-century Finnish *Kalevala* that it became a "rallying-flag for national aspirations, and is regarded as the 'national epic' by modern Finland"[2]; translator/scholar Dick Davis observes of the Persian *Shah-Nameh* that we are dealing with "the heroic history of the people" celebrated in a traditionally formal poem, thus a "national epic."[3] Epic poets have throughout literary history sought to define, legitimize, and inculcate a national "character" through the use of mythic, legendary, and historical tales of the founders and heroes of their lands, and their heroes have often inherited tasks the completion of which have exemplified that sense of character. However, the traits and themes that poets present as specific to their own national character have echoed remarkably consistently from country to country and age to age, suggesting that the epic impulse derives not from local custom and heredity alone, but also from a more generally human or global undercurrent that aims to understand the virtues that shape human growth and accomplishment. Above all those virtues, this one motif or theme emerges as perhaps most important and consistent — and most nearly universal — in the epic tradition: *duty*.

The heroes learn duty often through epiphany: an encounter with God or god (or in odd cases with infernal monsters) may hint, clarify, or even detail what the hero must learn, seek, or perform to find what his (or her) culture most needs, the answer that can point the way to advancement or perhaps even to survival.

The *Iliad* displays and deplores the "wrath of Achilles" that dooms many brave soldiers — until the hero, through the death of his friend Patroklos, remembers his nature, his duty, and his own humanity, with all its glories and limitations. Vergil wrote the *Aeneid* to legitimize Rome as imperial power, but also, in pious Aeneas, to create a character who fully embodied the essence of Roman virtue: devotion to family, the gods, the cause, the state. This pattern or theme, the "place" of heroic duty and action in our history and our present, began long before the Classical world, in the *Epic of Gilgamesh*: the hero-king through the life and death of his friend Enkidu learns the essential value of fulfilling one's place in world, of kindness and devotion to one's purpose and people. The practice continues into the modern age as we continue to seek our place and contributions in our respective societies.

In this chapter I intend to explore several examples, including the *Epic of Gilgamesh*, the Homeric epics, the *Aeneid*, the *Bhagavad Gita*, *Beowulf*, and the section of the Persian *Shah-Nameh* known as "The Legend of Seyavash" (with pauses upon some other historically significant epics along the way) to exhibit the consistent centrality of the theme of duty in national epics so as to argue that it potentially represents a historical rallying cry for humanity worldwide, regardless of political or national affiliation or our contemporary glorification of individualism. While devotion to duty in a limited political sense may suggest dangerous chauvinism, the devotion to more broadly *human* good suggested in the epic poems provides a

2. The "Duty" Theme in the Epic Tradition

globally unifying theme to connect cultures beyond the boundaries of place and time.

This point applies, I think, explicitly to the early epic poems, but at least implicitly to the later as well. Blake and Wordsworth, I believe, must have felt an obligation to express the rising individualism of their time: the revolutions of their age created public and private space for the individual, regardless of class, that had not existed before — though of course a good deal of time has passed since without our having yet completed the transition to full and universal social *equality*. Elizabeth Barrett Browning must have felt a duty to show that women can write epic poetry as well as men and thus can undertake any field of endeavor that a man can. Similarly, to name his epic *Omeros* and to use its pages to explore what it means to live as a Caribbean islander, Derek Walcott must have felt something more than the usual poetic desire to struggle with notions of individuality as they abut place, time, class, and varied and uncertain origins.

But for now let's begin at the beginning: what is perhaps our oldest extent literature, our first endeavor into the creative, literary expression of heroism, explores the implications of duty. The Mesopotamian *Gilgamesh* exhibits what happens when a king fails in his duty — and also what happens when he succeeds. The people of Uruk call upon the gods for help to ease the suffering caused by their hyperactive king, who insists on his first-night privileges, deflowering their innocent virgins, and leading their sons off to war. While the king has such rights, the ideal king would not insist upon practicing them; Gilgamesh becomes the ideal king when the gods answer the prayers of the people by creating Enkidu to serve as Gilgamesh's friend and partner in adventure. Enkidu's heroic presence inspires the king to acts worthy of his semi-divine origin and extraordinary powers — and also to acts exceeding them while showing their limits.

Gilgamesh must engage a series of tests on his way to the boon that his duty and fate urge him to seek. First, the two fast friends engage in battle with the guardian of the vast Cedar Wood, Humbaba the giant. By defeating the giant they not only gain unlimited access to the resources of the forest, but more importantly they defeat the paralyzing fear that prostrates anyone who would dare enter the giant's domain.

Subsequently they destroy the "Bull of Heaven," sent by the goddess Ishtar as a plague upon humans because Gilgamesh refuses to accept her as a lover and Enkidu taunts her for her failure. To punish the heroes for killing the bull and for their disrespect toward Ishtar, the gods infect Enkidu with a mortal illness, and Gilgamesh, grieving for his dead friend, seeks Utnapishtim, the Noah-like survivor of the great flood, to find the key to immortality. Along the way Gilgamesh meets Siduri, the divine wine-bearer, who prophesies Gilgamesh's failure in his quest, urging him instead to return home and enjoy his life, his family, his kingship: those things allotted him by life and fate. Gilgamesh, angered at the suggestion of his limitations, presses toward his goal across the waters of death with the help of the divinely appointed ferryman, Urshanabi, until he finds whom — but not *what*— he seeks. Untnapishtim requires that Gilgamesh merely remain awake for six days and seven nights, but Gilgamesh immediately falls asleep. Seeking redemption for his failure, Gilgamesh asks for a second opportunity, and Utnapishtim describes a flower that Gilgamesh may find beneath the waters, a flower which, when tasted, grants renewed youth. Gilgamesh finds the flower, but before he can return home, a serpent rises from the waters, consumes the flower, sheds its skin, and disappears back into the deep. The hero-king returns with this boon only: he writes down his story for all to read in ages to come, so that we may accept our own mortality and seek our own happiness within the limits of our talents and our fate. The best we can do in this life is to live well, care for our families and our peoples, and enjoy our particular lot of happiness: that is, fulfill our duties to ourselves and those close to us.

We must wait as much as two millennia to pick up the track where *Gilgamesh* leaves it. In the *Iliad*, as the epigraph above shows, Achilles fails his fellow pan–Hellenes by his inability to understand his place in the social structure and do his duty as the greatest of the Achaian soldiers. By casting himself, because of his greater martial prowess, as the social superior of his commander, Agamemnon, Achilles takes offense at the king's commandeering of his "prize," the lovely slave girl Briseis. Achilles takes offense not so much at the loss of the girl as at his commander's daring to demand repayment for his own sacrifice from his greatest warrior. In fact, while Achilles mopes in his tent, refusing to fight because of Agamemnon's slight, he fails in his duty not only to the king, and not even particularly to the king, but especially to all the other soldiers, leaders, and kings who because of their pact to protect Menelaos and Helen have gath-

2. The "Duty" Theme in the Epic Tradition

ered before Troy to raze the city and return the legendary beauty to her mate. Achilles fights, unlike the others, for fame and glory rather than to honor a pledge, but once he accepts the war as his own, his duty to his comrades and to his fate must overcome any petty insults. Finally, only his sense of duty to avenge his friend, Patroklos, killed and stripped of his armor by the Trojan hero Hektor, draws him back to battle to meet and defeat his opposite as fate and the gods command, and only his sense of duty to his father allows the white hair of the begging Priam to move Achilles to return Hektor's body to his parents for burial, as custom and the gods demand.

The *Odyssey* continues Homer's notion of heroic duty, extending the duty of the soldier to the duty of the veteran: Odysseus, having done his part as hero, must simply *get home*, a task complicated by the ill-will of gods offended by the razing of Troy and the lovesickness of sorceresses enticed and enticing.[4] The *Odyssey* begins:

> Tell me, Muse, of the man of many ways, who was driven
> far journeys, after he had sacked Troy's sacred citadel.
> Many were they whose cities he saw, whose minds he learned of,
> many the pains he suffered in his spirit on the wide sea,
> struggling for his own life and the homecoming of his companions
>   [lines 1–5][5]

Odysseus' success as post-war hero defines recovery from what we now call post-traumatic stress syndrome: the violence with which he kills the suitors who seek his wife's hand and his kingdom show the focused brutality of which the battle-hardened veteran remains capable, but also reopens the door to his old life on a peaceful if obscure Ithaka. Odysseus teaches us that with persistence and resourcefulness matching Penelope's patience and Telemachos' devotion to his belief in his father's return, the soldier may recapture his place in the world — the only duty that makes sense after twenty years of conflict and adventure. Finally he may temper violence with reconciliation and return from martial duty to familial duty and love — Homer shows us that we must never forget the danger such soldiers undergo and the price they and we pay for their sacrifice.

Vergil's *Aeneid* picks up where the *Odyssey* left off, though Aeneas lacks some of Odysseus' spunk. "Pious Aeneas" (he doesn't challenge the gods as Odysseus does) must put *duty* first, duty to the gods and duty to his

Heroes, Gods and the Role of Epiphany

people, since, for the Roman, that duty is both what produces heroism and what constitutes it. Whatever love Aeneas has for pining Queen Dido of Carthage, whom he leaves suicidal with love-longing, or for his doomed friend Palinurus, drowned off the coast of Sicily, fate and the gods require that he put foremost his fate to found what will become Rome. The irony that at the end of the poem our sympathies may pass at least in part from Aeneas to Turnus doesn't change Vergil's focus on the primacy of legendary Roman duty. The poet clarifies that for the Roman, no personal preference stands in the way of his execution of pious responsibilities. Vergil's theme lies in Aeneas's epithet: fighting storms along the Libyan coast, pious Aeneas mourns the loss of his faithful Trojan colleagues (Book 1, lines 307 ff.), even having assured the survivors that, should they recall their courage, Jove will bring an apt end to their suffering (ll. 278 ff.). Meeting his disguised mother outside Carthage, he even politely introduces himself as "pious Aeneas" who, surviving Troy, seeks Italy, led by fate and his goddess mother (ll. 531 ff.).

Vergil's proto–Romans hearken back to the *Iliad* in terms of the narrative necessity of their devotion to duty, but Vergil makes the point explicit: in Aeneas's piety — to the gods, to his father, to his followers — we find the essential Roman virtue. Vergil doesn't imply that Aeneas should be kind or even merciful to enemies: in Book 10, as the Trojans' battle with the Latins rages, Aeneas bloodthirstily slaughters four youths at once, then pitilessly beheads another who quivers supplicatingly at his knees for mercy. Soon he taunts another, thrown from his chariot, before slitting his breast. Even when he expresses pity, he shows no more than Achilles; as he kills another foolhardy youth, Aeneas speaks to the dying boy:

> Poor boy, for such an act what can the pious
> Aeneas give to match so bright a nature?
> Keep as your own the arms that made you glad;
> and to the Shades and ashes of your parents
> I give you back — if Shades still care for that.
> But, luckless, you can be consoled by this:
> You fall beneath the hand of great Aeneas.[6]

Like Achilles, Aeneas can fight enemies such as Turnus with all necessary commitment, even brutality, but like the post–Hektor Achilles he can understand human frailty: he willingly leaves behind those followers

2. The "Duty" Theme in the Epic Tradition

unable to complete the task (yet does not feel obligated to strip them of honor) and will pardon and mingle with the wayward Latins. Like Odysseus he can sail the world, from burning Troy to Buthrotum, then to Sicily, where his father dies, to Carthage and Dido, whom he readily leaves when duty calls him, to Sicily again with its games and where the women, tired of traveling, attempt to burn the Trojan ships, and to Cumae, where the Sibyl leads him to the Underworld and Anchises unveils for him the future of Rome, then finally to Latium and the recruitment of King Evander (by which we see Aeneas as accepted among Italian peoples), and finally into battle with the Latins. The adventures provide the backdrop for the theme: Aeneas's pious commitment to the duty the gods require of him and to the empire that will derive from his legacy. Further, his piety to his father urges him to the adventure of the underworld, partly for his advice, but mainly simply to see the beloved parent again. He leaves Dido purely at Jove's bidding, clarifying for Dido that he *may not* act according to his own will. Having discovered that they have finally arrived in Italy, Aeneas leads his followers in ritual and a series of prayers to the gods, "each in order" (Book 7, line 178). Meeting King Latinus to try to establish a peace through single combat with Turnus, Aeneas prays to the gods and pledges his word that should he lose, the Trojans will leave and seek no vengeance, and should he win, the Trojans will not subjugate the Latins, but accept them on equal terms — a pledge that Jove later confirms for Juno so that the gods will allow the conflict to take its course and Aeneas to succeed, the reward for his piety and persistence.

Piety, too, defines the duty of the great Indian hero Arjuna whose troubles inhabit the enormous *Mahabharata* in its epic centerpiece, the *Bhagavad Gita*. W.J. Johnson points out that to Hindus the *Gita* represents both "the word of God" and the "values inherent in Hindu culture"; it displays "the poetical history of mankind."[7] The *Gita* bears in its heroic theme a nearly exact parallel to Vergil's *Aeneid*. To Arjuna, the warrior-hero of the *Gita*, Krishna's revelations in the *Gita* define epic heroism because they specify his *duty* and urge him to focus on its performance rather than its results — duty, not its ends, emerges as theme. Beyond the *Gita*'s local context and social implications, the poem clarifies that for any human being to accept adult responsibility in daily life and yet retain spirituality defines both his place and his duty.

Heroes, Gods and the Role of Epiphany

Perhaps the greatest jewel in the crown of the larger epic it condenses, the *Gita* specifies issues at once social and spiritual, expressing the fullest possible epiphany, one that grants both a vision of God and a clear answer to pressing questions of duty: that is, the experience has both "theoretical" and "practical" implications, theological and "profane" applications. The composition of the epic as a whole nearly spans the time from Homer to Vergil. It recognizes (and re-cognizes) problems of class, family, individual achievement, how we locate truth and how we act on it[8]; it locates individual spiritual experience in the present while showing that spirituality incarnates as physicality in the observed world. A directive for peace springs amidst an appreciation of the glories of the warrior class; the soldier himself faces the conundrum.[9] The world of the text, like the human world, cannot separate questions of philosophy from those of quotidian life. Arjuna establishes the possibility of joining both duties, rather than fighting them, within the individual human being. Learning of the immortality of the soul, the insignificance of individual human worries, and the value of duty as part of the natural order, he ultimately takes up his rightful position at arms — and Arjuna acquires that lesson between the lines as the two massed armies prepare for battle. There Arjuna's charioteer, Krishna, reveals himself as an incarnation of Brahman and stills the hero's doubts. Whereas Arjuna, seeing family on both sides, shrinks from killing, Krishna confirms Arjuna's place in the cosmos. Following the events of the *Gita*, the Pandavas, led by Arjuna, win control of India from their cousins, but they too hold power only for a time, illustrating Krishna's point to Arjuna, that each of us participates but briefly, however seemingly significantly, in the dance of history that unfolds regardless of our individual wishes or troubles. All we have, all upon which we can depend, derives from our devotion to our own particular position, our own particular duty, according to how we choose to use our talents and how well or ill we choose to live. Krishna's revelation to Arjuna develops through the philosophical discussion that leads Arjuna to realize the epic theme of duty in renunciation: by engaging in our duty, but renouncing fixation upon any particular result, we accept our place in the dance of the universe, limit the amount of suffering we cause, and most readily find our true nature.

As Franklin Edgerton points out, "The *Gita* attempts no concrete definition of duty, but contents itself with saying that man should do his

2. The "Duty" Theme in the Epic Tradition

duty simply because it *is* his duty, and with perfect indifference to the results"[10]: that idea constitutes the doctrine of renunciation. And the *Gita* can counsel no particular duty, because Krishna's mode of action urges the individual to find his own *yoga*, the "disciplined activity" that in the *Gita* takes precedence over the quiet life of solitary, ascetic meditation.[11] That theme envelopes the *Gita* and connects it to the long, continuing line of epic tradition. The *Gita* appeared at a time of social and religious "tensions, the most significant being between those ... who enjoined the fulfilment of one's prescribed social and religious duties as a member of the class into which one had been born, and those who advocated renouncing that ascribed status altogether in favour of a life of homelessness and spiritual discipline."[12] The difficulty in resolving those two patterns probably generated the *Gita*'s particular epic question.

From Aeneas and Arjuna we move another millennium to that first great Germanic vernacular primary epic, *Beowulf*. Similar to Homer's Greek heroes and Vergil's Roman ideal, Beowulf, despite his appearance in Scandinavian rather than Anglo-Saxon domains, defines the Anglo-Saxon sense of duty: Old English literature does take its origin largely from the *Anglii*, the Danes settling in Britain from the region of Schleswig-Holstein. Regardless of our displacement to the Germanic world, *Beowulf* returns to an immediately post–Homeric and post–Vergilian concern: how one achieves and maintains heroism and how heroism defines duty. Beowulf, nominally the best of heroes and kings, must meet his mortality, and the Geats must live without him to meet theirs: they have duties of their own. Beowulf fights Grendel's mother to establish himself as a hero worthy of confidence, worthy to be invested with duties. Duty remains incumbent upon him to fight Grendel's mother and again, so many years later, to fight the dragon for the sake of self-defense as well as revenge. Beowulf's sense of duty draws him to Grendel: he wins youthful strength and daring support his commitment to duty. Grendel's mother proves a more formidable foe, buoyed by her own sense of duty to her son. Beowulf again gains victory by presence of mind with the assistance of fate and luck. The magic sword does not appear because Beowulf has courage, but he can find it and use it because courage, luck and duty converge, allowing the possibility (if improbability) of success. "Fate oft preserves the undoomed one, if his courage holds," Beowulf observes laconically. In the fight with the dragon that ends both the hero's life and the epic, Beowulf attacks alone not only because his followers, except for the faithful and courageous Wiglaf, fail in their explicit duty to support him, but also because he understands — and himself explains — that his duty requires him to do so: who else could? One may argue that Beowulf, by insisting on fighting the dragon himself, fails as a king, for his people will in his absence be overrun by invaders and lost to history; however, if Beowulf, the only hero able to do so, fails to fight the dragon, his people will not have the chance to muster their own courage against invaders, as they will not survive the dragon's wrath.

Beowulf certainly fights for honor and glory, praise and fame, but he fights more importantly out of duty. The dragon represents an immediate, deadly threat that he must quell, Grendel a debt that he owes the Danish king Hrothgar, and Grendel's mother the lawful *weregild* for the murder of Hrothgar's counselor Æscere. Beowulf fights not for bloodlust, but because nature has made him the best of warriors and circumstances have evolved to require duties that only his talents may achieve.

Adjacent to *Beowulf*, our explication of epic duty moves to the great Persian epic, the *Shah-Nameh*, or "Book of Kings," essentially contemporary with *Beowulf*, but much longer, perhaps in fact the longest of national epics. Of particular interest here, the fascinating, moving, and exemplary case of Prince Seyavash — an episode of the 50,000-line *Shah-Nameh* that itself runs to more than 2,500 lines, more than three-quarters the length of all *Beowulf*— explores the necessity, however difficult to maintain, of loyalty to one's king and duty to one's office alongside the primacy of ethical action. Davis identifies the "urgently ethical cast" of the poem, but notes that the "true battle" of this heroic poem, the one "waged between good and evil," occurs "in the souls of the heroes": moral heroism overrides physical heroism and represents one's primary duty and the essence of the particular ethnic character that the poem aims to inculcate (xii–xiii). The heroic "values" of the poem, "fierce loyalty to tribe and king, bravery, military prowess and the ability to trick the enemy" mirror those of Odysseus, but also urge resolution: one king asks his advisor to name the most desperate of men, and the advisor replies, "A good man whose king is a fool" (Davis x–xi). While the "poem's depiction of authority is profoundly ambiguous" (Davis xv), its requirement of virtue remains steadfast; Seyavash, son and prince of a bad king, Kavus, faces two tests: the first, sexual temptation, he passes, but the second, when his king requires him to commit the immoral execution of hostages, he fails in a historical if not moral sense.

First, Seyavash's stepmother attempts unsuccessfully to seduce him; to prove himself innocent, he passes comfortably through a wall of fire. Later, having lead the defeat of invading Turanian armies, he attempts to broker a peace his father will not fully accept, at which point he turns for help to the king of the defeated invaders. However, the Turanian king's brother betrays him and has him executed. The reader gains the consolation that Seyavash's son by the Turanian princess grows to avenge his compassionate father, but also from the fact that while ethical thought and action may not preserve one's life, adherence to moral duty lives on as heroism far greater and far more lasting than the exploits of battle or the petty demands of temporal kings: duty defines the hero's life and memory in the "Legend of Seyavash."

And beyond *Shah-Nameh*? Dante must learn that his primary duty lies not with Beatrice, but with God — and he does. The Romance Epics of the Middle Ages deal with the duties of chivalry (and thus to code, king, and beloved), but at the zenith of medieval quests, the Holy Grail story, duty turns once again to God. Edmund Spenser in the *Faerie Queene* defines the virtues — which one may see as the duties — of a Christian gentleman. John Milton in *Paradise Lost* simplifies the duty of fallen humanity: obey God. After Milton we fall upon the resources of a changed, "modern" world, but the power of the notion of duty remains with us even as we move into our own age, which may ultimately define itself by our unwillingness to accept responsibility for anything and our unavailability for duty that any culture may request of us: we have become first and foremost *individuals*, with all the ameliorative and pejorative implications of the term. However, even as individuals we remain "joiners," and joining implies responsibilities: we are born into families, communities, countries; we choose to become members of colleges, companies, clubs. The last century has certainly seen the evil that arises from conscienceless devotion to duties heartlessly imposed by selfish powers. But as members of more compassionate societies, perhaps we may yet find something of value in the historical devotion of brothers and sisters of religious orders, in the loyalty of Samurai, in the commitment of epic heroes; they model for us an understanding of duty that can balance praise and fame with belonging, complete individual accomplishment with a sense of belonging and continuity.

Blake exhibits a strong sense of duty to fulfill the talents and motivations God gave him to create. Wordsworth reports a devotion to nature little short of worship. Barrett Browning felt the tug of duty perhaps most of all: the need to create a space for women writers, an opportunity for creative freedom driven not out of Blake's bardic internality, but as direct evidence of ability and accomplishment in response to the Victorian "woman question." Walcott's drive again seems inward, though in response to the evils of colonialism, a living ghost that Caribbean and world culture alike had to face. Paradoxically, epic duty may actually free us for the ultimate achievement of self that our cultures allow, the heroic epiphany that creates an eternal present of fulfillment for both the individual and the culture.

Chapter 3

Epic Individualism

Gilgamesh, at the beginning of the epic, presents a problem for his people: though a sturdy, heroic warrior king, he insists on his right to deflower virgins before their marriage, and he leads the young men off to war unnecessarily. Because of his superhuman energies, he upsets the course of life for his subjects, who pray to the gods for a solution. The solution comes in the form of Enkidu, the gods' gift both to the people and to Gilgamesh. He becomes the king's friend, and in fact almost a personal as well as a narrative double, one who challenges him to new feats of heroic strength and accompanies him on adventures that stop him from bothering the folk who need him, but would prefer to keep him at a safer distance. Together Gilgamesh and Enkidu pursue adventures until Enkidu dies; Gilgamesh, broken-hearted and fully aware of his own mortality, travels to a distant land to learn if humans, bound by mortality, may find a way to live forever. He does so partly out of grief, but probably mostly for personal gain, to free himself of his own fear of death.

Achilles joins the Achaian princes in their war on Troy by choice — not because he vowed with the others to protect Helen and her successful suitor, but because he preferred heroic achievement and lasting fame to a long and pleasant but quiet life. When Agamemnon offends him, he retires to his tent to sulk and returns to battle only when his friend, Patroklos, dies on the battlefield at the hands of Hektor of Troy.[1] Having avenged his friend and killed Hektor, Achilles eventually releases the body (having disrespectfully dragged it around the battlefield) for proper funeral rites, but only after Priam has crept behind enemy lines to beg the killer of his son for mercy. In an instant Achilles experiences compassion, and he does give up the body, but only because Priam reminds Achilles of his own father: the hero can imagine his own old father weeping for *his* death at the hands of an enemy, and so recognizes Priam's suffering. Achilles weeps as much for his own father as for Priam, and he knows his own days will last but briefly.

Odysseus, by stratagem — one may also say trickery — brings about the end of Troy, but then he must get home. Not only his fellows' impiety, but also his own egotism make that path long and tortuous. When he gets home, he cleanses his house of Penelope's abusive but understandably persistent suitors by killing them all. The heroic goal of the *Odyssey*, to get home, with plenty of exciting adventures on the way, entails a sense of duty to family, to his chief goddess, Athena, and a connection to place. But more than anything else it derives from Odysseus' individuality as a person and his drive to find, make, affirm his place in the world. "Patient Penelope" waits chastely while Odysseus disports with goddesses: his duty allows more freedom than hers, and he enjoys it fully while never forgetting the purpose of his quest. The presence of Athena as Odysseus' divine patron connects wisdom to individualism: whether we describe the hero as crafty or resourceful, the fact that he stands out as an individual among his fellows determines his success.

Arjuna troubles over the matter of choice because his duty, his role as a soldier, defines him. The *Bhagavad Gita* teaches we must not shy away from our nature, but fulfill it. What must the hero do in time of war, since killing is wrong but a soldier's duty requires it of him? He must do that duty, but he may choose to do it only in the right place and at the right time and with lightness of heart, knowing that the course of the universe doesn't depend on his choices: duty still provides freedom to feel, to explore the nature of right and wrong (if they exist at all), and to learn what truths humans can. Arjuna not as soldier but as individual asks the "great question" and receives the great answer: he learns about the place of humans in the cosmos, and he experiences, as far as he can, the truth and expansiveness of Krishna's nature and power — only one acting as an

3. Epic Individualism

individual could ask such a question and have such an experience, and few but heroes could endure its grandeur and magnitude. The characters of Greek and Roman myth (or Hebrew, too, for that matter) seldom survive such encounters, which are tolerable for only the greatest spiritually as well as physically fit heroes. In general the Romans had more trouble with striving individuals than had the Greeks: Statius' Eteocles and Polyneices destroy a great city through their struggles for supremacy, and Ovid's characters repeatedly drive themselves to metamorphoses by pushing their desires to excess.

Paralleling the duty theme in epic poems we find the omnipresent problem of individual character and desire for personal gain: even while epic preaches devotion to duty, it paradoxically places increasingly powerful stress on the importance of self-assertion. All the epics have it: the heroes always want something, sometimes many things, and though a sense of piety often motivates or directs (and occasionally restrains) them, and they spend a great deal of energy — their own and others' — to gain what sets them apart as individuals among the consistent traits and patterns of the people of their cultures. The heroes create a dynamic between personal achievement and cultural duty: they must achieve personally, as representatives of their cultures though often servants of their own interests, to maintain the motivation to reach the goal, the courage to find the place of epiphany, the will to complete the task and return with the boon.[2]

Epics don't typically deal with what pop-psychology has called self-actualization. They stress not what separates the heroes from their contemporaries, but what connects them. While the heroes seek (and often accomplish) feats beyond those of their contemporaries, the feats represent something everyone wants or needs, but that not everyone has the wherewithal to accomplish. They require some degree of self-assertion — usually accompanied by difficulty, danger, confusion, and sorrow — but in the end, the boon applies to those others whom the hero represents at the boundary. Achilles would appear to have concern only for himself, for his pride and place, and perhaps for his most loyal friends (or even *friend*, singular: Patroklos). But he both represents and embodies qualities his author's society saw as essentially, even pre-eminently, Greek: he has strength, speed, tenacity, beauty, ability, all traits suitable to one of semi-divine origin, all traits the Greeks desired for themselves, sought in their endeavors, and depicted in their art as ideals. Achilles embodies $αρετε$, greatness, magnitude, devoted striving, the will for perfection in one's endeavor. The gods favor him, and in meeting and defeating Hektor of Troy, he surpasses all others of the warrior class of his time; in allowing Priam to conduct funeral rites for Hektor, he surpasses others in the gulf he must cross to learn compassion. But at least, if briefly, he crosses it.

Though we must term J.R.R. Tolkien's works novels rather than epics, his heroes intentionally parallel those of epic traditions, the author typically refiguring them to fit the needs of his time and his story. If, as Aristotle wrote, epic constitutes a more diffuse version of tragedy, the novel perhaps comprises a more emotionally diffuse version of epic, demanding not exclusively noble heroes, but merely a character or characters worth our interest and evocative of our sympathy. While Aragorn best fits the traditional notion of epic hero — Gandalf as a kind of minor deity fulfills more the role of guardian spirit, a gateway into the eternal, himself the presence of epiphany in the world for the other characters, rather than the actual of hero of the work — the true *protagonists* of *The Lord of the Rings*, Frodo and Sam, take the demands upon the twentieth-century person to the extreme. They wrestle with their world's biggest single problem: how to destroy the ring that will otherwise enslave all the world's creatures to Sauron. By means of the two hobbits Tolkien asks, how much can the "commoner" sacrifice to save his nation, his people, the world? How much can he endure, and can he allow himself to pass away? Can he keep his true self from disappearing into the horror of another's vindictive ego? Pursuing the necessary and ultimate good, tempted to submit to the greatest and ultimate evil, can the Hobbit, smaller, less warlike, but probably tougher than a human, complete his quest and survive? Burdened with the weight of the ring, Frodo at the last can't keep himself from turning into a smaller version of Sauron; fortunately for him Gollum can't either, and Gollum's ultimate demise prevents Frodo's. Frodo, having got himself to the brink of success, would have failed; returning to his old life becomes impossible, not so much because of the sufferings of the quest as from the knowledge of his insufficiency in the worst and greatest moment, the actual destruction of the ring. Faced with the completion of the task, he can't destroy the very device that for so long has plagued him.

Frodo, the ideal modern person — kind, loving, self-sacrificing,

3. Epic Individualism

unambitious, full of the joys of life, health, and youth — must bear an impossible burden. He carries it as well as anyone can, but for the modern world, that means not well enough. He serves the novel as common foot-soldier: what, Tolkien asks, would happen if we put that person in the position of holding the responsibility for saving the world? An American audience may ask, what would any other American have done in Harry Truman's place, faced with political pressure, the long sufferings of war, the bomb, his and his country's prejudices, the desire to save American lives and end history's most horrifying war, and limited knowledge of the full spectrum of consequences? Could any of us have had the courage, knowledge, wherewithal to have made better decisions than he did, faced with a war not of his own making and to the conclusion of which he came only by accident? No epic hero could have done better than Frodo does: exactly Tolkien's point. Low or high on the Great Chain of Being, all humans at some juncture, at the ultimate test, will fail. That Frodo gets to the Crack of Doom at all seems the unlikeliest of narrative events, but Tolkien needed him to get there, and we need him to get there, so that we may ask and answer questions of duty, individuality, and power. Even the most dutiful of heroes, those whose personalities most completely recede from their texts — such as Beowulf— still counterbalance the need for duty and responsibility with the naturally human desire to fulfill the ego.

Frodo better parallels another of Tolkien's favorite characters: Gawain of *Sir Gawain and the Green Knight*. He chooses to accept a quest out of a sense of duty, and he proceeds with the best possible heart. His quest bears the weight of mortality, and though not a specifically religious task, it resonates with spiritual purport. Gawain fails only the tiniest bit in courage, more significantly in faith; Frodo fails from something quite like the Christian notion of Original Sin: the constant presence of the ring and the increasing proximity to its creator (in a sense an "uncreator") drain his resistance to the ring's capability to inspire the desire to possess, control, and dominate. Falling to the ring, Frodo loses the individuality that defines him as a creature; when he wears the ring, duty departs as well, and enslavement ensues. An open bearer of the ring must devolve either to a slave of Sauron or his replacement. The presence of Gollum to save the day comes not from any sense of duty, but from other creatures' sense of

Heroes, Gods and the Role of Epiphany

the infinite value of individualism: not Bilbo, nor Gandalf, nor Faramir, nor Frodo will destroy him when they may choose otherwise. For good or ill, the individual must go to epiphany willingly to have success (the final ritual words preceding communion in many Protestant denominations often include, "Come not because you must, but because you will," or some close variation).

The greatest exception to this point, Vergil's Aeneas, does his best to subsume his ego in divine quest; he does so because Vergil designed him to embody that most Roman of virtues, *duty*, which, as we discussed in the previous chapter, the poet termed *piety*. Devotion to the gods, to family, to his appointed task gradually detract from the reader's ability to see Aeneas as Aeneas. The human sympathy we have for him as survivor of the destruction of Troy at the beginning of the poem declines when he leaves Dido and Carthage and again when he plunges his sword into Turnus to conclude the tale. We know he must behave as he does, choose as he does, but Aeneas becomes less the character and more the role. The sense of acts done by choice wanes, and while he becomes an admirable proto–Roman, he becomes a less living, breathing person, not a subject of tragic event, but an enactor of tragic consequences for others.

Aeneas exhibits individuality by choosing to subsume his desires to the will of the gods: he does what Milton's Satan cannot and what Adam can do only variably, but what Milton's epic teaches: the greatest freedom comes not in disobeying God, but in obeying willingly and lovingly. As an individual Aeneas falls in love with Dido, but as a proto–Roman he responds immediately to leave her behind to rejoin his appointed quest. Aeneas as character disappears from his epic as much as Beowulf does from his, though for different reasons. We learn from the texts little of their feelings and much of their sense of duty. But praise and fame, the desire for individual achievement, inspire Beowulf, while for Aeneas they have little importance: the fires of Troy have burnt any such motivations from him. And while both do respond to vengeance as motive, Beowulf's impetus comes from within rather than from any god or gods. Had Beowulf a wife, a hobby, a favorite color? Nothing in the epic tells us about his personality, and we learn only once of his feelings: after the dragon's attack, he has dark thoughts, and he wonders what he has done wrong to bring disaster upon his folk. But he rises *as an individual* to deal with the problem: the Anglo-Saxon ethos takes us to the great moment, epiphanal or not, as a lonely but brave soul facing mortality.

The same problem that makes Aeneas seem cold in Vergil often troubles readers of *Paradise Lost*, though more in its theme than in its creation of character: one finds, at least early in the poem, greater interest in and sympathy for the rebel than for the dutiful. Yet Adam's character (and Eve's as well: both serve as *PL*'s protagonists, if not its heroes) emerges more completely than does Aeneas's. Milton's Adam and Eve have far outgrown their originals in Genesis, and as C.S. Lewis argues in his *Preface to Paradise Lost*, they deserve greater audience interest than does Satan.[3] Satan, that pre–Romantic individualist, speaks of and thinks only of himself, and he acts only for himself, whereas Adam and Eve think of all sorts of things from God and their creation to cosmology, gardening, visitors, relationships, and of course sex — all of which are of no interest to Satan, who bears constantly in mind only his own wounded pride. When the possibility of epiphany presents itself to him in the form of the Stairway to Heaven, he knows he may climb it and return to God if he wishes. He refused to pay the price — his repentance — because he knows he will only rebel and fall again: he has chosen his own character and will not choose otherwise. Adam and Eve, once they have fallen, *will* choose otherwise: they will bow and humble themselves, accepting the choice Satan will not, so that they may retain what connection with God they may. In either case the quality of character, the ability to grow, to make better choices, to change, depends on individuality; the story of that choice, Adam or Eve's or Satan's, embodies a foundational myth that creates a pattern for a culture.

Long before he began *Paradise Lost*, Milton had thought to compose an Arthuriad, following Spenser. But he must have determined that he could do little there that Spenser hadn't done and that Spenser had so complicated notions of Christian virtue that a better task might involve simplifying the problem to the essential issue or issues that his own time needed to know or confront. The need for detailed accounts of Christian virtue, Milton must have thought, comes from Original Sin, and Original Sin, while it originates in pride, occurs as an act of disobedience: eating fruit from the forbidden tree. On that problem Milton focused his powers: how to narrate the magnitude of the human struggle with obedience in an epic format, at once showing his debt to the great epic masters of the past while also displaying the height of his own powers as "poet-prophet," the one who speaks out the necessary truth to his own time.

We have by the end of *Paradise Lost* a better sense of the individuality of Milton's persons than Vergil allows us of his, and for good reason, though both treat thematically variations on obedience. While Vergil deals with the relationship between humans and gods, he sought a secular point and a secular end: the virtues necessary to the efficient function and extension of the Roman Empire. Milton, while he had to accept and deal with the dangers of the Restoration of a king whose father's execution he had so strongly and publicly defended, aimed chiefly to point the way, as he saw it, to God's kingdom. Milton's idea of obedience as a subject meant supporting, to the best of his abilities and through Right Reason, what he saw as best for England, not for any specific leader or sect. He must have seen a parallel, but obviously not an equivalency, between himself and his Satan: Satan corrupts by false argument, leading people toward the thought of equaling, deposing, or replacing their "king." Milton sought through Right Reason (Classical reasoning ability supported by essential Christian doctrine and practice) to help both himself and his reader find a simpler way to understand and keep Christian faith. *Paradise Lost* not only *justifies* the ways of God to men; it also justifies or restores Milton's own understanding of obedience. "Henceforth I learn that to obey is best," Adam discovers, and of course he and Milton both mean "to obey God" and not necessarily any earthly interventions between oneself and God (Book 12, line 561).

That obedience comes about for Milton, as it has always done in essential Christian thought, through choice, that is, free will. Just as Adam and Eve fall by choice (and they must have the choice to fall, or they have no free will), so they accept God's judgment and make the choice to *justify* with Him: to pray, learn, and obey. The act of choosing exemplifies the essence of individuality: goodness comes through choosing good, not by standing idly by. Milton stresses this point with a painfully ironic oxymoron, when Satan, in the form of the serpent, momentarily disarmed by Eve's beauty, stands "Stupidly good" (Book 9, line 465). No more can we have stupid goodness than we can have darkness visible: goodness means facing the choice of good or evil, knowing the difference, and choosing the good. Satan not only opposes but fully defies goodness, though he has, as do all creatures in Milton's world, the opportunity to choose otherwise. As Milton's God explains, he made his creatures good but free, "Sufficient to have stood, though free to fall" (Book 3, line 99). Adam and Eve ultimately represent us pretty well: they fall where anyone would have fallen, they repent where few would have repented, and they learn enough to build a race that God considers worthy of saving with the death of his own Son.

Even Spenser's allegory allows for individuality, largely, as Milton perhaps learned from him as well as from the Bible, by personal choice. Allegory as a form would seem by its structure and purpose (a little story to represent a bigger story, characters who stand for other characters or even for inanimate principles) to resist individuality. Spenser, however, individualizes his knights partly by the discrete virtues they represent, but largely by the fact that they don't simply embody a virtue, but must learn it and others as they go, mostly through courageous and rational choices (though occasionally, too, through failures). In Book 1, for example, the Redcrosse Knight represents St. George the dragon-slayer and the individual on the lifelong quest to achieve holiness and to defeat the devil's terrifying wiles, but he gains a degree of individuality by choosing his quest, failing along the way (sometimes miserably), and eventually through instruction, encouragement, humility, and faith achieving his glorious end: the rescue of Una's parents in the slaying of the dragon. He errs where anyone may: in fearing his love untrue, in falling for another himself (and a duplicitous one, at that), in succumbing to pride and needing rescue. Having received instruction and epiphany on the Mount of Heavenly Contemplation, like Goethe's Faust he wishes to stay in the presence of that perfect moment; who can blame him? But his quest calls him away, and even afterward he must face two symbolic deaths before defeating the dragon on the third day of their battle. Most important, he does not even then win the peaceful enjoyment of his beloved, which he has earned: he must first fulfill his promise to the Faerie Queene, to return to her court to serve her as she will. The individual may choose the pleasurable solution at hand or may insist on living up to his responsibilities first. The key, as Milton learned, comes down to choice, and choice implies the primacy of individuality, since the individual must choose to accept and complete the duty.

Heroes, Gods and the Role of Epiphany

With the Romantics we have little trouble teasing out an almost defining sense of individuality. Blake's character Los affirms for himself that he must "Create his own system or be enslaved by another man's" (Jerusalem, plate 10, line 20). Still attracted to allegory, Blake represented in Los the fallen but still powerful state of the imagination. The Romantics responded to the clockwork rationality of the Enlightenment with a radical individualism that thrust forward budding ideas of human rights and solidified the tectonic shifts of Revolutions. Needing a nearly absolute sense of creative freedom, Blake created his own poetic universe, a shifting phantasmagoria of characters and ideas with few parallels in literary history— Tolkien may present the nearest comparison in the English tradition. Blake mediates between the allegory of the Middle Ages and Renaissance that precedes him and the often free-wheeling fictional universes of science fiction and fantasy that follow him. His work establishes a fulcrum point: before it the epic leans toward devotion to duty, while after it epic leans toward individual achievement and expression. Both ideas co-exist all along, after as well as before, but with Romantic epic, as in other genres and other media, self-fulfillment normally trumps social duty.[4]

Blake's world has a sense of duty: the part must not try to rule the whole, but must contribute its own talents to the health of the whole. The artist, however, must have creative freedom and freedom of life choices to explore and exhibit the gifts that come from God and that define the individual.[5]

In Wordsworth the issue of duty seldom arises; *The Prelude* deals specifically with the "growth of the poet's mind," implying an overriding significance of individual experience (especially in anyone interesting enough to have pursued creative endeavors). Oddly enough, the autobiographical epic, work essentially impossible for a writer of the ancient world, arises almost as soon as possible once the Romantic Age has turned primary attention to individual perception (no wonder Keats called Wordsworth's approach the "egotistical sublime"). Wordsworth follows the implications of Alexander Pope's assertion that "the proper study of mankind is man": to understand others we must first understand ourselves, and that understanding requires detailed examination of our own experiences. As "human in nature," Wordsworth beyond any other poet indulges in the act of sifting memory for every significant instance of how the epiphanal experience of the environment brought his poetic consciousness into being and nurtured his capacities to express it. Almost as soon as individualism gains control over duty in the epic, it rises to its zenith.

Aurora Leigh balances individualism with social duty while maintaining the need for self-assertion. Barrett Browning's heroine must assert herself, her talent, and her desire to create in a situation (both social and familial) that would stifle her own impulses beneath submission to elders, a strict code of conduct, and male relatives or lovers. Where poverty and social class could have worked together to limit Blake, obvious and nearly deadly sexism — from women as well as men — threatens to restrict Aurora's energies to helping the man who loves and claims her in his social schemes for helping the poor. While Barrett Browning and her Aurora may chiefly desire the opportunity for personal fulfillment in her poetry, they have a social goal as well: to free women to attempt whatever sort of work they choose, to show that neither poetry in general nor epic poetry in particular as fields of endeavor should devolve to men alone. Of course, the implications of that argument extend further: women should face no limitations beyond those men must also face, those imposed by the human condition rather than social expectations. Aurora acts, according to the constraints she faces, heroically, affirming herself even as her aunt discourages her from learning and from appreciating the Italian half of her heritage. She refuses the marriage proposal of her cousin, Romney, heir to the family estate, because in offering it he shows no love and no appreciation for her talents and her individuality. To Aurora he seems only to need a convenient wife to help with his chores and to support his plans — goals she doesn't disparage as such, but that don't apply to her as an independent person with her own mind. She doesn't know that even then he loves her and that she will grow to admit her love for him; at that point those eventualities don't matter. She has a personal duty to explore and expand her abilities and to create opportunities for other women: she walks point for what the Victorians called "The Woman Question," which she sees as a simple and obvious matter of human value regardless of gender.

As I've argued over the last two chapters, in epic poems protagonists represent their cultures, but Barrett Browning introduces a significant innovation: in *Aurora Leigh* the title character represents a particular group within her culture. Aurora stands not just for herself, but for women, particularly women who wish to develop their abilities but find them scorned by a male-dominated social structure. She pursues poetry because natural talents and inclinations lead her there, but her quest to become a poet launches her into the thick of social battles. Emerging from them stronger and better in her art, she supplies a boon: opportunity for others. But she achieves first singly, as an individual, in a strongly individualistic art form. Yet in saving Marian Earle (the girl who has been betrayed by Lady Waldemar and introduced into the company of an evil man who rapes, impregnates, and abandons her), making her a part of her family and providing her a means of living, Aurora stands up not just for women artists, but for women generally — again, a turn typical of epic but individualized by the poet to suit her time and its issues. Aurora gains fame, but she also gains love and magnanimity, expanding our sense of her not just as a poetic icon, but as a character. She has her flaws: even Aurora can't reach too far beyond her time; Marian lives with Aurora accepting her society's designation as fallen women, dedicated to bringing up her child to have a better life than she has had (her life, as a human being with opportunity for growth, pleasure, achievement, has ended, and she exists only as the "poor mother" happily befriended at last). But epic heroes do show, as part of their individuality, their limitations: Achilles remains petulant to the last, even in giving in to Priam's request; Aeneas coldly accepts the loss of Dido; Beowulf fails to leave his people a son to protect them in his stead; Adam and Eve — if we take them, rather than the Son, as the chief players in *Paradise Lost* — repent, but they repent because they have fallen.

In *Omeros*, the most individualistic of epics, Walcott undeniably connects his poem and its characters to the great tradition, but the postmodern polyphony of voices allows for a particularly broad and successful individuation of characters. The poetic voice, only one of the incarnations of Homer in the poem, seeks an identity for himself and for his birthplace, St. Lucia in the Caribbean, and his people that both links them to their heritage and frees them from it. While the poetic voice serves St. Lucia as its Homer, the narrator also meets Homer as a bust, as a disembodied head or voice, and in the old fisherman Seven Seas, who becomes in his age and experience a voice of wisdom and understanding. The poem addresses duty less than any other epic I know, yet many of the characters have a sense of it from their own point of view: the fishermen have

3. Epic Individualism

their task, Major Plunkett (feeling a duty to his wife and to his home) tries to write his history, and the narrator seeks to understand himself and his island. But the individual nature of those duties overshadows their public importance. Characters strive for or at what they value: that idea better than any other defines *Omeros* as postmodern, postcolonial epic; it takes the epic in the direction epic history needed to follow.

Aurora Leigh serves her society by freeing women to a creative avenue: women can and should write poetry, can and should write epic poetry if they feel moved to it, just as men should. *Omeros* creates characters both bound by their past and their culture and at the same time disengaged from it. The colonial/postcolonial person shares the epic traditions of the societies that populated the colonies, and he or she has the right to every bit of that tradition, should the motivation arise. The St. Lucians have a complex heritage: they suffer from the slavery in their past, but need to recover and understand the enslaved persons from whom they come; they feel both anger toward and reverence for the European traditions that have shaped their social institutions and interwoven themselves in their genetic material. The characters, all "castaways" in one sense or another, try to find their place, try to determine their identity, try to make sense of how they fit into the flow of life, culture, and history. Helen, aware and proud of her beauty, uses it to try to create a stable, secure relationship that will lead to a better life for herself and her children. Achille, the heroic fisherman, struggles against Hector for the love (or at least the temporary possession) of Helen, but he also has a deep need to connect with his African heritage, which he sees in a vision brought on by sunstroke. Plunkett, the Englishman with the Irish wife, loves St. Lucia enough to try to write at least a piece of its history, but he also seeks there his own familial connections: he finds among his ancestors a sailor who died young, someone he can think of as a "son," since he and his wife have no children. Even his wife, whom he neglects, though he loves her, to do his research, represents "colonial spoils": an Irish decoration for the Englishman.

The author's self-reflexivity reminds readers that we are following the stories of character, not persons, but that awareness doesn't spoil the characters: it intensives the individuation on the part of the author. For instance, Plunkett received a wound fighting in World War II: "This wound I have stitched into Plunkett's character./ He has to be wounded,

Heroes, Gods and the Role of Epiphany

affliction is one theme/ of this work."[6] Like Blake, Walcott praises, even places foremost, the act of making: "The worst crime is to leave a man's hads empty./ Men are born makers"[7]; the story has more to do with the narrator/author's working out his own sense of place than anything that "happens" in the narrative. The story takes place in the author's mind and in the narrator's words, and the voice sets sail with goals in mind: "he sends his narrator; he plays tricks with time because there are two journeys/ in every odyssey, one on the worried water,/ the other crouched and motionless.... For both the 'I' is a mast."[8] The author or narrator makes far clearer the themes or "intentions" of the story than the actual events themselves, which often fold into and out of dreams or reveries. Story had always guided epic; just as Aristotle places plot first among the hierarchy of elements that comprise tragedy (because it provided the biggest contribution to the cathartic effect), so plot has ruled epic, because it led the way to epiphany. For Walcott "thought" or idea trumps both plot and character, and language (Aristotle's fourth component of tragedy) nearly trumps thought because of the unflagging lyricism of the whole of the poem. Walcott therein asserts the originality and individuality of his own epic, even as he rejoices in its connections to Homer, Dante, Joyce, Milton, and any number of other epic voices. *Omeros* doesn't exactly equate with *Homeros*: the name implies an idea more than a man/poet. With an exclamation it locates the lives and struggles of the people of St. Lucia in and across the sea, and it remakes epic as their own — something upon which the great epic writers, despite their borrowings, have always insisted.

As with everything human, notions of individualism vary over time. Oddly enough, culture tells us how to be individuals, just as it tries to dictate our duties. Gilgamesh must learn to lead his people wisely and compassionately, and he must accept the limits of his own mortality. Achilles must win praise and fame; he must do heroic martial deeds beyond the abilities of his colleagues. Like Achilles, Beowulf comes from a heroic age: he too seeks praise and fame, but also to pay the debts of family and alliance, to know the tasks for which nature has made him and to attempt them unflinchingly. Aeneas must subsume his own desires to the task the gods have set for him; while maintaining the courage and tenacity of an Achilles or a Beowulf, he must show piety beyond the capacity of his fellows — only that far may we make claim to his individuality. He emerges

3. Epic Individualism

from the ashes of Troy and the maelstrom of searching because his mother, the goddess Venus, with the help and agreement of the other gods, helps him: a gift granted few humans. Spenser's heroes distinguish their otherwise allegorical selves by aiming for the perfection of a virtue, something to define and refine their character. Adam and Eve, given Paradise and sufficient instruction to know how to keep it, fail and fall, but they find within themselves the strength and humility to repent and to build together a new world flawed but redeemable. Blake sings for the glories of the individual imagination and the divine inspiration that sparks it. Wordsworth shows that Nature will inspire the heart that loves her, and he details how, through the course of a long life, She inspired him. Barrett Browning stood up for women's creative rights and wrote what her society said she couldn't; her poem, timely, lyrical, moving, now stands as one of the great monuments of the epic tradition. Walcott remakes a colonial tradition into a tour de force of person and of place; he re-colonizes a history with something essentially modern and postmodern, something Blakean and yet wholly real and local, a voice and a story both lyrically expressive and temporally definitive. The urgency of the epic impulse, foundational to a culture's imagination, inevitably incarnates as a heroic, individual act. Then tension between duty and individualism remains both motive for the hero and productive for literature.

In the next chapter we will move from the general history of epic and its themes to the English epic tradition as such. The "heroic world" of *Beowulf* takes us both back to Homer and forward with our epic concerns.

Chapter 4

Beowulf and Sub-liminal Epic Epiphany

All the great epic poems to some degree define or embody the essence of their culture. As the *Bhagavad Gita* incarnates both the values of Hindu culture and the essential questions of its time, and Homer's epics detail the Greek heroic ethos, and Dante's *Commedia* searches the heart of Florence on the brink of the Renaissance, *Beowulf* serves a similar function for the Anglo-Saxon world, both in its "Christian" and "pagan" aspects[1]: it explicitly enumerates proper behavior for hero, king, and thane, but it also implies that similar notions of propriety — and heroism — apply generally to human action.

As I've discussed in the earlier chapters, epic poets have always used *epiphanies* — traditionally, meetings with divine beings, crossings of significant liminal boundaries, or encounters with pure manifestations of essential aspects of nature — to provide their characters (and thus audiences) access to information or power necessary to their completing an essential task or to acquiring fundamental or crucial information. Epic poems offer, often in a monomythic Campbellian sense, that information as a boon: the epiphany unveils for the audience, usually in heroic trappings, its culture's wisdom — the audience learns what the gods want to tell them. *Beowulf* teaches us that we may make seek epiphany as a way to fame and

4. Beowulf and Sub-liminal Epic Epiphany

glory, but that course is accompanied by imminent mortality. Or, alternatively, epiphany may come to us: this unpredictable world presents just that sort of danger. Either way, the hero (and, by extension, the audience) must remain prepared for the encounter: that mental, emotional, and physical readiness represents the boon that stories such as *Beowulf* offer us. Much as in Spenser (as we shall see in the next chapter), where the individual knights represent either the quest for or the embodiment of each particular virtue, Beowulf as hero exemplifies the state of mind necessary for dealing with dangers of the world that may come only if we disrupt their existence or that may come simply of their own accord.

In *Beowulf* epiphanies involve no actual meetings with gods, as they do in Homer or Vergil — or *Gilgamesh* or *Mahabharata*, or even Dante or Milton — nor do they fall into the category of more esoteric manifestations of word or image that Joyce explores in *Portrait of the Artist as a Young Man* or *Ulysses*. The word *god* appears in *Beowulf*, used ambiguously by Hrothgar as well as the narrator with only the hint of the possibility of intervention, but scholars have argued at length for generations about the degree to which we may call the poem Christian or pagan. God or a god watches over the world, but that fact may not help the individual in a pinch. Fred Robinson draws the distinction between a Christian poet and pagan subject matter; Mary Parker has argued, as have I, that the poet interlaced Christian and pagan worlds comfortably.[2] The poem makes Old Testament allusions, and the physical details of Grendel's mere recall the vision of hell in *Visio Sancti Pauli*, as many scholars have noted. But the poet exploited neither the word *god* nor those allusions to introduce epiphanies, though they may inflect how we read the epiphanal passages.

Beowulf's epiphanies engage the tradition of a meeting with someone or something of a different order or existence — sometimes natural creatures, sometimes supernatural beings — with the unusual turn that those beings are exclusively monsters. Epiphanies in this epic occur with creatures that, though in many ways they have greater powers than humans, on the "Great Chain of Being" fall below us. The "rhetoric of epiphany" in *Beowulf* uses monster battles (which we may term sub-liminal epiphanies) full of suspense, adventure, and even horror to fix audience attention on the poem's themes: the need for steadfast courage, the glory of devotion to duty, immortality through *lof* and *dom*, praise or fame and glory. The poem's lack of insistence upon salvation intensifies those themes: one behaves well because duty and honor require it, not for any tangible gain. Spenser uses similar epiphanies — though paired with super-liminal epiphanies — in *The Faerie Queene* to inculcate ideas of Christian virtue; Milton uses biblical and apocryphal materials and allusions to reinforce the presence of divine instruction and the danger of demonic influence for Adam and Eve — and their children. But in *Beowulf* epiphanies equally (and in parallel) instruct Christian and non–Christian audiences: from the poet's point of view — and the culture's — both groups might derive benefit from the same themes. *Beowulf*'s monster-battle passages inculcate heroic attitudes and exemplify some of the essential concerns of Anglo-Saxon culture because either audience — and those on the fence between them — would see themselves as caught in a struggle with monsters for the survival of their world. Compare, for instance, Wulfstan's *Sermo Lupi ad Anglos*, one of the best and most historically important of the Anglo-Saxon homilies: the cleric exhorts his folk to defend themselves body and soul against Viking invaders who threaten the country because the people have neither the moral nor martial courage to defend themselves. If from Wulfstan's point of view we see the invaders as foreign monsters, the sermon makes emphatically the same point that *Beowulf* makes narratively: God doesn't solve all our worldly problems, which we must as a rule handle for ourselves with committed, courageous action. God may even make such demands of his Christian soldiers as self-sacrifice, in significant numbers, if we fail to show sufficient faith and virtue, Wulfstan asserts. The Christian soldier, he implies may, after many error of omission, bring piece only with a sword.

Beowulf as primary epic, whatever influence the poem may show from Vergil or homiletics, fits closer to Homer than it does to other epics before or after it: it takes place completely within a "heroic world." The hero does not rely on gods — they are untrustworthy in Homer and inaccessible in *Beowulf* — but on his own resources. Heroism and good governance alone may lead to praise, glory, and the immortality that story provides. No lesser behavior, the poet hints, deserves memorializing, and even the greatest heroic behavior may not keep one alive. The lack of epiphany stands, I think, as the chief problem some scholars have had in terming *Beowulf* an epic. Tolkien, for instance, calls it a heroic poem. It lacks the

4. Beowulf *and Sub-liminal Epic Epiphany*

invocation of Classical epic (the author's epiphany, whereby he or she requests and receives help from the appropriate, inspiring deity), it lacks the typical meeting with the divine messenger or counselor, and it doesn't take the hero to a temple or mountaintop, actual or symbolic, to receive a Grail — not to mention its relative brevity. But it has magnitude, the cultural gravity, the impulse to greatness, the essential theme — and its own sort of epiphanies.

Beowulf asks and answers a number of culturally central questions (about kinship and service, the goals of accomplishment, distinctions between Christian pride and a soldier's self-confidence), but, perhaps most importantly, *Beowulf* returns to a narratively more immediate post–Homeric and post–Vergilian concern with how the individual, having achieved heroism, maintains and enacts it — and what use he makes of it. Thereby *Beowulf* adds a refinement to the questions Homer and Vergil raised. The poet's answer crystallizes the epic's theme: we achieve significance (or salvation) and retain it only through steadfast courage and readiness to act in times of need. Given that lone, severe parameter, Beowulf must ultimately fail as king and hero, since he must finally, one way or another, die, leaving the people he has defended to defend themselves. In the first part of the poem he chooses to fight Grendel to gain *lof* and *dom*, praise and fame or glory; he may hardly refuse to fight Grendel's mother, having accepted the possibility of blood-feud by killing the son; in the final segment he must make certain that the dragon can no longer ravage Geatland. Against Grendel, Beowulf wins partly by strength, but mostly by superior courage and composure. In Grendel's Mother he finds a more courageous (or committed) adversary, but he maintains his own courage and prevails by keeping his wits and by the intrusion of fate or luck: finding the magic sword close at hand — though only the courageous could benefit from such luck. "Fate oft preserves the undoomed one, if his courage holds," Beowulf laconically observes, and that bit of gnomic wisdom typifies the thematic thrust of the poem's epiphanies. The course of the world may preserve us, but if our courage fails, it certainly won't. Later the dragon battles hinges on the hero's willingness to die in exchange for the opportunity to fell the enemy. Beowulf enters the battle knowing he will not survive it, yet among his folk he chooses (again, alone, though in this last adventure he gets help from one loyal thane) his place at the point of heroic epiphany. His choice comes up short of heroic fatalism: his efforts to stop the dragon, a figure of that represents greed and embodies remorseless, horrific destruction, resist chaos to the degree that the individual can, by example and to the extent of his power. Plus he wins a treasure, though, ironically, his folk refuse it and bury it with him. Epiphany may show us human or cultural limits — it need not *allow* liminal crossover, only unveil the limen and the magnitude of its potential.

The passages in which the battles occur show a good deal about how the Anglo-Saxons conceived heroic liminalities. The lines in which Grendel approaches Heorot unveil a mastery of suspense and horror:

> The truth is known,
> that mighty god rules always
> the race of men. In the dark night came
> striding a walker-in-shadows; the bowmen slept,
> those who were supposed to guard the horn-gabled hall,
> all except one....
> Then from the moor under the mist slopes
> came Grendel walking — he bore god's wrath.
> The evil-doer intended to ensnare one
> of the race of men in the high hall,
> came nearer under the skies until he most readily recognized
> the wine-hall, the gold hall of men....
> He came then to the hall, the warrior venturing,
> deprived of joys. The door, fast with fire-forged bands,
> at once gave way when he touched it with his hands.
> The ill-intended swung open the door of the hall,
> enraged [ll. 700–24].[3]

The tripling of the "then came" motif inches the audience toward the horror: "In the dark night came," "then from the moor came," "then to the door came." In an age before the Lancelot scene in *Monty Python and the Holy Grail*, where humor enters the picture, those lines create tension through pacing, repetition, and the suspension of the liminal breach that occurs when Grendel bursts into the hall and encounters the soldiers. "Then his heart laughed" (l. 730), says the poet, and Grendel, his eyes beaming a foul light, seizes a sleeping soldier, tears him, bites the joints, drinks the blood, swallows sinful bites — art short of contemporary horror film could hardly display a ghastlier series of cinematic frames. The sub-liminal epiphany appears suddenly and horribly of its own account,

4. Beowulf *and Sub-liminal Epic Epiphany*

and it occurs solely because the Danes dared to sing and enjoy themselves in the court they created as a meeting place, a stay against the chaos of the world.[4]

Once Grendel, having received his death-wound, has returned to his lair to die, his mother emerges to create the narrative's second epiphany, again sub-liminal:

> And his mother then yet,
> greedy and gallows-minded, wished to go
> on a sorrowful venture, to avenge her son's death.
>   She came to Heorot, where the ring–Danes
> slept throughout the hall. There was soon
> reversal of fortune for the men when
> Grendel's Mother entered....
> Then in the hall was the hard-blade drawn,
> swords over benches, and many broad shields
> raised.... One forgot his helmet
> and broad byrnie when the horror seized him.
> She was in haste, wished to go hence
> to save her life [ll. 1276–93].

The suspense in this passage falls short of that in Grendel's attack, and the poet explains why: her terror "was less/ even as much as is a maid's skill,/ that of a warrior-woman, to the weaponed-man's/ when the decorated sword ... shears through the boar upon the helmet opposite" (ll. 1282–87). Significantly here the passage moves much more quickly with less adornment than that of Grendel's attack: the she-beast comes for quick and dirty vengeance, not terror and feeding.

Later Beowulf breaches the liminal boundary into the monsters' mere, seeking his and the Danes' turn at vengeance:

> The surging lake received
> the battle-warrior. Then it was a time
> before he could descry the bottom.
> Soon she found out, who fiercely ravenous guarded
> the expanse of the flood for a hundred half-years,
> grim and greedy, that a certain man
> explored from above that home of alien-creatures.
> She grasped then toward him, seized the battle-warrior
> in horrible grips....
> When she came to the bottom, the sea-wolf
> then bore the prince of rings to her dwelling,

> so that he could not, no matter how brave he was,
> wield weapons.... Then the man perceived
> that he was in the enemy hall, he knew not what sort,
> where none of the water in any way harmed him,
> nor could it touch him, sudden rush of the flood,
> because of the roofed-hall. He saw fire-lights,
> gleaming flames, shining brightly [1494–1517].

Grendel's Mother actually totes the hero into her hall: having crossed the boundary into her territory, he hasn't the same freedom of action he had at Heorot. Epic epiphanies often impose restrictions to action, response, or even thought: seeing Achilles approach with Athena at his heels, Hektor, bravest of the Trojan warriors, turns and runs away. Aeneas, confronted with directions from Mercury to abandon his relationship with Dido and get to the business the gods have set for him, departs without a word of argument. Beowulf's confrontation with Grendel's Mother creates a distortion or disorientation that strains the hero's capacity for composure and forces him to rely more on wit than on the legendary strength of his hand-grip. The passage relies less on suspense and more on the creeping horror of one's being drawn out of one's own element into a slippery, slimy nest of water monsters and then into a den of human bones and who knows what monstrous acts. One feels claustrophobic disgust rather than the tingling terror of the hero who may stand on the verge of being eaten.

Beowulf's finding the magic sword even represents a kind of epiphany: it shines in the dark, a talisman first and a weapon second, a crossover artifact between the realm of the practical smith and that of the god-inspired smith. Only by means of that crossover does Beowulf acquire the instrument with which he may defeat the she-beast. *Wyrd*— fate, luck, the course of things, karma — preserves him because his courage holds; in a poem devoid of divine intervention, the material epiphany of the sword allows the hero to survive the sub-liminal epiphany with the monster.

In the final episode of the poem, the dragon's appearance, because of its overwhelming array of weapons, evokes another complex of emotions. The monster may attack from earth or air, and it may torch or crush or tear its victim to bits; as Tolkien argues, it represents the perfect final epiphany for Beowulf, though again a sub-liminal one.[5] The dragon

4. Beowulf *and Sub-liminal Epic Epiphany*

episode begins slowly, stealthily, as the thief breaches the boundary into the dragon's lair:

> he who in his high house watched a hoard,
> in a steep stone-barrow. A path lay beneath,
> unknown to men. There into the inside he went,
> I know not which man ... seized
> from the heathen hoard in hand...
> a shining treasure.... When the folk-burner
> discovered that, then he was enraged [ll. 2212–20].

Of course, the theft wakes the dragon, who wakes to assert a scorched-earth policy:

> Then the worm awoke — strife was renewed.
> It stalked then along the stone; the stout-hearted one
> found its enemy's footprint....
> [T]he hoard-guardian searched, wished to find the man,
> the one who had dealt foully with him in his sleep.
> Hot and fierce in mind he moved about the mound....
> But he rejoiced in war,
> in the work of battle.... The hoard-guardian
> waited impatiently until evening came;
> then the barrow-keeper was swollen with rage,
> wished to requite the enemy with fire
> for the dear drinking cup [ll. 2287–2306].

The dragon flies off, descends upon Geatish houses, and burns them to cinders: an epiphany devoutly to be feared in *Beowulf*'s world, because it comes from a source both unreachable by negotiation and barely subject to revenge by human powers.

The hero again initiates epiphany with the monster, arming himself and gathering a supporting troop, knowing he will die in the battle. After suitable speeches he strides out under the stone-cliff of the barrow, finds steam issuing from under the stone arch, and shouts a war cry to call out his adversary:

> Hate was roused; the hoard-guardian heard
> the man's voice. Nor was there a greater time
> to ask for peace. First came
> out from the stone the breath of the beast,
> hot battle-sweat; the ground resounded.
> The man under the barrow, lord of the Geats,
> swung his shield toward the terror-guest [ll. 2554–60].

Heroes, Gods and the Role of Epiphany

Of course, the "meeting of the two beings of different orders" occurs gruesomely and explicitly when the dragon clasps its teeth around Beowulf's neck, inflicting the wound by which the hero is poisoned and through which he will bleed to death. Together Beowulf and Wiglaf deliver the blows that destroy the dragon; literally they put his lights out, when after Wiglaf strikes and the "fire begins to abate," Beowulf slits him down the middle with his knife.

This last epiphany occurs beneath a cloud of grim resignation present but not so unrelenting in the earlier monster battles. Before fighting Grendel Beowulf jokes that if he loses, no one will need to perform funeral rights: the monster will consume him. Even the Grendel's mother adventure offers a touch of levity, whether the she-beast actually or only in the poet's pun sits on her adversary. No joke leavens the final battle, one that for characters and readers alike bears apocalyptic significance: the end must come, and if monsters can't bring it, we humans will inflict it upon ourselves — both Wiglaf and the Geatish messenger predict devastating invasion by foreign enemies. This final epiphany bears once again the persistent ameliorative theme of steadfast courage, but it shows that not even such a laudable quality can indefinitely postpone the great epiphany that climaxes life for everyone: death. There Christian and pagan audience alike may meet to drink to the memory of the hero, lament our limitation, and, as with all the great epics, praise the art that calls us to our liminal boundaries.

The monsters, for all their supernatural qualities, yet bear in Beowulf's world peri-natural status: they may suffer mortality if one knows how to kill them, and they arise as a part of nature, if one different from *common* nature. They exist, in part, because of human "sinfulness": the poet describes the Grendel-kin as "children of Cain," and according to Germanic folk (and literary) tradition a human may morph into a dragon as a result of a life of gross greed and violence (though the poem does not specify this particular dragon's origin).[6] Christian readers almost inevitably find in the dragon an allusion to Satan, common in the exegesis of the Apocalypse of St. John (or Revelation), medieval story, and manuscript illumination. Such a reading hints at the more common type of epiphany, though it remains sub-liminal. Readers familiar with the Old Norse materials will see an equally salient allusion in Beowulf's dragon battle to Thor

4. Beowulf and Sub-liminal Epic Epiphany

and Ragnarök, the battle that ends the current world in the Germanic cosmology.[7] But we need not read it that way, and the text gives us no super-liminal epiphany to balance it, either because a Christian poet must commit the pre–Christian Beowulf to the damned or because such a figure, symbolically redemptive to either Christians or non–Christians, noble in motivation to both, and exclusive of neither elicited a more positive response from audiences who wished to adopt him as their own.

The "rhetoric of epiphany" in *Beowulf* uses monster battles (*sub-liminal* epiphanies) full of suspense, adventure, and even horror to fix audience attention on the poem's themes: steadfast courage, composure in the face of one's own demise, devotion to duty, immortality through *lof* and *dom*—all that an individual may achieve in the Anglo-Saxon world. Spenser uses similar instances, though he pairs them with super-liminal epiphanies in *The Faerie Queene* to inculcate ideas of Christian virtue and to support Christian belief in the betterment of the soul. In *Beowulf* the hero's virtues may apply equally to Christian and non–Christian audiences, but their exhibition brings—at least as far as the poem tells us—only earthly fame, not spiritual immortality. As *Beowulf*'s monster-battle passages express those themes and show how they exemplify some of the essential concerns of Anglo-Saxon culture, so Spenser's concentration on stories to shape the moral life of a Christian gentleman—and the strategies by which one presents them—denotes a centerpiece of Renaissance thought: virtue as both physical and spiritual achievement.

Homeric epiphanies don't always help those who experience them: Achilles benefits from Athena's presence, but the goddess fools Hektor into confronting, one-on-one, an enemy too great for him alone, despite his own heroic qualities; Beowulf gains praise and fame for his exploits, the hope of the pagan warrior, but, as far as we know, not salvation, the hope of the Christian soldier. Vergilian epiphanies, too, depend on the gods' disposition toward the human in their presence: Turnus has no hope against Aeneas, driven by the gods to create the alliance that will one day emerge as an empire. The Anglo-Saxon Genesis, hardly an exact translation of its biblical source, brings humans into contact with both God and devils; they fail not because pride causes them to desire to emulate or become God, but because they trust their reasoning more than God's warning and fail to recognize the infernal messenger as a demon rather than an angel. Ever since *Gilgamesh* epiphany has presented problems as well as glories: spurned as a lover by the mortal Gilgamesh, Ishtar insists on vengeance. Arjuna has a brief vision of Krishna, but he will die before the culmination of the adventures of the Pandavas in the *Mahabharata*. *Beowulf* suggests that in this troubled world we must accept the far greater likelihood of deadly sub-liminal epiphanies rather than heavenly illuminations. In modern parlance we must find our mojo: there lies the basis of the other virtues that offer only brief, if admirable, and thoroughly earthly eminence.

In the next chapter I'll show how Spenser, fixing his sights on instruction in the complex nature of virtue, expands the potential for epiphanies to develop the wide array of qualities he found essential to the development of the Christian gentleman. In the magical world of epic Romance, as in the Romances generally, epiphany can happen nearly anywhere and any time: one need only find, by purpose or accident, the liminalities, both sub-liminal and super-liminal, that exist all around us.

Chapter 5

Epiphany and the Rhetoric of (Dis)Enchantment in Spenser's *Faerie Queene*

Scholars as well as poets and church officials have taken great interest in the history and use of magic. Lovers may call the power the beloved has over them *magic*. Readers still use the terms *magic* or *incantation* to describe the elusive mystical quality of even secular poetry or the power that poetry has over them. Poets, particularly in Romance or Romance epic, often project, either as part of the fiction or as a result of belief in the vatic property of poetry, a kind of magical power for their verse by conjuring up the dark side of the imagination or sexuality or forbidden pleasures or by reference to ancient religious practices. One would perhaps expect to find "magic" in dark Romantic poems (perhaps *Manfred* or "Kubla Khan" or "Lamia"), or in Marlowe's *Doctor Faustus*, or in Shakespeare's particularly otherworldly passages, such as Hamlet's "churchyard" speech ("'Tis now the very witching time of night") or Lear's speech as he carries the dead Cordelia on stage ("Howl, howl, howl! O, you are men of stones"), my own particular midnight favorites. An infusion of *poetic* magic, difficult enough to describe, let alone define, draws readers to poetry even more powerfully than do intellectuality and sensuality. In this chapter I hope to develop at least a partial "rhetoric of incantation" to help identify and illuminate techniques that contribute to the method of storytelling that Edmund Spenser used in the *Faerie Queene*. To create the majority of his epiphanies (in Spenser's case meetings between beings of different orders of existence as well as movements across boundaries that connect characters to other realms either superior or inferior to their own), Spenser calls upon traditions of magic that draw from both Classical sources and medieval Romance.[1] Indeed, epiphanies, both super-liminal and sub-liminal, occur with astonishing regularity in the *Faerie Queene*: one could write an entire book on them alone. Here I will select some representative examples to show how Spenser uses epiphany to address the most important epic question of his age: how in such a complicated world, so full of deceit, dangerous powers, and evil, does one find a way to live a virtuous, Christian life? Spenser shows that magic has power, but virtue has more: an essential message for anyone whose work grew out of the shadowy adventures of medieval Romance and Romance epic.[2] One may seek epiphanies or fall upon them, and they may present grave danger or illumination. A complex understanding of the virtuous life (and the ability to put that understanding into practice) determines whether or not one will pass the tests that both evil and epiphany present.

Spenser answers his great question, the next in our epic line of vision, how to live and grow in the Christian world, by laying out a baroque colloquy among knights and allegorical beings of all sorts. As Spenser explains in the letter to Sir Walter Raleigh that precedes the *Faerie Queene*, each knight either embodies or acquires though a series of adventures a particular virtue. Those virtues, fostered by the Faerie Queene, a figure representing Queen Elizabeth, all appear in Arthur, who has set out to seek the queen and who appears occasionally through the various books, helping knights in need as all pursue their quests, and who represents magnificence, the sum of the virtues that together describe the perfect knight. Unshrinkingly didactic, the book clearly expresses the views of Spenser's England on religion, politics, and behavior, but it exhibits an allegory much more complicated than, say, the late fifteenth-century play *Everyman*. Because Spenser died with *The Faerie Queene* well short of his goals for it, it leaves loose and tangled narrative strands that suspend the "ends" of his various stories and that muddy our understanding of his prescriptions for the

5. Epiphany and Rhetoric in Spenser's Faerie Queene

process of acquiring virtue and keeping it close enough to use its power. The presence of magic particularly encourages a state of irresolution in Spenser's fables; even obvious religious elements use an approach to magic common in medieval Romances to elicit epiphanies that teach, test, block, or confirm the knights in their quests. Magic and religion link inextricably.

Magic appears throughout the *Faerie Queene* as a means of getting us to boundaries where the most significant events can happen — Spenser sought it in his antiqued verse as well as his plot, I think. Incantation, the gift of the talented poet as well as the magician, serves a particular function within the range of phenomena we might identify as magical. I see incantation as a mode of discourse employed to change the quality (rather than merely the quantity) of someone's perception or to induce a sense that one's perception has changed, in lieu of altering physical reality. The speaker or magus creates either an altered reality or a believable illusion, and similarly the poet establishes a link between the reader and some vaster scale of passion, knowledge, or wisdom through the suggestion that by the power of the word one may subvert normal reality. As Northrop Frye notes, incantation normally uses the standard poetic devices of rhyme, alliteration, and repetition, attempts to "reduce freedom of action"[3] — or, I would add, to enable oneself to perform some special action — varies little from the "language of compulsion" or that of hymn or prayer or scripture, and is chiefly "reached through [the power of] imagination or belief."[4] Such passages appear often in the *Faerie Queene* for their poetic effect,[5] but also as part of the narrative progress of the poem to show how strong magic may overcome imperfect virtue. Perfect virtue, however, easily disempowers even the strongest magic: one of Spenser's major themes.[6]

Spenser's rhetorical turns come largely from the history of heroic poetry, current politics (especially religious politics), literary and folk legend, and from a natural, sweeping sense of the archetypal. They come also, I propose, from the Renaissance conception of magic. In *Occult Philosophy or Magic* Henry Cornelius Agrippa, sixteenth-century German scholar-magician, expounds on the virtues of astrology, herbs, magic rings, and on divining by thunder and lightning or by dreams or out of madness. Agrippa believed that incantation had the power to transform or metamorphose oneself or another by virtue of the "Passions of the Mind," power of the will or emotion or of suggestion: "the soul, being strongly elevated, and inflamed with a strong imagination, sends forth health or sickness, not only in its proper body, but also in other bodies."[7] Intense focus on one's work, or being passionately in love, or even being caught up in flights of imagine may produce, according to Agrippa, sufficiently powerful forces to transform and translate: "what force the imaginative power hath, not only over the body but the soul."[8] Passions of the mind, helped by the celestial season, supported by constancy of mind in every activity, can link one with the "Intelligence of the Celestials, and together with them Impress certain wonderful Virtues upon inferior Things."[9] But to do magic, one must first "know the virtue, measure, order and degree of his own soul, in relation to the Power of the Universe."[10] To Spenser virtue itself constitutes a kind of magic, allowing the possessor of a particular virtue to perform deeds impossible for the person lacking it or even the knight who, though otherwise good, doesn't serve as the special exemplar of it in the poem.

Agrippa provides vague directions on how to call up evil spirits (to do "sacrifice with shameful nakedness" or to indulge in the "detestable heresy of old churchmen") or good spirits (by "good works, pure mind, secret prayers, devout humiliation, and the like").[11] Ancient priests made statues and images and, he says, "infused into them the Spirits of the Stars," by which they might prophesy.[12] In addition to willpower, Agrippa lays great stress on the power of words and their delivery as well as on knowing the right names for things: "an uttered word hath a certain act in the voice and properties of locution, and is brought forth with the breath ... [and] the proper names of things are very necessary in Magical Operations."[13] Christ says that names are written in Heaven, and Adam named all things according to nature; thus, calling a person or thing by the right name invokes natural and celestial harmonies and connections. Further, words and names combined into sentences, verses, or charms with meaning and the "violence of the imagination" may provide enchantments with the power to "subvert all nature."[14] Agrippa's mention of writing, imprecations, inscriptions, and the relation of signs or letters to magical symbols valorizes the written as well as the spoken word.

Magical powers need not be used for evil purposes, and scholars such as Agrippa and Paracelsus saw the appropriate use of magic as desirable

5. Epiphany and Rhetoric in Spenser's Faerie Queene

and according to God's plan. Paracelsus asserted that "holy men in God who serve the beatific life ... are called saints" but "holy men in God who serve the forces of nature ... are called magi," and such magi are "'natural saints.'"[15] *Magic* often described what we would now consider primitive science or mathematics or what Giordano Bruno even termed "medicine and chemistry," plus such tricks (whether we call them incantatory or mnemonic) as Bruno used to accomplish famous feats of memory as well as astrology and other methods of divination.[16] Spenser's enchanters use the magic of incantation, but the most powerful magic of the *Faerie Queene* lies in the virtues of Spenser's knights and in the poet's own use of incantation to teach virtue. Most Renaissance treatises on magic and those from which Renaissance magicians drew their knowledge, such as the *Hermetica* of Hermes Trismegistus, stress natural magic rather than demonic magic, that is, moral magic used for good purposes rather than evil magic used to do harm or call up demons.[17] Neoplatonic magicians such as Ficino assert the greater power of natural magic, since magic, like mystical prayer, when used by the pure of body and spirit, can call down angels from Heaven.[18]

Natural magic might offer more uses than meditation alone, though; if one knew the right symbols and the right language, one might use it to act upon nature or other people. The use of Hebrew or of its letters might be sufficient to invoke "the powers of the angels ... to perform magical works."[19] Renaissance magicians seem to have relied on the power of ancient or archaic languages to empower their incantations, largely because they were the languages of sacred texts thought already to inscribe the words of God or gods, and also perhaps because ability in those languages was thought to denote learning or the learned. The language of the past recalled a mythical time of magic and romance when people were closer to God and to nature and knew how to invoke their aid, unlike the magician or poet's own mundane present. That reason perhaps accounts in part for Spenser's choice of archaic diction and syntax: the language of the past (even an invented language and an invented past) has a greater power to move the reader into a world where magic and epiphany are possible. And powerful language, especially that drawn from a respected (divine, semidivine, or learned) source, when accompanied by music, such as the elusive Orphic hymns, might prove especially efficacious.

Heroes, Gods and the Role of Epiphany

In *A General Theory of Magic* Marcel Mauss provides a modern commentary on incantation. He discusses "sympathetic magic," which involves puns on words such as *withdraw* and *reject* (as in exorcism), description of a rite corresponding to the desired result, or the use of the name of a rite or process to produce a particular effect.[20] Description of a similar situation or exemplar from epic or fairy tale or invocation of a divine or heroic character (such as calling the name of an angel) assimilates the exemplar to the actual instance at hand, making it a prototype or archetype and absorbing the power of that exemplar into the present circumstance.[21] Such metaphorizing exemplifies the formalistic aspect of magic, verbal or nonverbal: influence by association with or repetition of an effective activity. Startling or resonant metaphor such as that used in incantation constitutes an important aspect of poetry; the act of naming or renaming, figuring or refiguring gives the poet (like the magician) a degree of power over subject and reader.

Mauss also notes that "spells are composed of special languages," often a language of the gods (e.g., Church Latin), and they often exploit the value of archaisms and arcane terms; in essence, the language itself becomes a metaphorical structure for magic, such as the Greek *Ephesia grammata*.[22] Incantation also requires the attachment of apprehensions, emotions, and hope to rites or other formal verbal constructs; desire, re-creation, and uninterrupted attention permit the mind to focus on synchronizing events or converging spaces.[23] Personification and apostrophe are also important, as in the case of naming an illness so that it may be addressed and treated as a person — having recognized and named it, one may order it to depart.[24]

These methods seem to match those of the Renaissance and the Middle Ages (cf., for instance, the Anglo-Saxon charms), verifying a traditional or consistent rhetoric of incantation. The methods of incantation include: using proper names (Heaven, Hell, the Tetragrammaton, the names of heroes or villains); invoking actual boundaries (water, caves, forests, mirrors — Whitehead closes the Agrippa volume with an explanation of how to make a magic mirror) or metaphorical ones (death, rites of passage); calling upon the ancients (their customs, wisdom, or practices); making use of lore or arcane knowledge or using or perverting standard religious rituals; invoking nature itself (especially topographical or geographical extremes such as mountains, valleys, oceans); invoking biological meta-

5. Epiphany and Rhetoric in Spenser's Faerie Queene

morphoses (as parallel phenomena); attempting to merge discrepant times or spaces (to create a sense of infinity or contiguity); invoking mythological events (Creation, Judgment, Apocalypse); referring to holy books; approaching the invocation or incantation with aroused emotions such as fear, awe, a sense of the mysterious, or willpower; calling directly upon a god, spirit, or other supernatural being. The purpose of incantation is to establish super- or sub-liminal links or to move a liminal threshold (the brink of another level of perception or existence) and then cross it to make contact with some source of power. Common examples that we do not normally associate with magic include religious ritual and prayer, ritual drama, and epic or quest narrative. The invoker seeks inspiration, imagination, understanding—in short, some connection with God or gods.

A clear analogy between poetry and incantation arises, and examples abound. An excellent instance nearly contemporary with Spenser appears five lines into Scene 3 of *Doctor Faustus*, in which Marlowe's magician, by naming the appropriate demons and perverting Christian ritual, calls up Mephastophilis to do his bidding:

> Faustus, begin thine incantations,
> And trie if diuels will obey they hest,
> Seeing thou hast prayde and sacrific'd to them.
> Within this circle is *Iehouahs* name,
> Forward and backward anagrammatiz'd
> The breuiated names of holy Saints,
> Figures of euery adiunct to the heauens,
> By which the spirits are inforst to rise,
> Then feare not Faustus, but be resolute,
> And trie the vttermost Magicke can performe.
> *Sint mihi dei acherontis propitij, valeat numen*
> *triplex Iehouæ, ignei, aërij, aquatici spiritus saluete,*
> *Orientis princeps Belsibub, inferni ardentis monarcha &*
> *demigorgon, propitiamus vos, vt appareat & surgat*
> *Mephastophilis: quid tu moraris? per Iehouam, gehennam*
> *& consecratam aquam quam nunc spargo, signúmque crucis*
> *quod nunc facio, & per vota nostra ipse nunc surgat*
> *nobis dicatus Mephastophilis.*[25]

When the devil appears, Faustus cannot stand his ugliness, so commands him, "I charge thee to returne and chaunge thy shape,/ Thou art too vgly to attend on me,/ Goe and returne an old Franciscan Frier," and Mephastophilis obeys. Apparently Faustus needs the Latin to summon him, but believes he can command him afterward in his own tongue. Once summoned, though, Mephastophilis does not obey Faustus' commands, but simply distracts him to damnation, whether the incantations had power or not.

Marlowe's *Faustus* teaches a moral lesson against pride and conjuring, but it also demonstrates the power of the poet to move emotion: Marlowe's "mighty line," to use Ben Jonson's term. The purpose of Spenser's use of magic is the same as that of his use of the prophetic mode, to instruct the reader in virtue and in how to create an epiphany; that is, Spenser wants to help us improve not only in our own virtue, but also in our ability to experience religious mysticism, to bring us closer to God.[26] His goals parallel those of the natural magician, and the poetry directs our attention accordingly. Spenser intends to help the reader become, as he says in the introductory epistle, a gentleman, but he also hopes, I think, to help the reader become a *Christian* gentleman who can believe in his ability to experience God. His use of the rhetoric of incantation supports that end.

A number of scholars provide insights into Romance or Spenser that help open the *Faerie Queene* to a rhetoric of incantation. Most pertinent to my purpose here, Patricia Parker posits the "dilation" of being, process, and characters in Romance, explaining how the genre leads to the expansion of boundaries by metaphorical connections; characters wander between vision and fulfillment, quest and end.[27] Any trespass represents a dilation, the crossing of a boundary, but *naming* the trespass, or any object or concept (such as *Errour* in Book I) places it at a distance so that we are not part of it, but may resist it or act upon it (the power of naming). Parker identifies the veil of allegory in Renaissance texts, the desire to inform the few, but allegory also opens up potentialities by ambiguity and suggestion that direct discourse cannot.[28] She suggests the importance in Spenser of the Renaissance concept that God's Creation is continued in the creation of the poet. The poet's craft is not Archimago's craft; it adopts a different incantatory vocabulary for a different purpose: super-liminal rather than sub-liminal connection. David Bevington in his notes in *Medieval Drama* mentions the epiphanal potential of juxtaposing human drama and the allegory that infuses medieval drama[29]; Romance (Spenser in particular) fuses adventure and allegory to point the reader to epiphany.

5. Epiphany and Rhetoric in Spenser's Faerie Queene

Kenneth Gross suggests that the allegorical argument may depend on "images with an almost magical power to elevate and entrance the mind."[30] Though magic may be an untruth or profanation, it permits hierophany (or epiphany), and the forces of magic may represent what is "most difficult, mysterious, and necessary in Spenser's romance."[31] The magician plays more upon "memory and imagination" than "objective demons and cosmological sympathies"—Britomart's entrance into Busyrane's castle disenchants, but without intention to do so, because her presence and the progress of the adventure take precedence over the magical particulars.[32] For another example, the Garden of Adonis acts to "mediate the realm of time" between "secular history" and the "eternal timelessness of divine being"; it provides a "liminal space, suspended between potency and act" that "enlarges, challenges and chastens our desires for paradise, rather than simply flattering or mocking them as the Bower [of Bliss] does"— the allegory becomes a pointer, an "agent of divination."[33] To Gross, books themselves, their beginnings and endings, become liminal markers.

In *The Allegorical Epic* Michael Murrin characterizes Spenser's *Faerie Queene* as a "complex mental experience," an "unfamiliar reality" where nonconjunctive spaces and times meet synchronically.[34] But human perceptions have a natural discontinuity, a natural lack of closure that encourages the mind to its own imaginative/liminal leaps; Romance and allegory function to exploit the possibilities of suggestion and association. One moves easily with Spenser from the mundane to theological intuition by the juxtaposition of sacred and profane, a liminal threshold. In *The Veil of Allegory* Murrin again identifies allegory as a tool for liminality: it creates an analogy (as an incantation does) because one cannot reach equation with the holy, only likeness to or awareness of it.[35] The connection of author and reader is itself liminal, beginning a process of perceptions with epiphany as the goal[36]; allegory becomes a central technique of poetic incantation.

Allegory also represents a change in proportion: the allegorist provides moral instruction, seeking to create, extend, or increase the value of morality; it re-creates the scenes of our own world in such a way that we may fight our moral battles in miniature and thus, by metaphorical extension, fight them on a grander scale as well. Morality becomes a "product of language" by which we move toward epiphany.[37] The effectiveness of the poetry depends on the overflow of inspiration or moral furor. E.K.'s gloss on the "October Eclogue" purports the *enthousiasmos* of the poet-prophet, the presence of God or some divine interlocutor to guide poet and reader to epiphany; scholars' "levels of allegory" denote "attempts of critics to represent this truth in rational terms,"[38] in effect, to rational-ize inspiration. The ambiguity of the poet's expression of vision, which results in the critic's allegorical interpretation, forces the reader, because of the occasional ponderousness of the narrative thread, to focus on episodes, the elaborate and layered presentation of which, poet and critic hope, will lead the reader to epiphany.[39]

Douglas Brooks-Davies draws a connection between monarchy and magic.[40] In Book I Spenser conflates Elizabeth and the muse, thus connecting the two worlds and providing an immediate grounding for the liminal step: Elizabeth as temporal and spiritual leader, head of the state and the reformed church and also source of poetic inspiration.[41] Because magic seeks the mastery of the secrets of nature, and through nature a revelation of the affinity between upper and lower worlds, we pursue by it a link to Creation. Every change in perception that we experience through poetry becomes a potential source of inspiration, and every forest a gradient of symbolism, a refuge for dangers, demons, or gods (Cirlot 112).[42]

Spenser filled the *Faerie Queene* with incantatory passages. The desultory adventures of romance and the multireferentiality of Spenser's allegory provide rich opportunity for epiphany. In the introductory epistle Spenser calls upon the names of his predecessors, Homer, Vergil, Ariosto, and Tasso, and upon the ancient and legendary heroes, Ulysses, Rinaldo, Arthur, to initiate liminality: these names move us into the world of Romance where epiphany is not only likely but part of our expectation. By invoking the Muse in Book I (as he does before each Book), Spenser adopts one of the most common of literary incantations, the plea for divine inspiration, a turn both magical and religious. Since Spenser thought of himself as heir to the poet-prophet tradition, this step enfolds a supposition of liminality in the very presence of the book. Also in the invocation Spenser conflates Queen Elizabeth with Cynthia, the chaste moon goddess (and perhaps as chaste ideal also to some degree to Mary), and with the Muse (in the letter to Raleigh he equates her with Gloriana, the Fairy Queen, too), thus linking England, Heaven (or at least Olympus) and the

5. Epiphany and Rhetoric in Spenser's Faerie Queene

world of the text for the duration of the Romance, opening the text to the constant possibility of hierophany on many levels. Following the invocation Book I begins *in medias res*, already within Spenser's Faeryland; starting in an alternative world, we have already crossed a liminal threshold as soon as we read the book, so the act of reading begins with an epiphany.

For the sake of brevity and example, I will examine in detail three adventures from the poem for Spenser's incantatory rhetoric: Redcrosse's ascent to the New Jerusalem in I.10, Britomart's rescue of Amoret from Busyrane's lair in III.11–12, and Calidore's vision at Mt. Acidale in VI.10. Myriad possibilities present themselves; these three examples characterize Spenser's approach to several potentialities surrounding the epiphanal experience. Other obvious passages include the Garden of Adonis, Acrasia's Bower, the Cave of Mammon, Merlin's "epileptic" trance in III.3, Britomart's dream in Isis' church in V.7 — the list runs on, but the points they make converge: demonic magic and natural magic use the same techniques, but demonic magic has only limited power, while natural magic ultimately turns the soul inward toward virtue and upward toward God, whence true power comes. The practice of natural magic becomes the virtue itself, and ultimately the refined soul practices virtue and magic as one without even recognizing it, bent on the quest of eternal epiphany.

Canto 10 of Book I begins with a warning not to trust earthly strength. Then Una brings Redcrosse to the house of Holiness to "cherish him with diets daint" (stanza 2) to revivify him and prepare him for the great battle with the dragon to come.[43] The porter, representing humility, readily unlocks the door for them, and they soon meet Dame Caelia ("heavenly") and her daughters, personifications of faith, hope, and charity. The allegory connects the narrative directly to Biblical text (1 Corinthians 13) and to the goal of Book I: the attainment of holiness as directed by the one true faith, the highest Christian purpose of the poem and the major liminal step for the believer. The natural magic of Book I guides the reader, by example, to the same end.

"Strange thing it is an errant knight to see/ Here in this place" (stanza 10), Dame Caelia says, for Redcrosse has both wandered and erred, but he soon receives schooling from Fidelia in "celestiall discipline" to "open his dull eyes" from "her sacred Booke, with blood ywrit," available only through Fidelia's instruction: "For she was able with her words to kill,/

85

And raise again to life the heart that she did thrill" (stanzas 18, 19) — belief yields her magical powers. Redcrosse readily learns to despise earthly life, even to desire death. But by the encouragement of Speranza (hope) and the "Leach" Patience's application of his wondrous "salves and med'cines" (Greek magic often involved the use of a salve or an herb, plus a "magical tool" and a "god who reveals an important secret,"[44] and Milton's Michael is not above using a "magical" balm to help Adam see into the future), and finally through symbolic death and rebirth (Redcrosse lies in sackcloth in a "darksome lowly place farre in," where from treatment with "corrosiues," fasting, praying, and the plucking out of rotted "superfluous flesh" with "pincers firie whot"), he arises from his penance, "the pains of hell, and long enduring night," into the world once again, having undergone an ascetic cleansing not unlike that of the shaman (stanzas 25–32).[45]

Then in the "holy Hospitall" Charissa instructs the knight so that he becomes "so perfect" that he may ascend the steep hill to meet Contemplation, who leads him to the "highest Mount," whence he sees Heaven and the New Jerusalem. Redcrosse compares, of all earthly places, only "Cleopolis" (London, establishing a second connection of this world to the next, Jerusalem, London, the Holy City) to what he sees, and he compares Glorianna/Elizabeth to an angel. Contemplation urges Redcrosse to the holy quest and names him St. George (establishing again the historical-liminal and Christian-liminal connections), but he will not let the knight forgo his earthly quest, saving Una's parents, establishing the safety and reign of the one true faith. Contemplation identifies Redcrosse with the "ancient race of Saxons": Spenser places a charge upon the English to defend the one true faith. Redcrosse departs from the mountain, leaving the epiphanal vision to continue his quest, now purged of sin and the true knight of holiness.

Analogous visions are vouchsafed to Vasco de Gama in Book X of the *Lusiads*, to Godfrey in Book XIV of *Jerusalem Delivered*, and to Adam in Books XI and XII of *Paradise Lost*. Adam's vision compares directly, because it foretells a return to Paradise and portrays the recovery of humanity to God in the new Eden or New Jerusalem. The mountain, reaching to heaven, provides the earthly link to vision. Contemplation, meditation, and prayer do for Redcrosse what Michael does for Adam: mediate the vision. Strictures of time and distance fall, and the mysteries and powers of God open to view. Proper preparation plus use of the proper faculties plus an invocation produce an epiphany, as they do in natural magic. Like Adam, Redcrosse must then return to the world to the human quests that continue until Christ's redemption of humanity is fulfilled on the Day of Judgment. Redcrosse undergoes the great epiphany, the apocalyptic vision as space and time momentarily dissolve, and earth's rightful end appears before him. The rhetorical method—biblical allusion, allegory or an equating metaphor, followed by a symbolic ascent and vision—establish and fulfill the goals of the holy life and of Christian incantation: understanding and seeking to follow God's purpose.

Britomart's adventure in Busyrane's lair in Book III, Cantos 11–12, illustrates the rhetoric of disenchantment[46]; Spenser's incantation, essentially Britomart's strength of will drawn from her chastity, breaks Busyrane's spells so that she may effect Amoret's release. Having described her prowess in arms in Canto 1, Spenser recounts the beginnings of Britomart's adventures in Canto 2. Her quest issues from a liminal experience: a vision of Arthegall in Merlin's magic mirror. The time-honored motif of the mirror (self-revelation and prophecy) and the presence of the ubiquitous Merlin create her quest, provide vision and explanation, goal and purpose. Glauce tries to pacify Britomart's longings with potions and pomanders, but no magic has more power than love, that "most sacred fire, that burnest mightily/ In liuing breasts, ynkindled first aboue," not that which moves "base affections... In brutish minds, and filthy lust inflame" (Canto III, stanza 1). Britomart experiences virtuous love, "Whence spring[s] all noble deeds and never dying fame." Of course, in Romance, the heightened emotion one encounters most, and that which has the most power, is love. Then Merlin provides the history, the prophecy, the authentic prophets's trance, and the spur to arms that Britomart needs to take up the quest, and arrayed in the armor of the martial Angela, "terrible in fight," and with "a mighty speare,/ Which Bladud made by Magick art of yore" (stanza 60), she departs Britain for Faeryland.

As chaste love Britomart represents one of the highest of human virtues and of human powers that which most successfully defends one throughout life. As the British princess seeking Arthegall, Arthur's equal, she becomes also Queen Elizabeth seeking equal fame with Arthur for herself and her contemporary Britain. Through marriage with Arthegall,

Britomart becomes one with Arthur's equal and thus one with Arthur, inheriting his power and legitimizing the ruling line of Britain, linking chaste love to just governing, firm support for both human and spiritual empire. History, love, and the quest converge around her, and among the tests she successfully accomplishes is the rescue of Amoret, "lover" or "little loved one."

Britomart pursues the giant Ollyphant into a wood (threshold) and loses him but finds instead Scudamore, who tells of Busyrane's holding Amoret captive "by strong enchauntments and blacke Magicke leare" and of his inability to rescue her. Britomart, the "gentlest knight alive," undertakes her rescue, "resolu'd to proue her vtmost might" (Canto 11, stanza 25). Sulfurous fire surrounds Busyrane's castle; Scudamore cannot pass it, but Brimomart holds her shield before her, and the flame parts like the Red Sea for Moses — the shield of chaste love has more power than the "shield of romantic love," and virtue has more magic than romance, despite its emotional power. Entering the castle Britomart finds Cupid's tapestry, with its tales of lusty indulgence. She passes it and goes through a doorway inscribed "Be bold" and continues through a room of martial tapestries to a door inscribed "Be not so bold"; she easily passes the test and is not distracted by romance or battle. She waits patiently until with a rush of wind and smoke the door bursts open, and the figures of the "maske of Cupid" issue forth, representing Ease, Fancy, Desire, Doubt, Dissemblance, and others, all exemplary of the dangers and distortions of lustful erotic love. When they depart, the door locks behind them, and Britomart must wait again (the patience of chaste love not tempted by the erotic) until the next evening. When again the door flies open, she enters, "Neither of idle shewe, nor of false charms aghast" (12.29). She finds Amoret, bound to a brass pillar, and the enchanter, whose "thousand charmes" cannot "her steadfast heart remove"; Amoret's chastity is sufficient to resist the enchanter, but not to effect her own release from his spell. Busyrane sees Britomart and runs to kill Amoret; Britomart stops him and would kill him, but Amoret pleads that if he die, she will not be free of his enchantment (one must overcome temptation, not flee from it). At Britomart's threat, Busyrane reverses his spells, his horrible words causing "the virgins hart to perse,/ And her faire lockes up stared stiffe on end,/ Hearing him those same bloudy lines rehearse" (36). We never hear the

5. Epiphany and Rhetoric in Spenser's Faerie Queene

details of the spell (common practice also in works on magic, in which descriptions of spells rather than the spells themselves usually appear), but Amoret is released and restored to health. Britomart binds Busyrane and escorts Amoret to the woods without through the formerly rich, now blasted and decayed rooms through which she entered.

Britomart need work no charms, call no gods, nor speak any words; her actions work, literally, natural magic. Her presence alone effects the disenchantment. The strength of true love unhampered by lust remains immune to enchantment and can even disenchant others, since it works not for its own ends, but to benefit others. The difficulty of "thresholding" (e.g., Scudamore's) does not constrain Britomart, and the masque and the tapestry, while they pique her interest as curiosities, do not move her at all from her purpose. They seem simply perversions and powerless displays, pale imitations of her passions and martial skill, showing what the great Renaissance magi taught, that natural magic has much more power than demonic, and that the highest magic is virtue. The rhetoric of disenchantment requires only honesty, forthrightness, directness, and love, almost a separate incantation of its own because of its power to resist magic and bring about Christian ends. The incantation here lies not in what Britomart says, but in Spenser's elaboration of her virtue.

The episode of Calidore at Mt. Acidale exemplifies another kind of disenchantment. Spenser again directs the rhetoric of this incantatory passage at the reader, though the visual effects fall upon Calidore. Certainly Calidore's blundering interrupts the reverie of the vision for both himself and the reader. The Mt. Acidale scene, a relatively short one with a powerful message, stands out starkly amidst the rest of Book VI. Calidore, having presently given up the quest of the Blatant Beast to pursue his love for Pastorella, ranges over the open fields on a pleasant plain. The knight of courtesy, he has already made an error by abandoning his pledge to the Faerie Queene to pursue at all costs his quest for the Blatant Beast. He sees on the plain an abruptly rising hill bordered by a high wood and a gentle river (three thresholds) at which "Nymphs and Faerie's by the bancks did sit." The wood (cf. Book I: Redcrosse's adventures begin when he and Una enter a wood) and the river as thresholds border a land of nymphs and elves, which the poet asserts serves as a retreat of Venus. When Calidore approaches, he hears the merry sound of piping. He hides in the woods and watches "a troupe of Ladies dauncing," but does not enter the open circle "For dread of them vnawares to be descryde,/ For breaking of their dance" (6.10.10–11) — he does represent courtesy.

With Calidore we watch "An hundred naked maidens lilly white,/ All raunged in a ring, and dancing in delight" (11). Next we move inside the "girlond" of maidens to a ring of three more damsels, then to one amid the three, each ring a living threshold to greater beauty. The ring becomes metaphorically Ariadne's crown, a ring of stars and then a ring of flowers, then the three maidens become Graces, "Handmaidens of Venus" — Spenser conflates Faeryland, mythology, the firmament, natural beauty, goddesses who dispense charm and beauty, and a living, mobile magic ring, almost a Ptolemaic circle, all piping to one flute: poetry. The maidens dance to Colin Clout's piping; Colin, an old friend of Spenser's readers from the *Shepheardes Calender*, represents Spenser himself and the poet's magical ability to create levels of meaning and make them dance. Colin ceases playing for Elizabeth/Gloriana only to pipe in praise of his love, the country lass, handmaid to Gloriana, who dances in the center of the circle to the Graces' song.

This hypnotizing, whirling ring of grace and feminine beauty dissolves into air as Calidore steps from the wood into view. Here Calidore as Courtesy fails, since he does not step forward out of a chaste desire to do good, though his intention is not likely prurient. The intervention of mortality disrupts a paradisal dance, the only human link to which, the poet's rustic but inspired song, fades when imperfectly chaste thoughts enter. Calidore, "standing long astonished in spright,/ And rapt with pleasaunce, wist not what to weene" (17); he breaks the spell of the image the reader longs to visualize and participate in, which the human presence must drive away. As does Britomart, Calidore disenchants, but as with Redcrosse, the disenchantment comes to one who wishes to be absorbed into a divine vision, a vision which, as humans, however courteous, outside of prophecy we can glimpse but never enjoy long. We taste the awe of heavenly mead in the dance to honor Venus, but the desire fades with the imposition of our own humanity. Or perhaps the dance itself fails, since it honors romantic love (not courtesy's goal, either) rather than chaste love. As with Britomart, Calidore's mere presence disenchants, perhaps because his virtue fails — he does not courteously abstain from entering the circle — or per-

5. Epiphany and Rhetoric in Spenser's Faerie Queene

haps because the kind of Romantic love the dancers celebrate doesn't respond to courtesy. In a Christian Romance magic must seek just and holy ends, or its value and beauty will evaporate before our eyes.

Calidore then speaks with the piper Colin Clout, the one figure remaining after the disappearance of the dancers. Downcast at losing sight of his beloved, the maid "aduaunst to be another Grace" (16), Colin explains to Calidore what he has done; the knight, his courtesy returning, apologizes for the anti-epiphany his disruption has caused. Colin explains that the Graces, daughters of Jove, bestow all gracious gifts on humans, including courtesy and civility: again we see a knight imperfectly representing his future, but trying to do well even as he learns of his failure. We often need repeated tests to improve ourselves and achieve our goals. Unlike in Book 1, where from the mount Redcrosse has his vision of the New Jerusalem, an anti-climax culminates the narrative tension of Book 6. Blundering breaks the magic spell, a spell of great beauty and even artistic productivity, but not one essential to survival (such as Arthur's rescuing Redcrosse from Lucifera's dungeon) or human redemption. Spenser's magic may produce good or ill, but the knight who faces it must preserve the virtues, including wisdom and prudence, to dislodge bad magic or to avoid disenchanting the good — especially since one may not know at first glance one from the other.

Spenser's spells throughout the *Faerie Queene* rely not so much on nifty verbal play or on wild scenery — though we find both — or startling turns of plot as on the classical tropes of allegory and magic, Christian and mythological allusion, thresholding, the use of ancient knowledge and archaic diction, and the quest for virtue to establish the liminal connection. Virtue represents, for him, the proper goal of any liminal experience: the poet's as well as the magician's as well as the Christian's. George Luck points out that some scholars have found "no fundamental difference between religion and magic" except, perhaps, for religion's "consciousness of sin and the prayer for forgiveness."[47] For scholars in the Renaissance natural magic may have constituted an aspect of religion (using nature, ritual, and the power of the voice to invoke an epiphany), if one slightly removed from traditional Christianity. As a "prophetic" poet Spenser draws his magic from Romance, from a series of adventures converging and diverging, and from his use of the techniques of incantation to instruct the reader in epiphany and virtue: the goal that he sees as most necessary to his time and most appropriate to the epic medium. As a poet so unrelentingly interested in epiphany, he does more than link himself to one of the most important aspects of the epic tradition through a predominant rhetorical method of his age; he takes the approach to epiphany as far into baroque excess as a poet reasonably could. A complex system of virtue required a complex series of epiphanies — but it also introduced a great deal of confusion into the intellectual and spiritual life of the would-be Christian knight. When Milton took up the epic torch that Spenser had lit so brightly, he saw a need for a simpler solution and a simpler narrative, but with intricate tropes and complicated rhetoric of English Renaissance poetry still intact. How, Milton asked, can we, through the medium of epic poetry, most simply find our way back to God? That question takes us to the next point in our epic journey.

Chapter 6

Paradise Lost and the Resimplification of Epic Epiphany

In the ancient world *epiphany* had referred to the physical manifestation of a god or the sudden revelatory contact with a divine being (as especially in the Christian festival celebrating the Magi's visiting Jesus). The skepticism of the twentieth century has separated the religious vision of traditional epiphany from the secular "psychological phenomenon arising from a real sensuous experience"— the modern artistic epiphany, such as we find in Joyce,[1] and even from the "moral epiphany" of Spenser, to which Milton directly responded.

Spenser had complicated the problem of epiphany enormously. Returning with Milton to a more traditional use of the term *epiphany*, this chapter will consider the rhetoric of epiphanies in *Paradise Lost*, in respect to which the term does specifically denote human contact with God. As in Beowulf's battles with monsters, Milton does, though, include subliminal epiphanies as well: the reader's, the Son's, Adam and Eve's several encounters with Satan bear just as much if not more of the poem's creative weight. As Northrop Frye argues, Milton determined to "reconsider the epic theme of heroic action, to decide what in Christian terms a hero is and what an act is"; he lit upon "obedience, fidelity and perseverance" as "exemplified by Abdiel," the angel who removes himself from Satan's rebelling host to return to God. Yet we also find the "heroic quest of Christ"[2] and Milton's notion of fallen heroism in Adam and Eve as well: heroism has never left the arena, only transformed into something necessary to the audience of Milton's day.[3]

Spenser used Romance magic to invoke or disrupt epiphanies, and the epiphanies take us to the thematic points he wants his audience to recognize. In the old sense they prophesy, diagnosing the needs of the time. Milton's epiphanies relate particularly to the prophetic aspect of his work. *Prophecy* traditionally has not meant the same idea that riddles popular culture today, foretelling; rather, it denoted an outpouring of revealed, useful wisdom resulting from contact with a divine being or a being of another "order." Ancient prophecies differ significantly from uninformed readings of Nostradamus and the Apocalypse of St. John that seek to raise our fears of what dire events will come; they diagnose the problems of the present and warn what will come if people don't stop their current evil behaviors. Prophecy as an outpouring of divine inspiration represents a traditional form of epiphany: how the gods or their representatives teach us what we need to know. In Milton the contact with divine beings occurs literally; epiphany and subsequently prophecy result, those prophecies, if we pay attention, "justifying" (i.e., bringing back together, as would a carpenter) God and humanity, retelling the Fall story in the way Milton thought necessary to bring his audience closer to Christ. The attempt at heroic-prophecy explicitly comprises Milton's goal (that, along with his long-held hope of placing himself within the tradition of epic poets).[4]

Critics of twentieth-century fiction, perhaps accepting Eliot's move away from Miltonic influence, have focused their attention with Joyce on the literary epiphany — a "shift in perception" based on the creative imagination's "blending of sight and sound" resulting in the "modern sublime."[5] The perceiver (author, character, reader) achieves an instantaneous recognition of the "whatness" of an object, and this experience becomes "fraught with meaning beyond itself," precipitating a "revelation quite as valid as the religious."[6] The term *epiphany* has take this secular shape from James Joyce's work (particularly, from *Stephen Hero* and from Joyce's explication of *Dubliners* in his letters); whereas Yeats and Pater used art "to

6. Paradise Lost *and the Resimplification of Epic Epiphany*

bring us back to religion or mysticism," Joyce established art as a "rival to religion"[7] in its ability to evoke the epiphanal experience: the "pure but transient vision, the aesthetic or timeless moment ... of non-didactic revelation,"[8] a sensual anagoge imminentized yet secularized, "all symbols being united in a single infinite eternal verbal symbol."[9] Epiphany has come to mean the epiphany of the symbol, then finally of the words creating the symbol. And the epiphany lasts only briefly: it involves a flash of insight rather than a prolonged contact with a different-order being. While Milton must have sought that kind of linguistic power in his poetry, that turn of modernist thought, to the degree that it has infiltrated our reading practices, makes Milton's use of biblical epiphany feel all the more distant and unreal. Milton, I think, sought to make biblical epiphany as real, sensual, and immediate as he possibly could—that facet can make him feel dangerous, or obscure, or even sacrilegious to contemporary readers, depending on the biases we bring to the text, though it can also allot him a height from which we can better appreciate his accomplishment.

Milton's prophetic epiphanies, however, guide us through instruction in the nature of the world with the hope of helping us live in the world at hand. Joseph Wittreich and William Kerrigan, among others, have explored Milton's connections with the prophetic, and Leland Ryken has discussed the apocalyptic vision (revelation of the eschaton) in *Paradise Lost*. Prophecy, Wittreich argues,

> mediates between man and God, between fallen reason and the visionary imagination, and, liberating the mind, enables it to become the mediator between earthly and heavenly things, between time and eternity.[10]

Kerrigan notes the broad seventeenth-century definition of a prophet as a "teacher, preacher, poet, or inspired interpreter of the Bible" either "within or without the church," one who could be inspired to liberate a nation physically, like Samson, or intellectually and spiritually, like Milton.[11] Nora Chadwick defines prophecy as the expression of thought, whether of the present, the future, or the past, which has been acquired by inspiration, and which is uttered in a condition of exaltation or trance, or couched in the traditional form of such utterances.[12] Prophecy, for Milton as poet, becomes a justification, a bringing together of the inspiration of God and the perception of humanity in the poem. The present poem justifies, that is, makes synchronic, the past and the future, the eternal and the temporal.

Wittreich sees epic and prophecy "in union" in Milton's poetry, constituting the "ultimate transcendental form."[13] Prophecy begins with an epiphany, the moment of inspiration; so does the epic, often, with its invocation, and it often proceeds toward epiphanies: Gilgamesh's meeting with Utnapishtim, Hektor's battle with Achilles, Arjuna's talk with Krishna, the Redcrosse Knight's vision of the New Jerusalem. The invocation of the Muse, followed by the epic poem, asks the reader to accept that inspiration has occurred, that an epiphany has already taken place and is likely to again. The poet then relates the epiphany or its results to the reader, whereby the reader is also transported by the poem to a meeting with a being of a higher order or to a greater level of understanding of the nature of the world.

So, if we accept the conventions that the poet invokes, epiphany and prophecy both involve a link with the eternal. The point of contact or border-phenomenon of the epiphany is normally super-liminal, with a higher order or "unfallen" being. Milton's sub-liminal epiphanies (what Frye might call demonic epiphanies), human encounters with a fallen being, Satan, involve a sub-version of the epiphanal impulse, underwriting the human goal of submission to God. This kind of epiphany diverts, perverts, or seeks to subsume the human attempt to overwrite, wherein no insurance against the sub-liminal exists other than obedience to and faith in God.

To consider the rhetoric of Milton's epiphanies, I first address the differences between prelapsarian and postlapsarian contacts with divine beings, then show Milton's account of the decline of the epiphany from natural process to sparely occasional revelation, especially by focusing on how Milton's own epiphanies (those he claims as inspired epic/prophetic poet), the invocations to Books 1, 3, 7, and 9, reflect humanity's translation to the fallen state. Then I show how Milton's epiphanies seek to repair, through literature, the liminal link with God that was broken by the Fall.[14] The invocations serve a greater purpose in the poem than simply to link *PL* to the Classical tradition of invoking the Muse to begin an epic or re-invoking to prepare for a particularly dramatic episode; they suggest, at

6. Paradise Lost *and the Resimplification of Epic Epiphany*

least poetically, that human access to divine inspiration hasn't ended: if we remain true to our faith and our talents, we may yet, the blind bard Milton tells us, gain access to knowledge normally beyond mortal sight.

To proceed let us focus first on Adam and Eve's significant meetings with beings from a different order of existence, God, angels, Satan, beings from beyond a liminal boundary, existing in another state of being or perception.[15] *Paradise Lost*'s epiphanies uncover the process of humanity's Fall: Satan's whispering at Eve's ear in Book 4; Eve's account of her dream in Book 5; Raphael's approach and his subsequent discussion with Adam in Book 5; Adam's dream in Book 8; Eve's temptation in Book 9; the judgment scene in Book 10; Michael's approach in Book 11 and the subsequent prophecies. Following the discussion of the narrative scenes, I will address the invocations, Milton's attempt as epic poet to re-establish a connection with Heaven. To conclude the chapter I propose that Milton's epic landscape represents a significant step at once both backward and forward in our appreciation of epic epiphanies.

The first human contact in *Paradise Lost* with a being of another order capable of rational function occurs in Book 4, as Satan squats at Eve's ear, "Assaying by his devilish art to reach/ The organs of her fancy," to tempt her in a dream (ll. 801–2).[16] This event occurs first in the narrative, not chronological order, highlighting its importance as a foreshadowing of what the reader knows shall come. One would perhaps expect the first liminal connection established by the narrative to occur between Adam and God, but Milton relegates that scene to Adam's retelling his first memory in Book 8. The scene in Book 4 foregrounds the immediacy of the danger, the imminence of the Fall, rehearses the later temptation scene, and links humankind more closely to Satan than we have to that time been. Satan has overheard Adam and Eve's talk — a kind of epiphany for Satan, perhaps — and has immediately directed the thrust of his mission at the "weaker vessel."

Satan's speech attempts to pervert or subvert the word of God (the Word as active agent, creator) by setting up the fall of His creation, in effect, to deny humanity a future of super-liminal epiphany. Shortly he will succeed, partially. Ultimately, the Son, the true Word, will re-establish the link to the Creator as predominant to the sub-liminal connection to Satan, both by His mercy in judgment and by His sacrifice.

Heroes, Gods and the Role of Epiphany

A significant point of this first sub-liminal epiphany lies in its covertness: Eve is asleep during the contact. Prelapsarian super-liminal epiphanies are overt — they evoke no startle reaction, and one is aware of their approach. Though Adam and Eve do not yet feel fear, Eve's confusion as she relates her dream to Adam signals — though she doesn't know it yet — the sub-liminal epiphany; had the dream been a super-liminal epiphany, she would have recognized it as such, as Adam and Raphael do Adam's dream. In the postlapsarian world, sub-liminal epiphanies, such as human meetings with Sin and Death, which must enter the human world after the events of Milton's narrative end, will typically produce fear and at least temporary trepidation. Even Satan will be startled later in the poem by his own sub-liminal epiphany, when he too meets Sin and Death for the first time.

To return to Eve: this first contact could have proven instructive. We learn in Book 5 the contents of the imposed dream. Adam wakes to find "unawak'nd Eve/ With tresses discompos'd, and glowing Cheek/ As through unquiet rest" (ll. 9–11). Eve wakes "with startl'd eye," glad to see the morning, and immediately interprets the dream to Adam. A (deceiving) voice, sounding like Adam's, calls her to rise, and it begins the temptation with flattery, suggesting that Heaven remains awake hoping that Eve will come out so that all eyes may gaze on her beauty. She comes to the forbidden tree, "Much fairer to my Fancy than by day" — the appeal addresses not her reason, but her fancy. She sees a shape "wing'd like one of those from Heaven/ By us oft seen"; she assumes no ill, for super-liminal epiphanies are part of normal activity. The figure eats of the fruit, rejoices, then enjoins "angelic Eve" to taste and become a goddess. He holds the fruit to her mouth. Then she feels herself flying upward in "high elation," as though she had eaten, her guide having disappeared. "O how glad I wak'd/ To find this but a dream!" (ll. 92–93) she tells Adam, though of course we recognize it as more than it dream. She has had an epiphany, each of which serves as instruction.

Adam attempts to explain the dream, arguing that "what in sleep thou didst abhor to dream,/ Waking thou never wilt consent to do." Tears fall from Eve's eyes, and she remains, seemingly, unresolved by Adam's explanation, for "she was cheer'd,/ But silently a gentle tear let fall/ From either eye" (ll. 129–30), and she seems not to remember the

6. Paradise Lost *and the Resimplification of Epic Epiphany*

dream when later she is confronted by the serpent: that means of instruction hasn't worked. Raphael comes to explain fully the purport of Eve's dream. Through Adam's attempt, Raphael's more complete appraisal, and, most importantly, the dream itself, Eve gains instruction about what to avoid.

The overt instruction comes easily and palatably, even via super-liminal epiphany (that which comes from Raphael). The covert instruction, Satan's visitation, comes with a visceral rejection (that is why God permits it), since it should deepen Eve's rejection of the temptation, though the instruction fails finally. This episode establishes a pattern or rhetoric for the sub-liminal epiphany and shows the importance of that rhetoric: could Eve have used her instruction in it to avoid temptation, the fall would not have taken place.

The first super-liminal epiphany in *Paradise Lost* actually occurs with Raphael's approach, and it differs markedly from the meeting with Satan. Adam sees him from far off: "Him through the spicy Forest onward come/ Adam discern'd, as in the door he sat/ Of his cool bow'r" (5.298–300). Not until line 358 does the angel actually arrive, though, at which point Adam addresses him with a bow: "Nearer his presence Adam though not aw'd,/ Yet with submiss approach and reverence meek,/ As to a superior nature, bowing low." Adam and Eve have time to prepare for their guest, and they feel and show the appropriate reverence for a higher-order creature, though they feel neither awe nor fear nor suffer any confusion about how to act or how to interpret the meeting. The visitation is overt and appears to be as natural as the blooming of a flower: the appropriate rhetoric or pattern for super-liminal epiphany.

Adam and Eve converse with Raphael in matters weighty or friendly, proceeding with ease as friend to friend. The epiphanal quality of the encounter passes almost unnoticed, as the angel eats and drinks with them. Raphael even suggests that interaction between humanity and angels may one day involve a fuller experience: "time may come, when men/ With Angels may anticipate, and find no inconvenient diet" (ll. 493–95). He then narrates the war in Heaven (continuing through Book 6), warns Adam of Satan's presence, and recounts the creation (Book 7—the epiphany already in its third book will continue, showing the possibilities for epiphany that the fall will destroy). Adam, charmed by Raphael's discourse, asks astronomical questions, in answer to which the angel exhorts him to pursue matters worth his attention (Book 8).

Adam then offers to tell what he remembers of his own creation purely to prolong his exchange with the angel (pre-lapsarian epiphanies allow for a casual familiarity). Raphael assents, pleased too with Adam's words, and Adam relates his own dream-vision of God. Raphael leaves after a blushing allusion to angelic lovemaking in response to Adam's continued questions. This epiphany is long in Milton's telling, over three and a half books. The conversation seems much more to be that of near-equals than does that between Adam and Michael in Books 11 and 12. The postlapsarian world will broaden the leap necessary to achieve epiphany and make it an event of awe and even fear.

Returning to Adam's vision in Book 8, we find that Adam tells of his own romping about the banks of Eden, then sitting down pensive: "there gentle sleep/ First found me, and with soft oppression seiz'd/ My drowned sense, untroubl'd, though I thought/ I then was passing to my former state/ Insensible" (ll. 287–91). Though Adam felt no fear, God accommodated the vision to Adam's sight (by the "accommodation" of the Son, who acts as God's direct intermediary with His creation; even in the prelapsarian world Adam and Eve do not see the Father directly). Adam continues to the angel, recalling "suddenly stood at my head a dream,/ Whose inward apparition gently mov'd/ My fancy to believe I yet had being." The "shape divine" came (in the dream) in response to Adam's prayer, called him to rise, and took him by the hand, and, Adam explains, "Rejoicing, but with awe,/ In adoration at his feet I fell/ Submiss: he reared me, and Whom though soughtest I am,/ Said mildly" (ll. 313–17). Adam felt awe, but not fear or apprehension, for the "mild" vision (and audition) comes in answer to his prayer.[17] God then gave Paradise to Adam with "stern" warning that he not eat of the forbidden tree, but "soon his clear aspect/ Return'd" (ll. 336–37), and Adam named the animals and begged the boon of a wife. God (or the Son) even joked with Adam over his request, praised him for his deference, then returned him to unconscious, deathlike sleep after the creation of Eve from his rib. The fact that we are told the story in retrospect perhaps deepens our postlapsarian distance from God; we as readers do not interact with God through Adam except after the Fall, and that but once in a state of shame.

6. Paradise Lost *and the Resimplification of Epic Epiphany*

Though Adam feels awe toward God, he feels no longing to bring the contact to an end, no sense of anything unnatural in his discourse with God. This epiphany is one of sublime pleasure, "My earthly by his Heav'nly overpower'd,/ Which it had long stood under, strain'd to the highth/ In that celestial colloquy sublime" (8.453–55), bringing a sleep in which the epiphany may continue in a form which Adam will not find harmful or oppressive. Later, Adam suggests that God has "made ammends" for his loneliness by the creation of Eve; he unabashedly expresses his feelings to God, then forgets God's presence as he becomes enamored of Eve. Clearly prelapsarian Adam exhibits no shyness of God.

Next, in Book 9, we confront a fully conscious sub-liminal epiphany. Eve's temptation contrasts sharply with Adam's dream-vision. She clearly doubts the speaking serpent, though she quickly succumbs to its apparent though unwonted wisdom. This scene parallels the scenario of her dream. Satan, in the body of the serpent — "side-long he works his way" (9.512) — approaches Eve, curling wantonly, fawning on her.[18] Milton's use of *sidelong* and Eve's doubt reveal the nature of the sub-liminal epiphany: even an apparently overt approach couches covert intent. Then, when Satan speaks from the serpent's mouth, Eve, "not unamazed," answers "What may this mean? Language of man pronounc't/ By tongue of brute, and human sense exprest?" (9.553–54). Eve's amazement attests again to the problem, again cues the reader to the sub-liminal epiphany. When Satan begins to tempt Eve with the apple, she should immediately recognize the situation she has been schooled to resist.

She doesn't; she gives in to the same kind of flattery, the same appeal to pride. Perhaps that point attests as truly to the power of the epiphanal experience — to Satan's remaining power, despite his change of status in the Great Chain of Being — as it does to the failure of Eve's right reason.

The eating of the apple initiates a tremendous sub-liminal epiphany — the very fulcrum of the epic — as Adam and Eve descend from the blessed state to the cursed, face their subsequent awareness of Evil and suffer their abysmal mutual condemnation. I will pass over these scenes only in favor of staying more strictly with the boundaries of epiphany that I have set up previously: a meeting with a different-order being. This episode does constitute, though, an interesting narrative phenomenon: the characters create of themselves a sub-liminal epiphany in that Adam and Eve, having fallen, now live in a state inferior (sub-liminal) to that in which God created them. The scene, appropriately, ends in mutual accusation and quarreling, but not before Adam has observed that all subsequent epiphanies will change: "How shall I behold the face/ Henceforth of God or angel, erst with joy/ And rapture so oft beheld? those heav'nly shapes/ Will dazzle now this earthly, with their blaze/ Insufferably bright" (9.1080–84).

The judgment scene, which follows in Book 10, illustrates the first postlapsarian epiphany, a painful one for our first parents. Impending super-liminal epiphanies, up to the Fall, have signaled themselves clearly well in advance, and Adam and Eve have met them with grace and ease. The guardian angels forsake Paradise at the Fall, and the couple hear the Son, the "voice of God," walking in the garden. "They heard,/ And from his presence hid themselves" (10.99–100). The Son must call Adam forth. They come, but "discompos'd": "Love was not in their looks," but rather "shame, and perturbation, and despair,/ Anger, and obstinacy, and hate and guile" directed both at each other and at God. Now Adam and Eve fear both super- and sub-liminal epiphanies; Adam says, "I heard thee in the garden, and of thy voice/ Afraid, being naked, hid myself." He responds to the obvious question, "O Heav'n! in evil strait this day I stand/ Before my Judge, either to undergo/ Myself the total crime, or to accuse/ My other self" (ll. 125–28). What should be the greatest human triumph, meeting with God having obeyed His law, has become rather the confession of the greatest human failure: transgression of God's one prohibition. The rhetoric and the emotions that up to this point would have been appropriate to sub-liminal epiphany now accompany super-liminal epiphany. The world has changed. Humanity will henceforth doubt and fear the epiphany that to the innocent soul was pure mead. Humanity must henceforth question the source of each epiphany and come to long for contact with God, for epiphanies shall come seldom and will prove difficult to confirm.

The final epiphany of *Paradise Lost*, Michael's meeting with Adam to instruct him, occurs in Book 11, and again it is prefaced by fear: "Down from the sky of jasper lighted now... A glorious apparition, had not doubt/ And carnal fear that day dimmed Adam's eye" (ll. 209–12). Michael comes

6. Paradise Lost *and the Resimplification of Epic Epiphany*

in warlike array bearing, as Adam expects, "great tidings." For the fallen Adam to see the fullness of the vision that Michael will provide him, the angel must apply a balm to Adam's eyes; whereas Adam could before perceive at least a vision of God in a dream, now only artificial means can permit him to view even a prophetic vision. Even holy medicine proves insufficient, for Adam's strength fails, and Michael must tell the rest — the lost both need and love tales. With the knowledge of the murder of Abel and of the many woes to come into the world, Adam cries, "Alas, both for the deed and for the cause!/ But now have I seen Death?" (ll. 461–2); he has indeed seen murder, but has not had the sub-liminal epiphany of meeting Death himself. Adam plumbs the depths of despair as a result of this postlapsarian epiphany, but Michael, stern warrior that he is, proves able to recover Adam from simple blind submission to hope, by prophesying the Son's coming, and Adam, "with such joy/ Surcharg'd," responds: "'O prophet of glad tidings, finisher/ Of utmost hope!'" (12.372–76); "'O goodness infinite, goodness immense!/ That all this good of evil shall produce'" (ll. 469–70). Adam returns, through Michael's instruction, from despair to the greatest epiphanal understanding that fallen humanity can experience: redemption by Christ. Adam's joy doubles with the knowledge that the Son shall be incarnated through his seed (the *felix culpa*, true to some branches of the tradition, faulty though the reasoning be). Thus epiphany for fallen humanity may arouse fear and doubt, yet it retains its potential for raising the human spirit to a state of ecstasy — or at least to a state of understanding.

As Adam's prayer prepares him for the presence of God and essentially evokes an epiphany in Book 5, so Milton's narrator hopes that by his invocation the Muse may answer his prayer for inspiration and understanding, so that he may dare to "assert Eternal Providence" yet attract no censure for expanding his story. If the Muse answers, then he has experienced an epiphany. Invocations typically introduce epics of Classical heritage, but in *PL* they begin Books 1, 3, 7, and 9. The invocations gradually become less assured, less certain of answer, more human, but no less "epical" in their requests. They seek to create the potential for epiphany in the author as representative of fallen humanity who can return from the poem with the boon of knowledge derived from his literary/spiritual quest.

In the opening lines of Book 1, the narrator proclaims his epic purpose, to tell the tale of humanity's fall and "justify the ways of God to men." He calls upon the aid of the Heavenly Muse, the Holy Spirit, perhaps—"O Spirit! that dost prefer/ Before all temples th'upright heart and pure" (apparently the poet hopes to present the upright and pure heart)—to support his clearly stated intent, and lays out an outline for his request: the cause of the Fall and who provoked it. His invocation succeeds, for after an immediate answer to the second question, the passage slides directly into the narrative, which depicts Satan, already in Hell, regaining a sense of position. "Of Man's first disobedience" we do not hear the specifics until Book 9, and if Milton's muse takes her time about fulfilling the invocation, we do arrive there (despite Dr. Johnson's warning that no one ever wished *Paradise Lost* longer) none the worse for wear. Perhaps Milton decided that the limitations of fallen humanity best permit the muse's answer to begin with the sub-liminal epiphanal pole, that standing closer to our fallen state, or perhaps the fallen poet must accept the muse's answer as it comes, unsure of whether or not the request he made will be the one she grants.

A second invocation—or mini-invocation—occurs a bit later in Book 1, as the narrator asks the Muse to speak the names of the fallen angels (line 376). Homer, too, used the occasional or periodic invocation, and the need for a renewed request for help makes narrative sense at this point, given the horrors of the location and the company.

Milton begins Book 3 by hailing the "holy Light," the "Eternal Coeternal beam"—the Son, I think—but with a brief disclaimer: "May I express thee unblam'd?" Then "thee I revisit safe," the narrator says, "but thou/ Revisit'st not these eyes"—a kind of lament for, perhaps, a prayer unanswered. The narrator begins the poem in the fallen state (both physically and spiritually) and cannot be assured, but can only hope for superliminal epiphany. With "wisdom at one entrance quite shut out," the speaker depends so much more on the light to "shine inward" and illuminate the mind, "that I may see and tell/ Of things invisible to mortal sight." The prayer is immediately answered, as the narration begins anew with the next line, but the second invocation injects a more physical awareness of the speaker's inadequacy as a fallen man who laments his state: it reflects not so confident, even proud, a state of mind as the first; it indicates a character that questions rather than calls.

6. Paradise Lost *and the Resimplification of Epic Epiphany*

The invocation in Book 7 begins, "Descend from Heav'n Urania, by that name/ If rightly thou art call'd." The narrator suggests that the Muse has led him to the Heaven of Heavens, but he fears falling, and again he falls to complaining of having "fall'n on evil days ... and evil tongues ... with dangers compast round ... yet not alone" (ll. 25–28). He questions whether or not he calls the muse rightly and adds, "Fail not thou, who thee implores" and clarifies that he uses Classical machinery to invoke the Christian, not the classical muse ("The meaning, not the name I call"; 7.5). The narrator seeks to return to earth — "More safe I sing with mortal voice" (24) — for he must learn about the deep source of the Fall by the war in Heaven, as must Adam and the reader. The narrator learns that he may instruct people as Raphael instructs Adam — one hopes, to greater effect. Yet now he appears to stand more firmly on earthly, rather than Heavenly, ground than he did in the previous invocations: he battles rather than soars.

The Book 9 invocation takes on a darker tone. "No more talk where God or angel guest/ With Man," for in this part of the tale, humanity falls. "I now must change/ These notes to tragic; foul distrust, and breach/ Disloyal on the part of Man, revolt,/ And disobedience" (ll. 5–8). Not of military heroics would he sing, "yet argument/ Not less but more heroic.... [H]igher argument remains," which not only depicts the Fall, but will later build from the foundation of the Son's offer of sacrifice the future potential for humanity's redemption. The narrator claims to receive the Muse's "nightly visitation unimplor'd" to inspire his "unpremeditated verse," but adds, "unless [I be] an age too late, or [by] cold/ Climate... Deprest ... if all be mine,/ Not hers who brings it nightly to my ear" (ll. 4–47). The narrator here, not quickened by the Muse as he was early in the epic, expresses doubt of his inspiration, though then he plunges into the tale again. The nature of the invocation, especially of this invocation, implies uncertainty, the need for faith even (perhaps especially) in a fallen world, as the narrator attends to the Fall and thus becomes more caught up in his own fallen state. The work of art, Milton's rhetoric of his own epiphanies, stands along with the reader to address the question of the inspiration behind the epic. Milton's own participation in the Fall appears in the progress (or, perhaps, regress) of his invocations; as humanity through Adam and Eve proceeds toward the Fall and becomes less adept at epiphany in the narrative, Milton becomes less certain of his own claim upon poetic epiphany.

The critic's assessment of the poet's inspiration remains, of course, open to question, but I think Milton chose the epic not only as a test of and testament to his powers, but also because of its tradition as a medium of inspired utterance. As the Hebrew prophets' message proclaimed the mercy and righteousness of God,[19] perhaps prefiguring the Apocalypse but not expressly predicting its details, as prophets since have railed upon the sins of their culture,[20] so Milton embodied in a poem our mutual participation in Adam's fall and also in the potential for his redemption. Perhaps Milton represents a turning point in the tradition of English poetry in his "unity of aesthetics and ideology"[21] but he also forms a link in the tradition of the prophetic/epiphanal epic. As does Spenser's *enthousiasmos*, Milton's claim as epic poet to inspired creation sets in motion an attention to subsequent epiphanies: those of his characters, those of poets, and those of the reader. John Steadman suggests that *Paradise Lost* "portrays man's seduction as an archetypal epic enterprise."[22] Certainly, Satan undergoes an epic quest, but it is one of destruction, and not a human quest. Certainly the Son qualifies as the greatest hero of the poem, but only the Son of God could accomplish His quest.

Adam and Eve both serve, from our human point of view, as heroes of the poem, and their epiphanies become our own as we seek in our own spiritual quests to move from sin to redemption. To a degree, Adam and Eve fail, but many epic heroes fail partially or fully in their quests: Gilgamesh does not gain immortality; Beowulf dies and leaves his folk undefended; Achilles fells Hektor, but soon must die himself; in *Kalevala* Vainamoinen's songs finally fail, and he passes on, when a greater Hero enters the world. But Adam also succeeds: he submits to God's judgment and fathers the line in which Christ will be born and become second Adam, the source of the renewed Paradise. As Eve's temptation presents "a prototype of man's spiritual combats,"[23] so the entire poem fulfills the quest of Renaissance Christian culture: to understand the Fall into sin and the need for faith in redemption. The poet himself follows the quest in attempting to tell the story. The poem provides a medium for epiphany, wherein a reader may share in the pursuit and perhaps the achievement of that quest.

6. Paradise Lost *and the Resimplification of Epic Epiphany*

Wittreich argues that, finally, prophecy, not epic, is the "containing form of *Paradise Lost*"—that prophecy subsumes epic.[24] "Prophetic history" models the development of one's internal life, the "spiritual history of every man."[25] Epic and prophecy both traditionally find their source, sustenance, and survival in epiphany, both that of the poet-prophet and that of the reader. Tasso and Spenser in their epics anticipated what Milton achieved: the convergence of epic and prophecy, the new "heroic song" in which the "field of inquiry [is] the human mind,"[26] particularly as the mind seeks God. By taking the allegorical step in the epic, we link ourselves with Adam and Eve; we lose Paradise, but hope for its return. The reader is a type for Adam as Adam is a type whose antitype is accomplished in Jesus Christ. The reader who makes the equation participates in the Fall and the redemption, the *illo tempore*, the sacred moment, the epiphany. The presence of epiphanal potential as well as the priestly function of exposing the great cultural/religious quest marks in *Paradise Lost* the boldest victory that a literary text may accomplish. And part of our contemporary interest in epic, particularly Milton's epic, remains that it serves us as a source of traditional epiphany and prophecy: a way better to understand a principle central to Christian thought that the original text treats only with the greatest brevity. Prophecy implies an epiphany, and in the epic/prophecy we can find a world in which the possibilities of epiphany go beyond those of the modern to contemporary world, of the symbol or the word, to become again spiritual epiphanies (meetings with a higher-order being), something twentieth-century literature, criticism, and theory have downplayed. Our literary arguments have turned to polemics, politics, and cultural criticism (much like the pamphleteering of Milton's time), away from the Sidneyan sense that we read with the aim to learn, to improve our understanding and practice of virtue, a notion yet endemic to Milton's time. With such considerations the field of possibilities in Milton becomes grander. We need not believe in the truth of the Adam and Eve story to accept the possibility that inspiration from sacred text followed by dedication can lead us to artistic accomplishments worthy not only of helping to define our time, but also to last beyond it and provide some value for ages to come.

One continuing glory of Milton's epic rests in its belief in the human potential for meeting God, and perhaps this potential clarifies part of what returns us to *Paradise Lost* when the epiphany of word or image or art is not enough. Milton's accomplishment rests at the great literary historical fulcrum, the end of what the "old world" could do with epic and textual point from which later ages would rebel. Even someone as far-seeing as Milton couldn't have imagined the next great step in epic history, when William Blake turned the epic quest from Milton's cosmological playing field internally, to the microcosm of his own creative spirit.

Chapter 7

William Blake and the Personal Epic Fantastic

In the prophetic books, as he called them, William Blake creates a personal epic fantasy world in which *epiphany*, rather than the rare phenomenon of post–Neoclassical epic poetry and of our world, occurs naturally and consistently — and internally. In Blake's world epiphany — essentially an internal odyssey of epiphanies — defines the norm for the creative artist because through the imagination we (must) enter and participate in the creative principle of God and thereby work out our own process of rejoining the self-fragmented universe.

Blake expands his personal mythology and foregrounds poetic epic fantasy most completely in *The Four Zoas,* a lengthy, mythopoeic epic of more than 4,000 lines, but in the shorter poem, *Milton,* he most clearly establishes Wittreich's "line of vision," that vatic connection from the epic poets of the Classical world through Spenser and Milton to Blake himself and beyond. In *Milton,* "Blake"— much after the fashion in which Chaucer makes himself a character in the *Canterbury Tales* or Dante does so in his *Commedia*— as character, artist, and participant in his own epic/mythic world receives into himself the spirit of Milton[1] as source of inspiration, and he begins to revise for himself and generations to come the process of imaginative creation, to base it on what I'd like to call the "personal epic fantastic" rather than on obedience to a received tradition or a perceived external source or superior force.[2] While *The Four Zoas* (along with *Jerusalem*)[3] attains by its magnitude pre-eminence in Blake's oeuvre, as David Riede argues, "In *Milton* Blake made his most sustained, tortuous, and tortured attempt to examine the grounds of literary authority and to stake his own claims."[4] And Blake does, as did Milton (and Homer and Vergil before them both), "emphatically claim authoritative inspiration"—Riede adds, "even as he teaches us to suspect such claims."[5] In *Milton* Blake legitimizes his inspiration, his personal epic fantastic, by setting his mythic creation in eternal poetic history, confirming in his rewriting of *Paradise Lost* and *Paradise Regained* (and, thematically at least, his rewriting of all of John Milton's work) the validity and value of his internal world—and of its external, social message. For Blake the great epiphany comes through the creative act, the artist's continuing the act of God's creation according to his or her own inspiration. Creation for Blake means freedom and joy, not obedience, the conclusion to which Milton comes in *Paradise Lost*, or even in waiting for redemption (as in *Paradise Regained*), which for Blake already exists in eternity.[6]

By means of his source of inspiration and his own creative productivity, Blake as artist integrated himself amid the long, historical process by which epic illuminates how we meet our gods and how we achieve the quests required of us by our contemporary cultures: in Blake's case, the Romantic longing for simultaneous connection to both the natural world and the cosmology amid a concurrent desire for stark individuality and cultural criticism. As "prophet" Blake participates in the necessary social reform of his age, while as character in his own "prophesies" he simultaneously mingles with the powers of Eternity, aiming to legitimize and valorize poet and prophecy at once through his artistic media—for Blake, the mingling of word and visual art. Blake aims, finally, not like Milton to encourage obedience—nor does he insist that his mythopoeic world serve as our own—but rather to establish his prophecies "firmly rooted in the political and religious struggle of his time."[7] As prophecy has traditionally shown itself to work, Blake *models* the process for us. Like Los in *Jerusalem*, he asserts, "I must Create a System or be enslav'd by another Man's" (Chapter 1, Plate 10, line 20). He then confirms the act of prophetic modeling in the quotation that closes the Preface to *Milton*.[8] Following

7. William Blake and the Personal Epic Fantastic

the famous verses that begin "And did those feet," concluding with the resolution, through "mental fight," to participate in the rebuilding of Jerusalem in England, Blake cites Numbers 9:29: "Would to God that all the Lord's people were Prophets." Could any society bring about that juncture, Blake suggests, where all its citizens follow their inspiration and work together, each fulfilling all in the expression of his or her talents, then civil strife would cease, and peace and prosperity would reign: Albion as individual, country, and collective humanity would find health, indeed redemptive Apocalypse.

Before the turn of the nineteenth century, Blake had already busied himself constructing, in *Vala, or The Four Zoas*, his mythic-epic of "paradise lost" and "paradise regained." There he re-presented the Fall of Edenic humanity from a state of intellectual wholeness and passionate bliss into a state of fragmentation in which the powerful mental, physical, spiritually unifying (or compassionate), and imaginative faculties descend from a condition of healthy balance into war with one another. As each faculty strives to rule the others, Albion, the universal being—who is also symbolically England or the individual—"falls" into a faint, and the aspects of his being, the "Zoas" or "animal spirits" that combine to express the completeness of his healthy state, spiral into a chaos of deceit, egocentrism, and tyranny. *The Four Zoas*, however, points throughout its strange, thunderous narrative toward the passionate apocalypse in which it culminates, when the universe, the "human form divine," regains its natural, dynamic but peaceful unity: that apocalypse represents for Blake the creative Epiphany toward which the multitude of individual epiphanies throughout his prophet books point.

Albion falls because of the tyranny of, submission to, or worship of individual faculties, or more particularly when Albion seeks to embody divinity outside himself. As the epic begins, "Night the First," as Blake terms it, Tharmas (representing unity, or harmony, or compassion), feeling pity for the lost Jerusalem, quarrels with his emanation, Enion, who flees him, partly out of sadness, partly out of jealousy. Without the unifying force of compassion represented by Tharmas, Albion is doomed to fragmentation. Luvah, Albion's shadow, also his passion, is given the reins by Albion, and "like Phaeton, seizes the chariot of the sun, which belongs to Urizen the Price of Light [that is, reason]." But "[d]esire cannot usurp reason without disaster"[9]; no Zoa may take over the function of another with impunity. Luvah's attempt to tyrannize over Vala deepens Albion's illness, since "the tyrant cannot annihilate his counterpart and reign a lonely integral"; Zoa and Emanation must remain united, and all the Zoas must remain together in their proper places for Albion to stay whole and hale. But "Luvah's weakness, following his loss of Vala, subjects him to Urizen,"[10] and each struggles for "dominion over the Eternal Man as if he really and eternally were a separate entity."[11] Though passion must be buffered by reason (and vice versa), Luvah must assume his rightful place at the "terrible wine presses" whence flows the wine of passion that nourishes the heart for the continuing intellectual war: dangerous, even deadly unless its affects be tempered by Tharmas (compassion) and Urthona (imagination). Explicitly, the process of fragmentation results from a concatenation of anti-epiphanies, in which separate faculties reject or aim to control one another; healing or "oneness," the climax of the work and the goal of epiphany throughout literature, occurs when the "animal" faculties, imperfect but active in their organic forms, resume their harmony.

The sick Albion then turns over the ruling scepter to Urizen in "Night the Second." Urizen, the embodiment of reason, rationalizing the struggle, seeks to establish control by subjecting the imagination to an intellectual and sexually repressive religion.[12] Boastful Urizen removes intellect from the other faculties, establishing what Martin Bidney identifies as a darkly comic "intellectual distance,"[13] but the comedy quickly fades as Urizen, Satan-like in his fallen state, is also separated from his emanation, Ahania, because of his now overriding desire to rule over all. Without Ahania, a "total form of intellectual desire, which must express itself as sexual in the fallen world," Urizen becomes blind in "Night the Third."[14] By "Night the Fifth" Urizen realizes but exaggerates his error, claiming full blame for the evil of the fragmented and now oppressive world, though he remains unready for redemption, lamenting his loss of kingship rather than Albion's fall from unity.[15] Eventually Ahania returns to guide Urizen back to balance, but not until the apocalyptic "Night the Ninth" does Urizen, at Albion's bidding, give up deceit and tyranny to accept his proper place as the Man's guiding reason, not his sole ruler. Blake seems to be responding to Milton's idea of Right Reason, reason informed by faith, and suggesting instead that we must never allow the chains of constricting laws of any sort to prohibit the full experience of every aspect of life and the free expression of divinely inspired imagination ("One Law for the Lion & Ox is Oppression," the final line of The *Marriage of Heaven and Hell*). As long as any of the Zoas aims to control another, Albion, sick with struggle, can do little to heal; redemption begins after long argument (in both senses, "plot" and "spirited debate") as he gathers each faculty back to its rightful place within his being.

The process of anti-epiphany (or revolution and fragmentation), struggle, and epiphany regained (resolution and reunification) defines Blake's personal epic fantastic world. Each step in the "plot" of *The Four Zoas* exhibits Blake's concern — artistic as well as social and spiritual — with our need for constant epiphany. Through epiphany, which it is the responsibility of the individual to seek within, we regain our universality and embody the power of our own creativity, the joy of human existence. Failure to seek or experience or respond to epiphany, such as we find after the Fall in *Paradise Lost*, often directs the action in traditional epic poetry from *Gilgamesh* to the *Odyssey* to *The Faerie Queene*.

Though Los's recognition of Christ within the Man sparks the ultimate reunion of the fragmented faculties, imagination alone — especially the postlapsarian imagination, however willing — proves insufficient to redeem humanity[16]: "Night the First" presents Urthona dutifully working at his anvil, but he feels the crisis within Albion and collapses. His quick dispersal into the wily Enitharmon, the active but childish Los, and the powerful but directionless Orc proves unrestorable until late in "Night the Ninth," when finally the specter and fallen forms of Urthona reunite, and the compassionate, intuitive, and healing Tharmas assists him back to the Edenic state. Passion must not rule the brain, nor reason attempt to nullify the passions or stifle the imagination; with all faculties whole and governing their proper spheres, Albion no longer falls for the "soft wiles of deceit," nor does he worship any separate faculty or wish to find God outside himself. As the poem closes, Pastoral Eden reappears:

> The sun arises from his dewy bed, & fresh airs
> Play in the smiling beams giving the seeds of life to grow,
> And fresh Earth beams forth ten thousand springs of life
>   ["Night the Ninth," ll. 846–88].[17]

And finally

Heroes, Gods and the Role of Epiphany

> Urthona rises from the ruinous Walls
> In all his ancient strength to form the golden armour of science
> For intellectual War. The war of swords departed now,
> The dark Religions are departed & sweet Science reigns [ll. 852–55].

Comprising passion and imagination as well as reason and compassion, Albion must maintain eternal vigilance against the tyranny of any given faculty, a danger that remains given the state of flux that characterizes the world. Blake's world regenerates not simply from fragmentation to unity, but from the tyranny of Fallen fragmentation to the healthy mutuality of Redeemed pluralism, by means of the recognition of Christ within and the proper ordering and expression of all aspects of the human being.

The fragmentary nature of discourse, an axiom to contemporary theory, the Buddhist notion of the "dance of the universe" or the Hindu metaphorical plurality of the "ten thousand things" amid the experience of "the one and the many," the ceaseless interconversions of subatomic particles in modern physics: these many human expressions of the paradox of disintegration within a greater, restorative Unity haunt our imagination age by age. Yet Blake suggests that fragmentation, though an aspect of the nature of the world, need not precipitate a Fall — at least not a permanent one. As Coleridge's *fancy* merely shadows the *primary imagination*, still with some power to move us, but focused on fixities rather than on the "infinite I AM,"[18] or as Lacan's psychoanalytic subject keeps separate what he tells of himself from his own primary language,[19] Blake's eternal Zoas, a "mob of individuals," the "forces of fallen plurality," must willingly achieve their redeemed plurality, the apocalypse necessitated by Albion's own lack of vigilance.[20] Albion wills fragmentation and unification; the poet-prophet points to eschatological renewal, but cannot give a full account of it and defers its historical completion, which lies beyond vision, though its personal fulfillment rests in day-to-day action.

The Four Zoas achieves apocalypse, but not Apocalypse: reunified Albion renews the prelapsarian world, but can never foreseeably eschew Intellectual War — else we will fall again. The "strife of contraries," Harold Bloom comments, "enlivens [even] Blake's heaven, and forbids it to become static"[21]; though "sweet science reigns," Blake leaves us with no promise that we do not continue the cycle of birth and rebirth, fall and apocalypse. At that point, however, *Milton* intervenes, and with *Milton* even more than the other prophetic books Blake takes his place in the tradition of epic epiphany. It turns the prophecy to the quest motif as the poet looks to recover self, country, humanity to spiritual and creative health from the dangers of subservience and the worship of false or limited or failed models.

A work of the first decade of the nineteenth century, Blake's *Milton* assures us that we need not become tyrants, that the "line of vision" includes prophets who, even from eternity, look out for us, and we have deep within ourselves the capacity to free creativity in ourselves and others. Creative labor rewards us, as David Erdman suggests, with "instant *mental* liberation ... in the sense that the poem is a triumphant freeing of Los — not to escape the world's problems but to return to London to work."[22] The power, passion, and urgency of the Bard's song draw the spirit of Milton, who "descends to enter William Blake and learn the error of his tactics in the mental fight," to reunite with his Emanation Ololon ("history-as-it-should-have-been"), and to join with Jesus the Saviour.[23] Milton, like the offenders of Blake's own time, bears some responsibility not only for his own politics, but also for the subsequent political effects of his work, in some ways a greater responsibility because of his function as poet-prophet. As Blake knows and the character Milton must realize, the "sufferings poverty pain & woe" of the people remain real, oppression remains part of the social fabric, and "every revolution will turn to counterrevolution unless the guiding genius of man puts on a 'Garment of Pity & Compassion like the Garment of God.'"[24] For Blake, as Erdman shows, the result of the vision he and Milton share points to peace and justice: "The prophet's vision can *see* the mighty weeping of nations that will end the war: England repenting her cruelty toward America and India, the Germanic allies repenting their persecution of 'France & Italy.'"[25] As it had for Milton before, the connection to epic history gives Blake what Riede terms a "temporal, if not transcendent, authority"[26]; he works "in an ageless tradition and with timeless truths"[27] even as England, frightened of the possibility of the movement of revolution from America and France to its own shores, tightens its suppression of free speech (44).[28]

Blake as poet needed Milton as character for two reasons. Riede puts the first point this way:

Heroes, Gods and the Role of Epiphany

> [T]o establish his own poetic authority, Blake needed to subvert Milton's, to establish a difference between himself and Milton ... to repudiate what Milton saw as the essential structure of differences that constituted his cosmos and his text, the differences between God and man, soul and body, reason and sensuality, inspiration and imagination, man and woman.[29]

I would suggest that Blake gains authority by his poetic union with Milton in the same way that the Zoas, separated into fallen versions of themselves, Emanations and *Spectres* (Milton's specter in the poem is Satan!), gain power by reunion: Blake as Bard, as incarnation of the eternal poet-prophet, gains from his link with Milton a vein into the entire tradition of inspired poets. He, too, speaks at God's bidding, aiming like Milton to "justify," bring God and humans to rights, and history has given poets like Milton that power, if only in retrospect. The poetic epiphanal meeting with Milton, the great, looming symbol of the intellectual Englishman with whom the Romantic poets so struggled, redeems poetry and redeems England, now free of any of the bogies of oppression. The second reason involves Blake's sense of social responsibility: he perceived Milton to have fomented violence, to have encouraged an oppressive regime, and to have elicited a blind obedience to doctrine that he believed people did not understand. And therein we find the essential reason for Blake's *Milton*. The previous great poet-prophet returns to set right, through the current poet-prophet — and Blake must assert such authority, or his message will have no power to create change — his errors, so that he may through Blake re-engage the *mental* fight, encourage freedom of expression, valorize individual inspiration, call forth all people to the "Great Harvest & Vintage of the Nations" (*Milton* 50.1): Albion — England and each of its citizens — is once again rising. Once we realize, with Blake, Milton, Lucifer, and the Angels that "The imagination is not a State: it is the Human Existence itself" (*Milton* 35.32), we may finally establish "Jerusalem/ In England's green & pleasant Land."

Blake does not, however, detach his imagination from history, literary history, or Christian thought. As Thomas Altizer explains, Blake say himself not as rejecting Christian and epic traditions, but as inheriting them:

> Like his precursor, Milton, Blake became a biblical poet by choosing the prophetic vocation of recreating the form of the biblical epic — an epic that is

invisible in an age of unbelief—out of the materials of the history and consciousness of his own time and space. This vocation itself must remain meaningless both to those who reject the Bible as fable and fantasy and to those who believe that the literal words of the Bible are revealed truth.[30]

Whereas Milton's invocations call upon the Holy Spirit, and his epiphanies take place in the meetings among God, angels, Adam and Eve, and Satan, Blake begins, continues, and concludes amid a sustained, continuing, evolving epiphany available to anyone who would attend to the inspiration made available to the human imagination by God. What Milton finds in Adam's obedience at the end of Book 12 of *Paradise Lost*, Blake finds in the act of sub-creation and the acceptance of one's constant connection to eternity. Blake does not despise Milton; he revises him. The Milton in the poem returns to revise himself through Blake's offices.

Milton sought in his cosmological epic to simplify Christian thought so as to empower the individual Christian to accept the "justification" that God offers, to bring together God and person as we had been in the prelapsarian world; he did so in Adam's understanding that "henceforth I learn that to obey is best," to free the Christian from the oppression of sin and suffering, personal or political, by his or her direct attention to God's law. Blake responded to the poet Milton by bringing him as predecessor into his own epic fantastic world to praise Romantic freedom and imagination as powers fully as great as obedience—and to model for his age the ideal of free creativity. I have a sense that in that world what the man Milton would have found heretical, the poet Milton would have found glorious.

Blake, little noted by his poetic contemporaries, yet establishes the fulcrum of English epic history and its epiphanies: he turns them inward. Following Blake, Wordsworth finds his inspiration, the continuing source of epiphany, externally, in nature, but he turns that inspiration to detailed self-examination, specifically the growth of his own mind and poetic imagination. In a sense Wordsworth buffers the "excesses" of Blake, and while the source of epiphany returns to the outside world, the goal of epiphany remains the improved ability of the self to find and practice his or her place in the world.

Chapter 8

Wordsworth's Spots of Time: Romantic Epiphany and Nature Spectacular

With the Romantics epiphany took a turn inward, through Blake's building his personal mythology. Later, in the hands of Byron epic turned to mock-epic (*Don Juan*), and for Keats it entailed an attempt to reach back to old mythologies to metaphorize the nature of the poet's struggles with mortality, fame, and the location of personal imagination (*Endymion* and *Hyperion*). For Shelley the epic took up the subject of Greek myth and the form of closet drama (*Prometheus Unbound*), but also symbolized the overthrow of powers past in favor of the generation that had, presumably, suffered at their hands (Neoclassicism in its reliance on the formal and traditional). Wordsworth straddles the barrier between internal and external, just as he retains something of the Neoclassical emotional distance (at least from a post-modern perspective) while allowing himself extensive autobiography — but his autobiography is as a *poet* rather than as a human being. "The Growth of a Poet's Mind," Wordsworth's subtitle, clearly implies the Romantic fascination (even obsession) with the internal workings of the imagination, but the poet makes explicit that he found his inspiration in intense experiences of natural phenomena and

8. Wordsworth's Spots of Time

that they moved him in a thoroughly religious way. In "Tintern Abbey" his narrator calls himself a "worshipper of Nature" (line 152) and claims that "Nature never did betray/ The heart that loved her" (ll. 122–23). *The Prelude*, in many ways "Tintern Abbey" writ large, details all those incidents of natural inspiration that, to Wordsworth's understanding, built him into the man and poet he became.[1] Wordsworth didn't inherit his task from Blake, nor did he inherit it from the Neoclassicals, whose epic ventures largely involved translations of the Classics. He does, though, embody the ideals of "Romantic" in his epic: the poem focuses on him, and on him as poet, as well as on the power of nature that so inspired him and his contemporaries. Wordsworth takes the epic torch, as does Blake, directly from Milton.[2] In the last lines of *Paradise Lost*, Adam and Eve depart Paradise,

> The world was all before them, where to choose
> Their place of rest, and Providence their guide.
> They, hand in hand, with wandering steps and slow,
> Through Eden took their solitary way.

The Prelude begins there, moving into the wide world, from the poet's humbler and somewhat more joyful perspective. "Escaped from the vast city," he returns to the rural landscape he loves:

> What dwelling shall receive me? in what vale
> Shall I take my harbor? underneath what grove
> Shall I take up my home? and what clear stream
> Shall with its murmur lull me into rest?
> The earth is all before me. With a heart
> Joyous, nor scared at its own liberty,
> I look about; and should the chosen guide
> Be nothing better than a wandering cloud,
> I cannot miss my way. I breathe again [Book First, 1850, lines 10–19].[3]

Wordsworth practically paraphrases Milton, but unlike Adam and Eve, he returns to rather than departs his garden. With the world as garden he enters rather than departs his epic, beginning joyously to reminisce rather than wondering, sadly but resignedly, what comes ahead. As prophet of the individual in nature, he joins Blake, prophet of the individual imagination, plotting the identity of self and of his time:

> to the open fields I told
> A prophecy; poetic numbers came

Heroes, Gods and the Role of Epiphany

> Spontaneously to clothe in priestly robe
> A renovated spirit singled out,
> Such hope was mine, for holy services.
> My own voice cheered me, and, far more, the mind's
> Internal echo of the imperfect sound;
> To both I listened, drawing from them both
> A cheerful confidence in things to come [Book First, 1850, lines 50–58].[4]

He has already "shaken off" the "burden of my own unnatural self" to seek

> Dear Liberty! Yet what would it avail
> But for a gift that consecrates the joy?
> For I, methought, while the sweet breath of heaven
> Was blowing on my body, felt within
> A correspondent breeze, that gently moved
> With quickening virtue, but is now become
> A tempest, a redundant energy,
> Vexing its own creation [ll. 31–38].

From that liberty he hopes to produce something of value, and the desire and inspiration to write rises within him, he says, with almost annoying intensity. He clarifies later, and expands on the nature of the of poetic gift (including another Miltonic echo):

> The Poet, gentle creature that he is,
> Hath, like the Lover, his unruly times;
> His fits when he is neither sick nor well,
> Though no distress be near him but his own
> Unmanageable thoughts: his mind, best pleased
> While she as duteous as the mother dove
> Sits brooding [ll. 135–140].

Like Milton's Creator, who "Dove-like sat'st brooding over the abyss/ And mad'st it pregnant (*PL* 1.21–22), Wordsworth's "mind of the poet" broods over Nature, from experiences of which it builds a world in a poem. That process of mind becomes the epic adventure:

> When ... I through myself
> Make rigorous inquisition, the report
> Is often cheering; for I neither seem
> To lack that first great gift, the vital soul,
> Nor general Truths, which are themselves a sort
> Of Elements and Agents, Under-powers,
> Subordinate helpers of the living mind:

8. Wordsworth's Spots of Time

> Nor am I naked of external things,
> Forms, images, nor numerous other aids
> Of less regard, though won perhaps with toil
> And needful to build up a Poet's praise [146–57].

No wonder Keats saw in Wordsworth the "egotistical sublime," but we may find that as well in Blake: the Romantic Age was to a large degree about the exploration and glorification of self (cf. Whitman's *Song of Myself*). Then, from the experience of self and the place of the self in Nature, epiphanies must come. They came, and if we may believe the poems, often, from Blake's immersion in his own poetic world or from Wordsworth's "Truth that cherishes our daily life" (Book First, 1850, 230), the (Keats-like) "passions that build up build up our human soul" (407), resolving into "the story of my life" (640). Romantic epiphanies lead to self-understanding and self-definition.

One danger arises in how we as readers — and Wordsworth as poet — may distinguish, without a "meeting with a god," between false and true epiphanies, how we may survive the unruly or vexatious roil of thought and emotion to reach something of truth and value. He explains:

> Thus oft amid fits of vulgar joy
> Which, through all seasons, on a child's pursuits
> Are prompt attendants, 'mid that giddy bliss
> Which, like a tempest, works along the blood
> And is forgotten; even then I felt
> Gleams like the flashing of a shield;— the earth
> And common face of Nature spake to me
> Rememberable things; sometimes, 'tis true,
> By chance collisions and quaint accidents
> ... yet not vain
> Nor profitless, if haply they impressed
> Collateral objects and appearances
> Albeit lifeless then, and doomed to sleep
> Until maturer seasons called them forth
> To impregnate and to elevate the mind [ll. 581–96].

The process took him years of rumination: he had to practice and grow into a poet ready to deal with the product of his illuminations. But moments of inspiration began with nature, sunk into his mind and spirit, took time to grow, and flowered when he reached sufficient maturity to recognize them and their value to him.

Heroes, Gods and the Role of Epiphany

As did Blake with his prophetic books, Wordsworth worked on his epic, *The Prelude*, over many years. He originally intended it to serve as an introduction to an even larger work—much as Blake's long poems fit into one fairly consistent imaginative system. Wordsworth produced three significantly different editions of *The Prelude* (1799—only a two-book version—1805, 1850), the third appearing well into the Victorian period, published just after his death. While we think of Wordsworth as a Romantic poet—perhaps, for his particularly potent and omnipresent love of nature, even as the quintessential Romantic poet—his epic epiphanies look forward, more than do any other poet's, to Joyce's. While for Joyce the epiphany takes place in the momentary but full, clear perception of the image, instance, or word, Wordsworth's epiphany take place as we might expect of a writer so much the prophet of Nature: in the full, even ecstatic perception of and participation in natural scenes or phenomena. Those moments of intense clarity and pleasure reinforce for the poet the human need to avoid distancing ourselves from Nature, our best source of peace but also the best venue from which we may learn virtue.

In *The Prelude* Wordsworth calls those moments "spots of time" ("The soul when smitten thus/ By a sublime *idea*, whencesoe'er/ Vouchsafed for union or communion, feeds/ On the pure bliss, and takes her rest with God" [Book Eighth, 1850, lines 672–75]), and they form the focal points around which he collected the memories of the scenes and events that punctuated—as he tells us in his subtitle to *The Prelude*—the growth of his mind and spirit.[5] Following *Paradise Lost*, where Adam and Eve experience the epiphany of their own creation out of Nature, but also the grandest of all possible epiphanies, the immediate presence of God, Blake and Wordsworth came to what we might call the Romantic fork in the road, and each took his own direction from there. As Blake was turning epiphany wholly internally, into his own imagination for the spark through which he connected with deity or eternity, the line of vision could move inward no further. With Blake's entire mythic world coming from his own imagination, that artery of epic exploration—we might, Hopkins-like, call it *instatic*—reaches its logical end. Wordsworth, working at the same time as Blake, follows Milton more explicitly, to an experience more in the traditional sense of the word *ecstatic*. His epiphany shares a great deal with that of Adam's and Eve's waking into Paradise. It remains personal, as to some extent epiphany had always been. It need have no relation to others, yet it still provides knowledge essential to his people and his time: we can regain something of the humanity we have lost through connection to and love of nature ("Nature never did betray the heart that loved her" ["Tintern Abbey," lines 122–23], a Romantic notion in an ironic as well as historical sense). But Wordsworth focuses much as did Blake on the effect of epiphany on the individual: the growth of his own mind, rather than more fully, as did, say, Spenser, on what his contemporaries could learn from his experience, how they could use his epic epiphanies to grow into virtuous lives.

For Wordsworth the natural scene, and the presence of the human (though not always the humane) within the natural scene, may arouse an extreme emotion, nurture clearer perceptions, and allow the self as full an actualization as humans can achieve: manifest awareness of the self, another, the world. Those moments of clarity and full realization of his presence in nature represent for Wordsworth the poet the greatest of human experiences and our highest achievements as creations of God. By implication in *The Prelude*, not only he but also the reader may gain access to the same kind of experience; he makes that point explicitly in "Tintern Abbey."

Wordsworth clarifies the *idea* of the spots of time before *The Prelude* in "Tintern Abbey," which serves in retrospect as a "mini–Prelude," summarizing the "growth of the poet's mind" and explicating the experience that will unfold often and fully in the spots of time of the epic. "Tintern" shows how for Wordsworth natural scenes can evoke ecstatic responses, reinvigorate the senses, or produce gratified calm. Natural beauty refines the character and prepares the observer for later times of trial, but most importantly it connects the viewer to other persons and to eternity. "Tintern" begins as does *The Prelude*, with an "escape from the vast city." The experience of the wildly beautiful landscape remains powerful years later; memories of it recall ecstasy, but bring calm in stressful times, allowing him to mature without losing his appreciation for the beauty that inspired him. Upon revisiting the scene that meant so much to him, the second time with a dear "friend" (his sister, Dorothy), he experiences it differently, with less youthful exuberance, but with a power more subdued and intellectual, refracted by age, time, revision. But on the second visit he adds a new facet to the experience: the original thrill at the scene he recalls vicariously through his companion, whose first experience of the scene mimics his own. Whether we call it compassion or empathy — I allow myself here the dangerous step of equating author and narrator — he experiences great joy when he sees in Dorothy the pleasure that had meant so much to him, and the experience gains another layer of meaning for him as he recognizes her emotional response.

The Prelude aims, I think, to recreate in many and evolving forms something of that same epiphany for the reader that the friend experiences in "Tintern." As Wordsworth recorded and embellished the spots of time that meant so much to him, he must have hoped that his reader would to some degree share those perceptions, either through visualizing the scenes in response to Wordsworth's *poiesis* or through remembering equivalents in his or her own experience and allowing them range to evoke their own ecstatic effects. Before we relegate such notions to Romantic drivel, recall the last time you had (or watched someone else have) the Faustian experience, as Goethe casts it: this moment is so beautiful that I wish it could last indefinitely, so moving and new that I would live a lifetime within it. The beauty of such an instance transports us for a moment beyond ourselves, and the almost unbearable lightness of being of that results releases the senses, at least until self-consciousness occurs, from the burdens of fleshly identity and singularity. Even Milton's Satan, in the shape of the serpent watching Adam and Eve for the first time, stares for a long moment, rapt in that impossible oxymoron, "stupidly good": in the unexpected, instantaneous experience of beauty (and the perfection he has lost) he detaches from his absolute commitment to evil because he detaches from the lonely pain of the self— sadly, briefly. Beyond the pleasure he must have experienced in reminiscence, what a great service Wordsworth would perform for the reader, if he could succeed through his recollections in stimulating the reader's freedom from the cares of self-imprisonment.

"Tintern," beyond its greatness as a poem with integrity of its own, serves as an explication of the idea of the spot of time; it gives us a way, and a way thoroughly of Wordsworth's time and method, to read *The Prelude* beyond autobiography and within the epic line of vision. Wordsworth diagnoses a longing for natural beauty, much as does Blake, who brooded over the "dark Satanic mills," while equally loving "England's green and pleasant land," though he prescribes not mental fight, but flight (both in body and memory) from the city back to the grandeur that so moved and shaped him.

Wordsworth's magical phrase appears in the 1850 version in Book Twelfth, lines 209 and following (see also the parallel passage in Book Eleventh, line 208 ff., 1805 version). Over the next few pages I will indulge in some lengthy quotation from Book Twelfth so that we may parse idea and examples thoroughly:

> There are in our existence spots of time,
> That with distinct pre-eminence retain
> A renovating virtue, whence — depressed
> By false opinion and contentious thought,
> Or aught of heavier or more deadly weight,
> In trivial occupations, and the round
> Of ordinary intercourse, our minds
> Are nourished and invisibly repaired;
> A virtue, by which pleasure is enhanced,
> That penetrates, enables us to mount,
> When high, more high, and lifts us up when fallen.

First, the inspiring moments remain with the person who experiences them, gradually promoting a virtuous life as one learns to remember them and appreciate their value — so much of poetry before the twentieth century dealt with ideas of virtue and how we acquire it, and Wordsworth falls within the center of that tradition. Next,

> This efficacious spirit chiefly lurks
> Among those passages of life that give
> Profoundest knowledge to what point, and how,
> The mind is lord and master — outward sense
> The obedient servant of her will. Such moments
> Are scattered everywhere, taking their date
> From our first childhood.

The spots of time will teach us, he suggests, that we may master ourselves and practice the best part of ourselves, and if we pay attention, such moments will happen often. He immediately follows that description with an example, in fact a double example, with two spots of time juxtaposed, thus clarifying what he means and reinforcing their effect:

Heroes, Gods and the Role of Epiphany

> I remember well,
> That once, while yet my inexperienced hand
> Could scarcely hold a bridle, with proud hopes
> I mounted, and we journeyed towards the hills;
> An ancient servant of my father's house
> Was with me, my encourager and guide;
> We had not travelled long, ere some mischance
> Disjoined me from my comrade; and, through fear
> Dismounting, down the rough and stony moor
> I led my horse, and stumbling on, at length
> Came to a bottom, where in former times
> A murderer had been hung in iron chains.
> The gibbet-mast had mouldered down, the bones
> And iron-case were gone; but on the turf,
> Hard by, soon after that fell deed was wrought.
> Some unknown hand had carved the murderer's name.
> The monumental letters were inscribed
> In times long past; but still, from year to year,
> By superstition of the neighborhood,
> The grass is cleared away, and to that hour
> The characters were fresh and visible:
> A casual glance had shown them, and I fled,
> Faltering and faint, and ignorant of the road:
> Then, reascending the bare common, saw
> A naked pool that lay beneath the hills,
> The beacon on its summit, and, more near,
> A girl, who bore a pitcher on her head,
> And seemed with difficult steps to force her way
> Against the blowing wind. It was, in truth,
> An ordinary sight; but I should need
> Colors and words that unknown to man,
> To paint the visionary dreariness
> Which, while I looked all round for my lost guide,
> Invested moorland waste, and naked pool.

These two sufficiently ordinary instances, an old gibbet inscribe with the name of the man who hung there, and a girl bearing a water pitcher on her head, struck him with such a strong sense of dreary sadness that they stuck with him, barely beneath the surface of his consciousness, coming back to thought to inform him about the constant sorrows of life. Yet one may alleviate those sorrows with remembrance not only of the beauties of nature, but also of its magnitude and of the human capacity to understand and appreciate both pleasure and suffering as inseparable from daily experience. He adds, then, to that reminiscence of the hills and its characters past and present another image, following the pool and dreary crags:

> And on the melancholy beacon, fell
> A spirit of pleasure and youth's golden gleam;
> And think ye not with radiance more sublime
> For these remembrances, and for the power
> They had left behind? So feeling comes in aid
> Of feeling, and diversity of strength
> Attends us, if but once we have been strong.

The mixture of beauty with suffering adds depth to the experience and keeps us from passing too quickly over either. He reflects then that, as he ages, he sees but glimpses of the reserves of power that lie within us, yet he feels moved while he still can to "give life" to those feelings, to record "the spirit of the Past/ For future restoration." Reflecting on the action leads him to reconstitute another memory at the end of Book Twelfth, another spot of time:

> One Christmas-time,
> On the glad eve of its dear holidays,
> Feverish, and tired, and restless, I went forth
> Into the fields, impatient for the sight
> Of those led palfreys that should bear us home;
> My brothers and myself. There rose a crag
> That, from the meeting-point of two highways
> Ascending, overlooked them both, far stretched;

The crag serves here as a natural stepping-off point for epiphany, and the epiphany again serves to heighten the sensory experience of both the landscape and one's self-conscious place in it:

> Thither, uncertain on which road to fix
> My expectation, thither I repaired,
> Scout-like, and gained the summit; 'twas day
> Tempestuous, dark, and wild, and on the grass
> I sate half-sheltered by a naked wall;
> Upon my right hand couched a single sheep,
> Upon my left a blasted hawthorn stood;
> With those companions at my side, I sate
> Straining my eyes intensely, as the mist
> Gave intermitting prospect of the copse

Heroes, Gods and the Role of Epiphany

> And plain beneath. Ere we to school returned —
> That dreary time, — ere we had been ten days
> Sojourners in my father's house, he died.
> And I and my three brothers, orphans then,
> Followed his body to the grave. The event,
> With all the sorrow that it brought, appeared
> A chastisement; and when I called to mind
> That day so lately past, when from the crag
> I looked in such anxiety of hope;
> With trite reflections of morality,
> Yet in deepest passion, I bowed low
> To God, Who thus corrected my desires.

The epiphany need not prove a happy one; it need only bear truth and power and the ability to shape the character as well as future judgments and interpretations of experience. In that instance what may partially echo Adam's ascent with Michael to see the future turns quickly to an image of personal desolation: the death of his father and its effect on the family. We may expect that Wordsworth as "nature poet" and "Romantic" would prefer epiphanies that exhibit positive emotions, even ecstatic joy. In the epic tradition (as in the mythic one) epiphanies need not, for character or reader, be wholly and exclusively positive. Many of the spots of time dredge up negative emotions, sometimes extremely so, either sorrow or fright, much as epiphanies may do in *Beowulf,* Spenser, and Milton, where there are plenty of examples of subliminal epiphanies.

    The important aspect of the spot of time, as epiphany, is that it moves the observer exceedingly: it makes us new, "re-novating," repairing, pulling us from depression and triviality. It is both miraculous and ready at hand. Better yet, such moments retain that virtue over time: their power tends not to fade, if anything to increase, particularly as one later shares them with another person. A "penetrating virtue" (presumable one that cuts through the worries and squabbles of quotidian life), which enhances the pleasure of experience, lifts us when we have fallen or even allows us to mount higher yet when we have already risen beyond our usual levels of competency and pleasure — that passage explicitly defines epiphany for the narrator whose touchstone comes from natural phenomena rather than from explicit meetings with gods. The "spirit" here refers neither to the narrator nor to some divine meta-observer, but to the process of the epiphany: it works when the mind, its awareness heightened by the epiphany, teaches us that sense serves the will (compare the 1805 version, which has somewhat greater clarity on this point). Such moments, the spots of time, begin, Wordsworth suggests, early in life and continue throughout — if we remain attentive and willing — and they will remain available in the memory to ease and heal us in times of worry and trouble. They make us more rational, more fully human, more aware of the world, better able to deal with it — and love it.

Epic epiphany, at its best and happiest, has always appeared naturally, and, within the context of the great narrative events, commonly enough. When they meet their gods, Homer's heroes give them their full attention without fainting or groveling; even Milton's Adam and Eve, at least in the prelapsarian world, feel comfortable walking in the Garden with God or preparing dinner for a visiting angel. For Wordsworth that fact comes to the forefront: the attentive lover of Nature may find epiphany just over the hill or beyond the bend. And once one experiences it, the epiphany may return to memory — sensory memory as well as thought — during any number of times of need: wild Nature teaches, corrects, soothes, nourishes the mind and spirit better than can any other perception.

The first example that follows the term and its explanation, his spotting the gallows during a childhood adventure, seems an odd one to illuminate what the definition would lead us to expect to be a sanguinary experience. A monument of torture and superstition, the gallows and the name of the executed man, once carved into the ground and still cleared by locals, inspire fear, and along with his having got separated from his adult guide, the experience makes him sufficiently weak to stumble. The second, immediately appended example does nothing to alleviate his discomfort. The sight of the girl bearing a pitcher on her head as she fights through the wind to get water at the naked pool afflicts him not with fear, but with dreariness, partly because of its starkness and his recognition of the girl's suffering, but also because it imprints in his youthful thoughts the fact that much suffering in life goes unalleviated — if one has the strength of mind to accept the lesson. No foolish notion here of a benign Nature, nor any romantic insistence on the natural goodness of humanity: those instances show that epiphany instructs us as at least as commonly, persistently, and powerfully in the pains and sadnesses of the world as it does in beauty, continuity, and divinity. We may recall here *Beowulf*, where we find only subliminal epiphanies: the only boundaries the hero (or anyone else) crosses this side of death place him face to face with monsters. Wordsworth's gibbet, especially in the eyes of a child, serves as just such a monster, but the poet does not let us drift into the realm of Romance or myth; he returns us immediately to the common reality of the difficulties of the poor or ultimately of anyone—life binds us all sooner or later to suffering and mortality.

The next epiphany comes with his return to the scene of the pool later in life, the second time, as in "Tintern," with a beloved companion, but with a different emotional effect: "so feeling comes in aid of feeling," as the new experience builds on the old. Pleasure attends the presence of the beloved, and strength and maturity come from observing (and absorbing) the scene literally in a different light. What can at one time nearly induce despair can at a later time refine the thoughts and feelings by showing us the range of responses available to us; the scene itself has no inherent emotion—no pathetic fallacy—but evokes and inflects the humanity of the observer, changing persons willing to accept change, willing to attend and weigh the feeling and ruminate on the results.

That point Wordsworth makes clear in the Preface to *Lyrical Ballads*, in the often underquoted bit of that often overquoted passage, where he writes that poetry comes from the "spontaneous overflow of powerful emotion recollected in tranquility." The sentence does not end there. He adds, that point (emotional overflow) being so, it tends to happen only in one who has thought long and deeply—Wordsworth stands historically not so far from the Age of Reason or from the Victorians as we often place him. No Nobodaddy (to borrow a term from Blake) descends to engulf the observer in divine wisdom; no angel appears to instruct the supplicant; no vision of the New Jerusalem rises from atop a mountain. Wordsworth's epiphanies come from the conjunction of moving scenes and observers attentive enough, willing enough to feel moved. They require someone attuned (or as we used to say in the romantic idiom of the 1970s, at one with Nature) to the free-flowing act of subcreation, not lingering in the slavery of subdued imitation. No pedagogue sits watching, waiting to pass judgment on the human observer to determine the quality of his or her response; the epiphany teaches the person sufficiently sensitive to respond to it. It instructs both in feeling and in thought, refining us for finer, more varied, more meaningful and more permanent experiences.

The third example similarly melds two experiences into one, this one more painful yet because it blends expectation of something better with enduring loneliness. Prepared to return home for the Christmas holiday, eagerly expecting the joys of the season, he waits atop a crag at a crossroads, (only) "half-sheltered by a naked wall" (nakedness comes up often not as a human image but to stress the starkness of the scene), a single sheep standing on one side of him and a blasted hawthorn tree to the other: the first, of course a seasonal image, represents peace, but also loneliness and sacrifice, and the second, thorny and possibly dying, also resonates with sacrifice and suffering. Pursuing that image no further, he jumps ahead ten days, through any pleasures of family reunion, to his father's death, an event that orphaned him and his siblings, a death that brings extreme sorrow without redemption. The 1805 version appends to that story an apostrophe to the friend to whom he addressed the poem (Coleridge), in which he reflects how in later years his thoughts returned to those events or others and find from them, where they could not find peace, at least instruction and strength, as well as a greater facility for "devout sympathy"—a useful point oddly omitted from the 1850 revision. Again we find an epiphany hardly pleasurable, but one that even more thoroughly—perhaps with the growing strength of the poet to endure and express it—teaches the need for patient resolution, compassion, and willingness to learn from all facets of life.

Epiphany serves to inform not always what we want, but what we need. "How strange," he reflects later in Book First, that

> The terrors, pains, and early miseries,
> Regrets, vexations, lassitudes interfused
> Within my mind, should e'er have borne a part,
> And that a needful part, in making up
> The calm existence that is mine when I
> Am worthy of myself! [344–50].

The early epiphanies, despite Wordsworth's occasional assurances to the contrary of a more benign Nature, normally exhibit the painful process of growth and moral transformation. The "stolen birds" and "stolen boat" incidents provide two clear and memorable examples. Here is the first:

Heroes, Gods and the Role of Epiphany

> Sometimes it befell
> In these night wanderings , that a strong desire
> O'erpowered my better reason, and the bird
> Which was the captive of another's toil
> Became my prey; and when the deed was done
> I heard among the solitary hills
> Low breathings coming after me, and sounds
> Of undistinguishable motion, steps
> Almost as silent as the turf they trod [317–25].

The theft weighs not only internally, but externally: Nature takes a ghostly form as physical avenger of the deed. And then again, more fully and powerfully, Nature intervenes to instruct:

> One summer evening (led by her [Nature]) I found
> A little boat tied to a willow tree
> Within a rocky cave, its usual home.
> Straight I unloosed her chain, and stepping in
> Pushed from the shore. It was an act of stealth
> And troubled pleasure.

But Nature will not permit his conscience freedom from the emotional and moral consequences of the act:

> I fixed my view
> Upon the summit of a craggy ridge....
> She was an elfin pinnace; lustily
> I dipped my oars into the silent lake...
> When, from behind that craggy steep till then
> The horizon's bound, a huge peak, black and huge,
> As if with voluntary power instinct
> Upreared its head. I struck and struck again
> And growing still in stature the grim shape
> Towered up between me and the stars, and still,
> For so it seemed, with purpose of its own
> And measured motion like a living thing,
> Strode after me. With trembling oars I turned,
> And through the silent water stole my way
> Back to the covert of the willow tree;
> There in the mooring place I left my bark,—
> And through the meadows homeward went, in grave
> And serious mood [ll. 357–90].

The image of the watchful peak striding after him has almost Tolkienian fantastical echoes, but it has a specific purpose in the poet's mind: to

8. Wordsworth's Spots of Time

instruct in virtuous behavior. Natural phenomena undergo a transformation not merely in the subject's imagination: they bear that quality as an aspect of their creation, inherent for our pleasure and instruction. We walk ever on the verge of epiphany as long as we open our hearts and senses to its instructive capacity. Of course the image stays with him, as such images will. The frights of childhood may shape us indefinitely, for good or ill, though Wordsworth calls attention to them to show not merely their terror, but more permanently their salubrious effects, if only in the long run.

Not all of Wordsworth's epiphanies bring with them fear and pain; some bring great and lasting beauty, though even they retain the indelible imprint of moral as well as poetic authority. One of the most beautiful and memorable occurs (fittingly, after much time and rumination to prepare the soul for it) nearly at the end of the poem, in Book Fourteenth, in the ascent of Mount Snowden (beginning with line four, and following):

> I left Bethgelert's huts at crouching-time.
> And westward took my way, to see the sun
> Rise from the top of Snowden....
> It was a close, warm, breezeless summer night...
> But undiscouraged, we began to climb.

The mountain peak and the poet's movement towards it recalls Spenser's Mount of Heavenly Contemplation and the vision through contemplative prayer of the New Jerusalem. The walk up allows for "suspense" or preparation for the moment, and the peak makes the perfect natural spot for epiphany:

> And, after ordinary travellers' talk
> With our conductor, pensively we sank
> Each into commerce with his private thoughts:
> Thus did we breast that ascent....
>   ... With forehead bent
> Earthward, as if in opposition set
> Against an enemy, I panted up
> With eager pace...
> And as I chanced, the foremost of the band;
> When at my feet the ground appeared to brighten,
> And with a step or two seemed brighter still;
> Nor was time given to ask or learn the cause,
> For instantly a light upon the turf

Heroes, Gods and the Role of Epiphany

> Fell like a flash, and lo! as I looked up,
> The Moon hung naked in the firmament
> Of azure without cloud, and at my feet
> Rested a silent sea of hoary mist.

The moon, so often an object of mystical reflection, greets his ascent, but his presentation of the image immediately connects heaven and earth, the epiphany that Nature has provided him all along, as he recasts the sky as sea:

> A hundred hills their dusky backs upheaved
> All over this still ocean....
> Not distant from the shore whereon we stood
> A fixed, abysmal, gloomy, breathing-place —
> Mounted the roar of waters, torrents, streams
> Innumerable, roaring with one voice
> Heard over earth and sea, and, in that hour,
> For so it seems, felt by the starry heavens [Book Fourteenth, lines 11–62].

The reader may begin expecting a sunrise, the idealized experience suggesting movement to a new day. The narrator sees, of course, not sunrise, but moonrise, and its unexpected effects move him—with another Miltonic echo—to reflect on the nature of the mind:

> When into that air had partially dissolved
> That vision, given to spirits of the night
> And three chance human wanderers, in calm thought
> Reflected, it appeared to me the type
> Of a majestic intellect, its acts
> And its possessions, what it has and craves,
> What in itself it is, and would become.
> There I beheld the emblem of a mind
> That feeds upon infinity, that broods
> Over the dark abyss, intent to hear
> Its voices issuing forth to silent light
> In one continuous stream; a mind sustained
> By recognitions of transcendent power [ll. 63–75].

Milton's dove over the pre–Creation abyss converts to the poet's presence before the abyss of night, which brings not fear and mystery, but rather understanding, though in a necessarily duller light, given our human limitations to climb and to perceive. The vision metaphorizes both the individual mind and eternity: unexpected light rises amid the darkness, and time and experience flood and roll like a sea, powerful and only vaguely determinable, infinitely varied and yet ultimately unified.

For Wordsworth the mind functions, though, as more than a mere part of Nature: it transcends Nature, trumps Nature, since it has inherently greater divinity. Thus he concludes *The Prelude*:

> Then, though (too weak to tread the ways of truth)
> This age fall back to old idolatry,
> Though men return to servitude as fast
> As the tide ebbs ... we shall still
> Find solace — knowing what we have learnt to know....
> Prophets of Nature, we to them will speak
> A lasting inspiration, sanctified
> By reason, blest by faith: what we have loved,
> Others will love, and we will teach them how;
> Instruct them how the mind of man becomes
> A thousand times more beautiful than the earth
> On which it dwells...
> In beauty exalted, as it is itself
> Of quality and fabric more divine [ll. 435–56].

Wordsworth and Coleridge, prophets of Nature, find their prophecy affirmed and made holy by reason: if we attend to what Nature can teach us, it will direct us to the most permanent and glorious element of our humanity, the mind, closer yet to God than is the Nature it observes. The stress on reason may seem out of character for a Romantic poet, but it persists in Wordsworth's thought, for instance both in the Preface to *Lyrical Ballads* and with increasing importance (along with greater emphasis on religious faith) in the subsequent drafts of *The Prelude*. Beauty alone never dominates the poem: it serves to inspire and refine the poet's ability to speak out. Reason, faith, and love ultimately work together, especially spurred on by attentiveness to the source of inspiration that lies all around us. They guide us to integrate the aspects of ourselves and our time into as complete an understanding as humans may experience, and that experience creates a virtuous character which can lead to loving and virtuous actions: Wordsworth's understanding of the prophetic tradition.

The idea of beauty and prophecy merging in the province of the poet occurs elsewhere in the poem. In Book Eighth he describes how, once he had freed himself of the dizzying crowds of London, the landscape taught him to speak out poetry:

> Once — while, in that shade
> Loitering, I watched the golden beams of light
> Flung from the setting sun, as they reposed
> In silent beauty on the naked ridge
> Of a high eastern hill — thus flowed my thoughts
> In a pure stream of words fresh from the heart:
> Dear native Region, wheresoe'er shall close
> My mortal course, there will I think on you [ll. 462-69].

Here the sun directly prompts the "flow of words." Yet those meditations lead him back to the concern for humanity in Nature, for our need to attend to what Nature can teach us about mind and virtue: the potential for goodness that lies within us.

The essence of that experience remains with him even as he struggles with "a sense/ Of what in the Great City had been done/ And suffered, and was doing, suffering, still" (Book Eighth, lines 625-27). But because his awareness of human nature had been nursed in the "Wilds," and "then my young imagination found/ No uncongenial element" (ll. 639-40), a belief in the potential for goodness remains with him even in the City:

> The effect was, still more elevated views
> Of human nature. Neither vice nor guilt,
> Debasement undergone by body or mind,
> Nor all the misery forced upon my sight,
> Misery not lightly passed, but sometimes scanned
> Most feelingly, could overthrow my trust
> In what we *may* become [ll. 644-50].

The prophetic vision says not "Woe to you O Israel," but "Believe in the good you may learn to do." And, he continues, some good comes from mixing in the teeming multitudes:

> Add also, that among the multitudes
> Of that huge city, oftentimes was seen
> Affectingly set forth, more than elsewhere
> Is possible, the unity of man [ll. 665-68].

Many of the spots of time, in the city or in rural landscapes, reinforce that theme, the point of much of Wordsworth's "prophecy" (how he diagnoses the ills of his time), that we live never far away from someone else's suffering, if not our own, and that suffering eventually returns to us. However, we may find not only ease, but glory more than sufficient to master suffering in the pre-eminence of the mind in Nature. The mind, the ability to perceive and reason and create, marks the human as God's special creation; its growth defines the great human adventure, the quest to toward fuller if not full awareness of Nature, self, others, the divinity that flows through each of us ("feeling has to him imparted power/ That through the growing faculties of sense/ Doth like an agent of the one great Mind/ Create, creator and receiver both,/ Working but in alliance with the works/ Which it beholds," Book Second, lines 255–60), and, finally, God:

> Wonder not
> If high the transport, great the joy I felt,
> Communing in this sort through earth and heaven
> With every form of creature, as it looked
> Towards the Uncreated with a countenance
> Of adoration, with an eye of love [Book Second, 1850, lines 409–414].

What moves beyond our understanding may yet evoke our love and encourage us to speak what perceptions of it we can understand. Wordsworth has no trouble labeling the imaginative response to inspiration as *prophecy*:

> I had a world about me — 'twas my own;
> I made it, for it only lived to me,
> And to the God who sees into the heart.
> Such sympathies, though rarely, were betrayed
> By outward gestures and by visible looks:
> Some called it madness — so indeed it was,
> If child-like fruitfulness in passing joy,
> If steady moods of thoughtfulness matured
> To inspiration sort with such a name;
> If prophecy be madness [Book Third, 1850, lines 144–53].

That sense of prophetic impulse and power allow the poet to present dreams, visions, and observations as equal sources of understanding, refinement, and instruction. In Book Fifth he recalls how once, sitting in seaside cave and reading Cervantes, he fell asleep and dreamed of an Arab who carried beneath one arm a stone and in the other hand a bright shell. The man identifies the stone as Euclid's *Elements*, then he holds the shell to the poet's ear: it speaks in an "unknown tongue" the story of Noah's Flood. The Arab says that he will bury those two books, and he flees the

Heroes, Gods and the Role of Epiphany

poet, who desires to follow him, and as he flees he becomes Don Quixote. The poet wakes in terror to find before him the sea and the book he had been reading. Often, he says, books have produced such dreams; he wishes to share the "maniac's" vision and "errand," to escape disaster carrying with him both science and poetry to safety, to some place where one may speak them effectively and productively.

He comments similarly prophetically, if less happily and more discursively, in Book Tenth, responding to his experiences in France at the time of the Revolution:

> But as the ancient Prophets, borne aloft
> In vision, yet constrained by natural laws
> With them to take a troubled human heart,
> ... when they denounced
> ... punishments to come;
> Or saw, like other men, with bodily eyes,
> Before them, in some desolated place,
> The wrath consummate and the threat fulfilled;
> So, with devout humility be it said,
> So, did a portion of that spirit fall
> On me uplifted from the vantage-ground
> Of pity and sorrow to a state of being
> That through the time's exceeding fierceness saw
> Glimpses of retribution, terrible [ll. 437–52].

The prophet's message tends not to bring happiness, but warning of dangers and suffering — one must be willing to deliver the message as it appears, from waking or sleeping source. It humbles rather than glorifies the speaker, but it brings something necessary to the individual and the time.

We may compare and contrast, for both method and theme, a vision from later in Book Fifth, the recollection of the drowned man in Esthwaite Water (1850, lines 426 ff.). Walking by the Lake the poet finds a abandoned pile of clothes. The next day

> At last, the dead man, 'mid that beauteous scene
> Of trees and hills and water, bolt upright
> Rose, with his ghastly face, a spectre shape
> Of terror; yet no soul-debasing fear,
> Young as I was, a child not nine years old,
> Possessed me, for my inner eye had seen
> Such sights before, among the shining streams
> Of faëry land, the forests of romance.

8. Wordsworth's Spots of Time

> Their spirit hallowed the sad spectacle
> With decoration of ideal grace:
> A dignity, a smoothness, like the works
> Of Grecian art, and purest poesy.

Considering the fright he has taken from other visions, we may feel surprise that he disclaims fear on that occasion; the incident serves to show the power of imagination and reflection to prepare one for the experience to come, so that if one has adapted the mind for shocking spots of time, it can endure them not without sympathy, but without collapse.

In Book Seventh he recounts how, during his residence in London, he was once walking among the "overflowing streets," feeling oppressed by his own thoughts, when he found himself

>   smitten
> Abruptly, with the view (a sight not rare)
> Of a blind Beggar, who, with upright face,
> Stood, propped against a wall, upon his chest
> Wearing a written paper, to explain
> His story, whence he came, and who he was.
> Caught by the spectacle my mind turned round
> As with the might of waters; an apt type
> This label seemed of the utmost we can know.
> Both of ourselves and of the universe;
> And, on the shape of that unmoving man,
> His steadfast face and sightless eyes, I gazed
> As if admonished from another world [ll. 637–49].

Spots of time can occur even among the human bustle, if one attends to them, and they can refine the spirit just as do those that occur amidst natural beauty. They show us our mutual humanity and our human limitations, take us — even someone focused on the growth of his own mind — outside ourselves, confront us with suffering, urge us to appreciate our own gifts.

Another urban spot of time appears in Book Eighth, with the poet's first sight of London, recounted in a prosopopeia:

> But how could I in mood so light indulge,
> Keeping such fresh remembrance of the day,
> When, having thridded the long labyrinth
> Of the suburban villages, I first
> Entered thy vast dominions? On the roof

Heroes, Gods and the Role of Epiphany

> Of an itinerant vehicle I sate....
> When to myself it fairly might be said,
> The threshold now is overpast...
> A weight of ages did at once descend
> Upon my heart; no thought embodied, no
> Distinct remembrances, but weight and power,—
> Power growing under weight: alas! I feel
> That I am trifling; 'twas a moment's pause,—
> All that took place within me came and went
> At a moment; yet with Time it dwells,
> And grateful memory, as a thing divine [ll. 539–59].

In this spot he crosses a liminal boundary, a significant one for him, and the significance weighs heavily beyond the bounds of thought, moving him to the core: he has entered not only a new environment, but a different realm of living where stimuli will have equal power to those of his beloved natural scenes, but different emotional effects that will teach their lessons—though not greatly differing lessons—differently. In the city he confronts the smallness, though not insignificance, of the self against a background not of mountains and lakes, but of the great number and array of human persons.

One last example requires our attention here, because it shows the vastness of the poet's vision as prophet, his place in the expanse of history. In Book Thirteenth he explains how as a child, he saw a vision:

> as I ranged at will the pastoral downs
> Trackless and smooth...
> Time with his retinue of ages fled
> Backwards, nor checked his flight until I saw
> Our dim ancestral Past in vision clear;
> Saw multitudes of men, and, here and there,
> A single Briton clothed in wolf-skin vest,
> With shield and stone-axe, stride across the wold [ll. 315–23].

Speaking later to the Friend to whom he addresses the poem (Coleridge), he adds, closing Book Thirteenth:

> I seemed about this time to gain clear sight
> Of a new world—a world, too, that was fit
> To be transmitted, and to other eyes
> Made visible; as ruled by those fixed laws
> Whence spiritual dignity originates,

8. Wordsworth's Spots of Time

> Which do both give it being and maintain
> A balance, and ennobling interchange
> Of action from without and from within;
> The excellence, pure function, and best power
> Both of the object seen, and eye that sees.

As the mind grows sufficient to communicate the ideas that Nature inspires, internal and external meld in the poet's process of communicating the vision.

Wordsworth sums up the point of observation, vision, and poetry — and of his epiphanies — in a passage in Book Eleventh in which he resolves his feelings about the French Revolution:

> What delight!
> How glorious! in self-knowledge and self-rule,
> To look through all the frailties of the world,
> And, with a resolute mastery shaking off
> Infirmities of nature, time, and place,
> Build social upon personal Liberty [ll. 235–40].

Through connectedness comes not compulsion, but freedom of thought and experience, awareness of the state of the human in the world. By recognizing the glories of Nature and the sufferings and potentials that mix and moil either to encourage or restrain our individuality, we may extend the value of liberty from the creative to the social sphere.

And there, with the conjunction of Romantic personal creative liberty and Victorian concern with social structure and hierarchy, Elizabeth Barrett Browning enters the epic tradition.

Chapter 9

Aurora Leigh: Victorian Epic and Woman's Social Epiphany

With Elizabeth Barrett Browning and the Victorian period, the epic poet, like those before her, turns her attention to the sweeping social questions endemic to and definitive of the age. The focal character remains, as with Wordsworth, intent upon, even fascinated with, personal development — hardly a flaw, since in Christian epics heroes often direct their attention largely if not entirely to their own salvation. But Barrett Browning uses her protagonist to call attention to the great issues of the position of the individual in her society: the "woman question"; the effects of the Reform Bill of 1832, which began to unsettle notions of class, law, and human dignity; advances in learning and cultural exchange that, against stiff resistance, would gradually change England (and the world) more completely and rapidly than anything humanity had seen to that point in history.[1] In Blake's work epiphany remained, as it had turned since the christianization of English literature, thoroughly religious, if religious in a personally creative and internally mythopoeic turn; with Wordsworth we experience the divine in intense perception of our connection to Nature, its beauty, power, sublimity. Barrett Browing produced an epic fully grounded in Christian culture and explicitly Christian in its trappings, yet in which epiphanies occur outside traditional religious experience.[2] Her

9. Aurora Leigh

epiphanies occur when characters cross social classes, leap social boundaries, or experience brilliant, disruptive, or even convulsive meetings with one another. With *Aurora Leigh* epiphany lands both feet fully on the ground, moving the perceiver (character or reader) from isolation into the throng of human struggle and commerce, and it incarnates in a thoroughly Victorian way.[3]

Working with a self-consciously female epic allows us to consider some significant structural questions as well, such as how, at least incidentally, does the innovative women poet approach epic differently than does the traditional male poet?[4] Most male epics follow Joseph Campbell's monomyth[5] pretty neatly; can we expect Barrett Browning to do the same? Is the monomyth a male construct, the "male-myth" rather than the unified myth that speaks for all, and did Barrett Browning follow it as a result of the weight or inertia of the tradition, did she point a direction toward a "female monomyth," or did she disengage from the tradition entirely? This consideration deserves some discussion not only for its intrinsic value, but also because it will help us identify epiphanies in Barrett Browning's text just as Campbell's points out their likely type and location in male epics: epiphanies tend to occur at the structural nodes Campbell identifies as the definitive points in the monomyth.

Campbell illustrates his monomyth with dozens of examples that stack up according to the following steps: "call to adventure"; "refusal of the call"; "supernatural aid"; "crossing the first threshold"; "belly of the whale"; "road of trials"; "meeting with the goddess"; "woman as temptress"; "atonement with the father"; "apotheosis"/achievement of and return with the boon.[6] The hero's story often begins with some sort of miraculous birth, and it ends with his gaining "mastery of two worlds," achieving a "freedom to live," and sharing some knowledge or wisdom essential to his culture. Hundreds of stories worldwide follow most to all of that model — no wonder, since it essentially traces (if in a romantic way) the basic processes of a busy private and public life, through coming of age, finding one's place in life, and seeking immortality. Epics follow the monomyth partly because Campbell follows epics, but partly because they tend to trace archetypal patterns. But does the woman's pattern mirror the man's?

In *The Heroine's Journey* therapist Maureen Murdock attempts to draw a similar female monomyth, but she argues that it takes the form of a circle, a symbol she finds more complete, natural, and healing: "I knew that the stages of the heroine's journey incorporated aspects of the journey of the hero, but I felt that the focus of female spiritual development was the heal the internal split between woman and her feminine nature"[7] — a split caused by unsatisfying, even dangerous, cultural models and expectations. While Murdock's steps don't actually trace a circle — the heroine doesn't end up where she began — they do provide a parallel alternative to Campbell's monomyth that we may try to apply as we observe the shape of Barrett Browning's narrative: "separation from the feminine"; "identification with the masculine and gathering allies"; "road of trials: meeting ogres and dragons"; "finding the boon of success"; "awakening to feelings of spiritual aridity: death"; "initiation and descent to the Goddess"; "urgent yearning to reconnect with the feminine"; "healing the mother/daughter split"; "healing the wounded masculine"; "integration of masculine and feminine."[8]

Aurora's separation from the feminine comes with the death of her mother, resulting in an identification with the masculine: her father becomes the center of he world until he also dies. She then has difficulty gathering allies — that problem in part contributes to her devotion to learning and poetry. Accustomed to Mediterranean warmth, she can establish no spiritual connection with her stodgy, cold, English aunt, and though she loves Romney (Aurora's first description of Romney calls him "cold" as well), she can't accept him because of the demeaning words and tone in which he shapes his proposal: as a woman she can accomplish nothing significant on her own, but should instead serve as helpmate to a man's greater mission.[9] As she matures, she begins finally to acquire as allies Lord Howe, Carrinton, and Marian Erle — a small but loyal coterie — along with the growing number of critics who favor her work. The road of trials involves not only her growth toward literary success and some degree of financial independence, but also her encounters with lesser ogres (recalcitrant critics and her own prejudices), greater ones (Lady Waldemar and her confederates — indirectly Aurora suffers through sympathetic response to Marian's trauma), and her need to gain confidence in her own accomplishments. The boon of success comes first with the publication and popularity of her poetry, but later and more particularly as the men she knows and trusts learn to see her not as a "mere woman," but as a talented, productive human being. Spiritual aridity, if not death, follows, though, as Aurora admits to herself her love for Romney and realizes that she wishes for its fulfillment as much as she does for success as a writer — the "death" comes, perhaps, in her belief that Romney has married her enemy, Lady Waldemar, placing him beyond her reach. I see no exact descent to the Goddess, unless we may call that her return to Florence — the city's capability to inspire her truest and most powerful work — or the exploration of the "goddess within," the self, through which she comes to grips with her true feelings and desires. We may call her attraction to motherhood through Marian's relationship with her child, her caring for Marian and the child, and her renewed consciousness of her feelings for Romney the reconnecting with the feminine and healing the mother/daughter split. She literally reunites with the wounded masculine when the blind Romney appears in Florence, Aurora learns his circumstances, and the two are finally able to express and pledge their mutual love. Their new bond will integrate the masculine and feminine, as each better sees the heart and value of the other.

We may safely say that Murdock's pattern, though intended for psychological rather than critical application, fits *Aurora Leigh* pretty nearly, yet neither does the poem fall so distant from Campbell's model, though there we must read the stages even more metaphorically — in either case epiphany remains. We may see the call to adventure as Romney's proposal, which Aurora refuses. Lord and Lady Howe provide friendship and encouragement. Aurora crosses the threshold by striking out on her own to make her way as a writer, finding herself in the belly of the whale as she learns her craft, growing from versifier to true poet (though that stage may better fit her journey from Italy to England and her sentence under her aunt's tutelage). The road of trials includes her meeting and befriending Marian, encouraging the young woman's love for her beloved, Romney, as well as her own internal struggles with her vocation. Again, the meeting with the goddess proves difficult to identify, unless we accept the muse-like influence of her parents on her early childhood: her mother died when Aurora was four and her father when she was thirteen. As she matures, Aurora doesn't find a mentor, instructor, or woman guide; she does, however, maintain a strong religious faith, and the memories of her father continue to instill love and hint at the possibility that she will one day find a fulfilling love relationship. Lady Waldemar tempts Aurora, though entirely unsuccessfully, to betray both Marian and herself. Aurora seeks a kind of atonement with the father through her return to Italy. She gains apotheosis through literary success and then finally again in reuniting with Romney, thus winning the ultimate boon: she retains her independence and the ability and opportunity to do her work while joining with her beloved as well — thereby she will cross the second threshold (marriage) and master both worlds, professional and personal, gaining the freedom to live a complete rather than truncated life.

While neither pattern fits perfectly, both fit reasonable well. Not all male heroic stories fit Campbell's monomyth exactly: it defines a composite, an ideal, not a series of constraints. We should expect a single, female monomyth to work no better: in any given story most particulars, but not all, will approximately match the pattern.

If we look at Aurora's story as an incarnation of a kind of archetypal tale, rather than by the light of a more modern psychological model, we may propose for it a fairly simple series of steps to mark the nodes of its foundational myth. As we often see in hero tales, Aurora does have a type of miraculous birth: she comes from what to her aunt should constitute a forbidden match, of English man to Italian woman, but her parents do give her love, and from them she draws inspiration. Misfortune then casts her into a period in which she is secreted away for special training: while her aunt would confine her, as we learn in the marvelous passage satirizing the "proper" education for an English girl, amid time-consuming and growth-limiting busywork, Aurora uses every opportunity to acquire learning from books and to extend her imagination and retain a sense of individuality and self-worth. She emerges into public life with a first trial: receiving a sufficient but hardly impressive inheritance and rejecting Romney's proposal (as well as the much more substantial monetary gift he tries to give her), she undertakes the life of the writer. Though she loves Romney, she will not give up her sense of self— despite her society's desire to quash it — to have him. She won't even admit that love to herself, though her aunt points it out to her, because it can mean nothing to her until she achieves a fuller sense of herself as individual human worthy of praise for her abilities. Aurora has a version of the traditional "meeting with the goddess," if we wish to call it that, with the noble but manipulative Lady Waldemar; the goddess turns out infernal rather than divine — another (subliminal) test that Aurora passes. Perhaps instead we find a symbolic "meeting with a god": Romney, who sets out to recover the worst-off and worst of his fellow Englishman and sacrifices a great deal in the attempt. While Aurora needs a female mentor and friend, she doesn't find one but instead becomes one to the hapless Marian — Aurora asserts herself as strong, capable, and good. She accepts a course of life indicated by her talents and energies, pursues it, and succeeds, finding that success only partly fulfilling. A greater sense of wholeness comes from her growing relationships, first with friends such as Lord and Lady Howe, later and closer with Marian and her child, then culminating in the ability and opportunity to share love with Romney.

At the risk of falling into a dangerous stereotype, I find this latter point essential to the "female story" in a way that it isn't to the male, whose apotheosis historically often separates him from others, whether family, society, or world, though it may join him to God or gods (consider for instance *Jane Eyre*, *Wuthering Heights*, Madame de Staël's *Corinne*, George Sand's *Consuelo*). The female journey usually ends with a joining, either with the heroine's mate or family or a group of friends or (as in the case of public leaders) a people — apotheosis or fulfillment of the journey comes as much from that joining as from personal accomplishment. Perhaps the female monomyth involves less seeking and finding and more giving, expressing, and sharing. Pop culture sources as well as traditional (religious or mythic) and literary sources tend to bear out that same result — whether they echo a truth or reinforce a stereotype I can't say. And yet Aurora undergoes a kind of gender reversal, at least for her time, in that she becomes not only caregiver but provider.[10]

Epiphanies in *Aurora Leigh* come at those nodal plot points that mark Aurora's personal rather professional crises and achievements: they stem particularly from the human interactions that punctuate those instances. Much as in earlier epics, Barrett Browning begins the poems with muses, though she need not invoke them. Aurora says she will "write my story for my better self" (Book 1, line 4), probably Romney, who thus serves as her muse in the poem's "present."[11] Her first muses, though, her parents, began the process that led to Aurora's desire to express her creative nature, so that she comes to define herself by that activity: "I write" (l. 29). "O my father's hand" (l. 25): the gentle caress represents the caring strength and true but cooler love of the father; however, "[w]omen know/ The way to rear up children ... kissing full sense into empty words ... children learn by such,/ Love's holy earnest in a pretty play,/ and get not early over-early solemnized.... Such good do mothers" (ll. 47–60). Once her mother has died, a painting, at which she would gaze for hours, remains to remind Aurora, both immediately and through its evolution in her imagination, of her mother's face and its inspiring qualities:

> still that face ... which did not therefore change,
> But kept the mystic level of all forms,
> Hates, fears, and admirations, was by turns
> Ghost, fiend, and angel, fairy, witch, and sprite,
> A dauntless Muse who eyes a dreadful Fate,
> A loving Psyche who loses sight of Love,
> A still Medusa with mild milky brows [ll. 151–57].

The face induces both love and terror, as the early death of a parent will, so that "I felt a mother-want about the world" (l. 39). While first experiences with and later memories of her parents inspire Aurora, their deaths act almost as anti-epiphanies, placing her in a situation where love is hard to find and to identify (though, ironically, her father's last word to her is "Love," seemingly a directive). What we may call social or interpersonal epiphanies return with her ensconcement with the Leighs in England, yet they come with complications for both Aurora and the reader. Her aunt, a sub-liminal influence in her eagerness to hold back Aurora and punish her for her father's marriage to an Italian, yet says clearly and simply to Aurora that she recognizes her love for Romney and can't understand her rejecting his proposal.

Romney, in social terms a super-liminal epiphany in that he has higher status and presents the opportunity for both security and true love — something missing in Aurora's world since her parents' deaths — functions narratively because of his blundering proposal as though he were sub-liminal, pushing Aurora away from a source of happiness and fulfillment. Missing the possible epiphany of romantic love, Aurora finds her joy in books and, like Wordsworth, in the growth of her imagination: that epiphany occurs inwardly as she recognizes — if not yet realizes — her talent and potential as a complete human being. Another epiphany occurs when, after a time of learning, she asserts her identity *as writer*, when she emerges into her professional self—the importance of that assertion overcomes the power of romantic love that will have such importance at the end of the poem. Her early poems do well with readers even though Aurora herself feels they have little value: she knows that they don't express her full talent or speak to her identity as a significant human being, not just a "mere woman" playing at poetry, as Romney suggests (she once describes a book she finds Romney reading as "mere statistics," I, 525). Aurora expects no less than epiphany from her work:

> Fame itself...
> Presents a poor end...
> And the highest fame was never reached except
> By what was aimed above it. Art for art,
> And good for God Himself, the essential Good!
> We'll keep our aims sublime, our eyes erect....
> ... Let no one till his death
> Be called unhappy. Measure not the work
> Until the day's out and the labour done....
> Deal with us nobly, women though we be,
> And honour us with truth, if not with praise [Book V, lines 64–83].

She believes epic lies within the potential of poets of her time; admitting herself as poet allows her the option of epic, something Victorian critics, even those willing to admit women as lyric poets, thought beyond women; epic provides a means to reach God. At times she questions whether, having gained admiration, finding love remains within reach, and having made poetry, epiphany remains available in her time:

> Books succeed,
> And lives fail. Do I feel it so, at last?
> Kate loves a worn-out cloak for being like mine,
> While I live self-despised for being myself,
> And yearn toward some one else, who yearns away
> From what he is, in his turn. Strain a step
> For ever, yet gain no step? Are we such,
> We cannot, with our admirations even,
> Our tip-toe aspirations, touch a thing
> That's higher than we? is all a dismal flat,
> And God alone above each [Book VII, lines 704–14].

Heroes, Gods and the Role of Epiphany

But Aurora expresses heroism at least as the best and truest of realism and as ready for epic in her time as in any other:

> The critics say that epics have died out
> With Agamemnon and the goat-nursed gods;
> I'll not believe it. I could never deem
> As Payne Knight did...
> That Homer's heroes measured twelve feet high.
> They were but men: — his Helen's hair turned grey
> Like any plain Miss Smith's....
> And all men possible heroes; every age,
> Heroic in proportions, double-faced,
> Looks backward and before, expects a morn
> And claims an epos....
>   But poets should
> Exert a double vision; should have eyes
> To see things as comprehensively
> As if afar they took their point of sight....
> Their [poets] sole work is to represent the age....
>   Never flinch,
> But still, unscrupulously epic, catch
> Upon a burning lava of a song
> The full-veined, heaving, double-breasted Age....
>   [T]his is living art,
> Which thus presents, and thus records true life [Book 5, lines 139–222].

We see here a vision Yeats will echo later in "Sailing to Byzantium," the magic figure who speaks "Of what is past, or passing, or to come" (l. 32), perhaps the clearest rendering of *prophecy* in the history of poetry. The epic poet particularly prophesies, looking back, looking forward, then defining her Age:

> What's done at last?
> Behold, at last, a book.
> If life-blood's necessary, which it is,
> (By that blue vein athrob on Mahomet's brow,
> Each prophet-poet's book must show man's blood!)
> [Book 5, lines 352–56].

Aurora produces a book, and by the end of the poem a book that not only the reading public like, but of which she can hesitantly feel proud and which wins the approbation not only of her friends, but finally of Romney as well. That moment, when Romney, physically blind but artistically

9. Aurora Leigh

at least partially awakened though not fully enlightened, admits that Aurora's latest book has moved him. His epiphany becomes Aurora's; once he appreciates — with a notable remnant of reluctance — the talent of the woman he has loved all along,

> in this last book
> You showed me something separate from yourself,
> Beyond you, and I bore to take it in,
> And let it draw me. You have shown me truths...
> truths not yours, indeed,
> But set within my reach by means of you,
> Presented by your voice and verse the way
> To take them clearest. Verily I was wrong [Book 8, lines 605–13].

she may, particularly after she learns of his blindness, and after Marian relieves him of any sense of obligation to her, allow her love for Romney to take shape in words:

> "Is there hope for me?...
> I love you, Romney."
> "Silence!" he exclaimed.
> "A woman's pity sometimes makes her mad...."
> "But I love you, sir;
> And when a woman says she loves a man,
> The man must hear her, though he love her not,
> Which ... hush! ... he has leave to answer in his turn."
> [Book 9, lines 601–15].

The greatest epiphany of *Aurora Leigh*, an epiphany of empathy or compassion or recognition as well as the resolution of the love relationship that has sat tacit through nearly the entirety of the poem, occurs as Romney accepts Aurora as complete, talented human being, which ironically frees Aurora to emerge as complete, fully loving human being. Much as in *Jane Eyre*, the male has lost strength but gained love, and the female has gained strength which she then sacrifices — or at least shares — for the sake of love.

Several other epiphanies in *Aurora Leigh* deserve our attention, some in the form of interpersonal exchanges and some in the form of recognitions or ideas. For instance in Book VII Aurora, having returned to Florence and noticing the snakes, frogs, and lizards like "green lightnings on the wall" (1080), recalls her childhood and observes an "epiphany lost":

Heroes, Gods and the Role of Epiphany

> How last I sate among them equally,
> In fellowship and mateship, as a child
> Feels equal still toward insect, beast, and bird,
> Before the Adam in him has foregone
> All privilege of Eden, — making friends
> And talk with such a bird or such a goat....
> But now the creatures all seemed farther off,
> No longer mine, nor like me, only *there* [ll. 1087–1100].

As her human sympathies grow, the old epiphanies with other creatures depart. Her memories float to her father and then to a Wordsworthian spot of time, a detailed recollection of a mountain-house, which unfolds until the memory grows too strong for her, and she must abandon it. It reminds her too powerfully of her parents' deaths, causing her to keep that sort of epiphany at a distance: "That was trial enough/ Of graves. I would not visit, if I could,/ My father's, or my mother's any more.... [L]et me think/ That rather they are visiting my grave,/ Called life here" [ll. 1142–1151]. As the tradition of epic epiphany has long shown, epiphanies need not always bring pleasure. They can, as when the young Aurora cracks the liminal threshold of her books to find worlds and ideas that liberate her from her dull and dreary present, but they can as well bring sorrow, pain, or even terror.

The same point holds true for the interpersonal epiphanies in *Aurora Leigh*. Through the course of the poem Romney as epiphany transforms imagistically from fire-starter to audience to king to angel. When they are still teenagers, Aurora says, "I used him as a sort of friend" (I, 512), and "Once, he stood so near/ He dropped a sudden hand upon my head/ Bent down on woman's work, as sort as rain —/ But then I rose and shook it off as fire" (I, 542–44). The fact that "[a]lways Romney Leigh/ Was looking for the worms, I for the gods" (551–52) separates them: neither can experience the epiphany of love and compassion since each seeks something the other can't yet give.

Later, when Aurora is twenty, Romney comes upon her suddenly as she strolls in the garden playing with the idea of her identity as poet-in-the-making: she passes the laurel (symbol of the poet) and the myrtle (symbol of love) and ties a wreath of ivy (growth and fecundity) around her forehead and

9. Aurora Leigh

> turning faced
> ... My public!—cousin Romney—with a mouth
> Twice graver than his eyes.
> I stood there fixed —
> My arms up, like the caryatid, sole
> Of some abolished temple...
> Yet my blush was flame [Book II, lines 58–64].

The fire image returns, but with the addition of Romney as Aurora's "adoring public," but Romney proceeds with terrible blundering gravity to insult first Aurora and then all women and then to propose marriage. He has neither a clue to her character nor a chance of success with such an approach; she replies, "What you love,/ Is not a woman, Romney, but a cause" (ll. 400–401) and "You misconceive the question like a man" (l. 433). An epiphany that could have ended in mutual love fails, and only at the end of the poem do the two set things right.

Romney appears again to Aurora in Book VIII, stepping into her fantasy, as she sits at night on her terrace in Florence looking over the city and imagining it as a vast sea-kingdom:

> Methinks I have plunged, I see it all so clear...
> And, O my heart ... the sea-king!
>   In my ears
> The sound of waters. There he stood, my king! [ll. 58–61].

Aurora has often thought of Romney and even scolded herself for doing so, particularly after she believes him to have married lady Waldemar. Because of the darkness and because he remains fairly still, she doesn't notice his blindness. Even before she experiences the revelation of his blindness, Romney transforms metaphorically into an angel. He praises her and her work warmly and lovingly, to the point that Aurora, believing him married, grows angry with him. He assures her he remains single, and he gives her Lady Waldemar's scathing letter (surely another sub-liminal epiphany) then announces that he has come to make good his earlier promise to marry Marian. Marian rejects the proposal, but not the goodness that elicits it: "I haply set you above live itself,/ and out of reach of these poor woman's arms,/ Angelic Romney" (Book IX, lines 367–69). Twice the angel who tried to save Marian from poverty, loneliness, and disgrace, Romney gains the freedom to express love to Aurora—and Aurora has learned enough about herself as well as him that she may finally and fully declare her love for him as well. Blinded trying to save Marian's father from the fire that the poor started and that burnt down Leigh Hall, Romney now symbolically looks to Aurora as his dawn, his light, his angel: the two of them have traded roles.[12] We may say in a sense that now Aurora descends to meet him, though neither character in the poem expresses that sentiment. She names him king, and he names her goddess — not exactly figures to encourage a healthy relationship, but each an epiphany to the other.

Other significant interpersonal epiphanies occur in the poem, for instance, as I have briefly mentioned, Aurora's meeting and subsequent friendship with Lord and Lady Howe, but more particularly her first meetings with Lady Waldemar and Marian Erle (both in Book III) affect the course of the narrative and Aurora's development as a human being. Lady Waldemar, above Aurora in social rank, immediately uncovers the scheming and manipulative nature of her character. "Is this ... the Muse?" she asks (l. 363), but Aurora, feeling her insincerity, will play no game with her, eliciting a change in tone from fawning to direct insult: "Ah — keep me ... to the point/ Like any pedant" (ll. 378–79). Despite the woman's superiority by class, Aurora does not submit to her, refuses her suit to talk Romney out of marrying Marian. What would appear by class to be a super-liminal epiphany turns out a subliminal epiphany, since Lady Waldemar attempts by charm and guile to get Aurora to betray her principles.

Meeting Marian Erle, on the other hand, appears, socially, as a subliminal step for Aurora, but the poor young woman has exactly the opposite effect of Lady Waldemar. Later, in Book IV, Aurora will even call her "noble Marian" (l. 313). Having been forced to run away from her parents to avoid being sold by her mother to a pedophile, Marian seeks socially what Aurora seeks artistically: by her own virtue to raise herself to some form of laudable, livable circumstance. Aurora succeeds, not only in gaining status and satisfaction as an artist, but in using her position to save others (both Marian and Romney) rather than to condemn or use them (as would Lady Waldemar). Marian rises, falls, then rises again — her fortunes rise as she relies on the Leighs, falls as she depends on or is thrust into the hands of those of her own class. Barrett Browning shows no interest in social *equality*, nor any trace of belief that we can ever achieve it;

she does see and express a human obligation to help those in need, as individuals, when they merit it. The social epiphanies in the poem lead to those ends. Marian has passed a liminal boundary into a life of security and friendship for her and her child — in her world she can rise no higher. Aurora has achieved the goal of self-actualization and the dream that for so long lay beyond her ability or willingness to express it, romantic love. As epic heroine she crosses those two liminalities, epiphanies greater than those achieved by anyone else in the poem, great enough that at the end of the poem she not only becomes Romney's "morning-star," but also feels confident enough to assert her vision of the great chain of love: "First, God's love" (Book IX, line 881). The epiphany of their love produces at the end of the poem a mutual vision of eternity: as dawn crests into "the first foundations of that new, near Day" (9.956) and Romney stands still, as though gazing through blind eyes, Aurora "saw [that] his soul saw" (9.962), and she quotes from Revelation 21: 18–20, naming the stones that line the foundation of the New Jerusalem, from the earthy brown Jasper to the blue sapphire to the white chalcedony to, finally, the purple amethyst. Love of art (Aurora) plus social love (Marian) plus romantic love (Romney) equals the joining of heaven and earth, the Great Epiphany, moving us all from earthly dust to a state of purity and ultimately to a state of spiritual nobility. Here we find the fulfillment to which even *Paradise Regained* only points, only as a vision, yet promising the greatest joys this life can offer. The heroine, together with hero (and we may also include Marian as child, ward, friend) has found the boon, hopes to keep it, and has at least temporary apotheosis.

Throughout the English epic tradition epiphany, if the protagonist responds to it correctly, both instructs and elicits growth. In each case in *Aurora Leigh* the epiphanies allow Aurora the opportunity to grow, and through their artistic, social, and romantic implications they point the reader to ways of considering the great Victorian questions.

The epiphanies in *Aurora Leigh* support complex layers of social themes: the value of the self, of the individual; the importance of finding and following one's calling or vocation and the centrality of work to one's life and character; the power of poetry to refine the mind and spirit; the value of a woman's soul, and its equality with the man's; the dangers of the tragic and heroic masks we choose to wear, aggrandizing our own accomplishments or sufferings; the inestimable value of compassion; the need for the poet and philanthropist to work together to reform society; the fact that class does not equate with character; the need for completeness (life means learning, work, and accomplishment, but also and especially love, generosity, and spirituality). We could hardly expect such a significant Victorian poem to lack didactic purpose, and Barrett Browning's epiphanies support them all. Further, by breaking down — or at least peeking over — significant barriers in the epic tradition (gender, class, subject matter such as notions of declining heroism), the poet creates space for even bolder experiments to come.

Chapter 10

Walcott's *Omeros*: Postmodern/Postcolonial Epic Epiphanies

The history of epic poetry continues following Wittreich's consistent "line of vision"[1]; as I've shown in the preceding chapters, from its beginnings we may trace a predictable course of themes, concerns, constructs and quests even into our own time. English epic (or epic poetry *in English*) takes up that course with *Beowulf*, where one expects and finds, didactically, a hero fighting monsters, a hero to embody courage, loyalty, and duty and to earn *lof* and *dom*— but without the explicit Christianity that characterizes most of the poem's literary milieu. The hero undergoes *sub-liminal* epiphanies[2] in his battles with infernal monsters, but experiences no *super-liminal* epiphanies, or meetings with gods, to offset them or prepare him for his *agon*. We may suspect the resulting *aporia*, no matter how we read it, to enhance the elder poets' themes: (1) the pagan warrior had no certain access to divine intervention, and so had finally to fall; (2) doomed or not, one follows one's calling unflinchingly; (3) glory comes more from process than result. From *Beowulf* forward we may trace the English line of vision, allowing for a little selectivity, through Spenser, Milton, Blake, Wordsworth, Barrett Browning, and Joyce, watching how the

Heroes, Gods and the Role of Epiphany

various poets' preferences for themes and approaches to epiphanies evolve age by age — at least we may do so into the early twentieth century. From there where do we go, in an age when the poetry "establishment" has decentralized epic as its culminating form of expression, its summit of respect and poetic power?

I would like to suggest that the natural evolution of English language epic concerns leads us next, even necessarily, to Derek Walcott's *Omeros* as its current *terminus ad quem*, not as the definitive end of epic history, but as the pole toward which epic would logically migrate in a postcolonial world. As conscious inheritor of, participant in, and re-shaper of the tradition, Walcott takes up the methods inherent in his genre; as innovator and epic-spokesman he must almost certainly stamp the form with the predispositions and anxieties of his age, though filtered through and informed by his own genius (both in the personal and Classical sense of the word), inflected by national (in this case international) and autobiographical concerns. In *Omeros* we find not only a plethora of themes central to diagnosing if not healing the twentieth century's postcolonial abuses and obsessions, but also a renewable revision of our understanding of epiphany. *Omeros* structurally and thematically fits the line of vision even as it uniquely incarnates late twentieth-century epic sensibility, born of individual but culturally extrusive perception and expression.

Walcott transports both reader and narrator to his native St. Lucia, where polyphonic voices syncopate the wounds of colonialism with brief but recurrent pulses of joie de vivre. Polychronic viewpoints sometimes suture, sometimes reopen those wounds for examination. Rinsing to the ear and variegated to the eye, *Omeros* does not easily unfold its literal fable to traditional exegesis: any given narreme may imply but not specify its connection to vision, dream, symbol, fact, play, or several layered readings. To say it simply: I don't always know what "happens" in the story. The movements of the narrative elements cross boundaries and each other constantly and symphonically, so that one seldom feels confident separating drama from dream. That difficulty seems central to Walcott's plan: to undermine what we *know* about the colonies, race, one another, ourselves. Epiphanies occur in the poem not to clear up doubts, but to provide one a way to appreciate and live with them, to encourage a Keatsian "negative capability" beside a Gandhian composed resistance beside a Homeric pugnacity that destabilizes a stereotypicalized Caribbean warmth, balancing history and race against a struggle for identity building.[3]

Epiphanies arise in *Omeros* like riffs across a clef of characters: the "I" who may well stand for the poet, and who not only recapitulates Homer, but also converses with him and counterpoints him; Achille and Hector, sailors and fisherman and rivals for the heart of the beautiful Helen, who embodies the maddening beauty of the island—to her own detriment as well as theirs; Major Plunkett and his wife, Maud, the benign, doomed colonists; "foam-haired" Philoctete who seeks healing from the shamanic/sibyllic Ma Kilman, who "glimpsed god in the leaves" (48.1) and, possessed by a spirit, heals Philoctete's wound; the blind, bardic Seven Seas who, "moved by a sixth sense," stands in for Homer, but can accomplish nothing; the recurring swift, the bird so eminently symbolic as the movement of sea, time, memory, and experience that it almost emerges as more character than symbol; the trees that, like the swift, take on several lives, moving and growing like life itself, looming over everything like gods; canoes that have their own often telling, often sadly humorous names (e.g., Achille's *In God we Troust*, the misspelling individualizing the name but undermining the trust).[4]

The thematic threadings that outline the epiphanies emerge almost as a floating tapestry of their own, each clear and discrete, yet woven almost into gnomic desideratum: in the face of declining empire, the colonists' need to redress the "desolate beauty" of the island and its people; the poet's duty to the people, because from them come his rhythms, his sense of poetry; the contrast between the penury of the folk—and even of the colonizers' sailors—and the wealth of the colonizers and slavers, and the lie that imperialism intended to help those colonized; that "History earns its own tenderness in time ... for the V of a velvet back in a yellow dress"; the people's loss of their past, and yet their continuing exuberance in the face of despair; the "epical splendour" of the slaves' surviving the journey to the island; the human as maker, thus the necessity not "to leave a man's hands empty"—the poet's labor continues even more than it deconstructs the creation of empire, connecting, recording the evolution of race and culture; the sea as life, as clock, as mother, as priest, as divinity; the search for the "light beyond metaphor"; destruction by tourism, but, despite it, the fact that the sea goes on, taking us with it or not—finally, one has the need, the obligation, to feel, to record, to *tell*.⁵ Plunkett, the descendent of the colonizers, must have an injury, says the narrator, working out his plan, because "affliction is one theme/ of this work, this fiction, since every 'I' is a/ fiction finally. Phantom narrator, resume" (5.2). The poem disgorges themes as Poseidon does waves, and its epiphanies wrestle with those themes as did Jacob with the angel, for a name and a place and a conviction of truth, the author's and his island's.

The themes congeal around this firm, epiphanal statement of purpose in Chapter 58:

> Therefore, this is what this island has meant to you,
> why my bust spoke, why the sea-swift was sent to you:
> to circle yourself and your island with this art.
> In Chapter 2 the narrator requests of his mentor an
> epiphany with this invocation:
> O open this day with the conch's moan, Omeros,
> as you did in my boyhood, when I was a noun
> gently exhaled from the palate of the sunrise.

Later he explains,

> and *O* was the conch-shell's invocation, *mer* was
> both mother and sea in our Antillean patois,
> *os*, a grey bone, and the white surf as it crashes.

A successful invocation would in a book such as this one call forth lamentation and activity, origin and continuity, the structure of things and any living structure's inherently shifting variations—and so it does, to begin the process of "circling" self and island, molding the autobiography that comes from the history.

One may argue that epiphany occurs as the fishermen battle the elements or even in the moments of intense sexual love: though not enough in themselves to resolve human questions, those moments at least have beauty. But more specific epiphanies from a variety of perspectives punctuate the narrative. Achille's vision of drowned bodies rising by the hundreds (24.2) not only encapsulates the danger of the fisherman's life and the sickening slaughters wrought by imperialism, but also prepares the reader for the long dream-vision of Chapter 25. That extended epiphany serves as a "descent into hell"—in this case a crocodile-infested African mangrove swamp—and also supplies super-liminal and sub-liminal voices that reconnect Achille to name, family, history, and myth. He meets his dead father, who cannot remember the name he gave his son — neither can Achille remember. In losing his name, he has lost his past, accepting a present and future imposed upon him by others: "In the world I come from/ we accept the sounds we were given" (25.3). "You, nameless son," the father replies, "are only the ghost/ of a name." He adds, "Why haven't I missed you, my son, until you were lost?" But he teaches Achille myths and rituals, as he "walk[s] there for three hundred years" (26.3), seeing even a group of captured slaves yielded up to the slavers, learning the Faulknerian lesson of endurance and passing out of time. He returns, of course, to the pleasure of his seafaring present, finding there another epiphany, his connection to the past in the practices of the present (30.2):

> Then an uplifting oar is stronger than marble
> Caesar's arresting palm, and a swift outrigger
> fleeter than his galleys in its skittering bliss.
>
> And I'm homing with him, Homeros, my nigger
> my captain, his breastplates bursting with happiness!

Both the creations (epic and culture) and the horrors (slavery and racism) of the past flood away in the wake of the necessity of the present: since we must go on, we must find joy in the going. Achille allows space in his soul for the echo of the canoe's wash and for Marley's reggae, and the poet mirrors, repeats both Achille and himself in the American Indian, the cowboy, and even the Conquistador, until the quotidian voice of Seven Seas wakes Achille from his dream to rake the leaves in his yard: Walcott leaps from sublime to mundane as though each instance of either one serves as a stepping-stone to keep writer and reader from drowning in time.

The narrator hops such stepping-stones in his own epiphany: "I crossed my meridian," he says (37.1), to the "mud-caked settlement founded by Ulysses ... Ulissibona ... 'Lisbon' as the Mediterranean/ aged into the white Atlantic," to find "this port where Europe/ rose with its terrors and terraces." "We had," he adds, "no such erections/ above our colonial wharves" (37.3), where three empires, "London, Rome, Greece," met and where they retain more than a mere shadow of their ancient power: "Who decrees an epoch? The meridian of Greenwich" (38.2–3). The colonizer still names the center of the world. The Caribbean remains to some degree stripped of regenerative or reproductive energy, chained in time and space to the vast, skeletal fingers of imperialism and colonialism, its energy squeezed in a death-grip of cloying traditions and a present both unwilling and unable to sacrifice its taste for blood, with no place to flee amidst a wide world addicted to wealth and power. The character Helen stands for the island, its life force, but the other characters fight over her or turn her into symbol or dream, neutralizing her humanity or individuality. Poet engages poetic past to help him answer his questions both personal and racial.

Not only Homer, but also Joyce, "our age's Omeros" (39.3), serves as Muse, "undimmed Master/ and true tenor of the place!" as the narrator, a sort of international Leopold Bloom, walks dreamily along the Liffy. "I blest myself in his voice," he says, and he even sees and puns on Joyce's ghost, "the wick-low shade.... Then Mr. Joyce/ led us all," but that image disappears, re-emerging in the Aegean, where "[o]n the scorched deck Odysseus/ hears the hill music through the wormholes of the mast" (40.1), until the Greek's wanderings, drawing themselves from the Irishman's, return the narrator's thoughts to Africa, whence the sea-swift catches and flings his imagination to Caribbean currents, Istanbul spires, Venician gondoliers, and as far as "the scraping cellos in concentration camps" and the "mausoleum museums" of modern art (40.2-3) — a swift with powerful wings, certainly, and one that exhibits for the narrator his love/hate relationship with art and with the past, the "slave from the outer regions/ of their fraying empires" who still sees "what power lay in the work/ of forgiving fountains with naiads and lions" (40.3).

Yes, the narrator does have his encounter with Omeros, Homer, but in an unexpected locale. He reports that, in the Dakotas, at an Indian camp, through a tent door, "I saw the white-eyed Omeros" (43.2), who speaks in the voice of a Sioux warrior, observing that "Whiteness is everywhere" (43.3). That image, too, rapidly gives way to the memory of a lost love. In this epic, as in imagination, politics, or life, no voice, no image, no assurance lasts long as anything other than recorded vision, and most, as one would expect of postmodern epic, produce self-reflexivity:

> When would it stop,
> the echo in the throat, insisting, "Omeros":
> when would I enter that light beyond metaphor?

10. Walcott's Omeros

> But it was mine to make what I wanted of it, or
> what I thought was wanted.

Even the poet is enslaved to his visions, though he has some choice in their explication and application.

Chapters 56 and 57 unveil another dream vision. The narrator walks "out onto the balcony/ of my white hotel" in view of the sea, and there drifts a floating head "as the surf hissed: 'Omeros.'" But Omeros becomes the character Seven Seas, who shifts into a shadow, then a driftwood log, then a plaster bust of Homer, which then takes on the features of a black man, then becomes a foam-headed fisherman, and then a dog, leaving its pawprints on the sand: The narrator explains, "I was seeing/ the light of St. Lucia at last through her own eyes,/ her blindness, her inward vision as revealing/ as his [Omeros'], because a closing darkness brightens love,/ and I felt every wound pass" (56.2). Self-exegesis gives way to a conversation with Homer: "'I saw you in London,' I said 'sunning on the steps/ of St. Martin-in-the-Fields, your dog-eared manuscript/ clutched to your heaving chest'" (56.3). The Greek replies, "The Aegean's chimera/ is a camera, you get my drift, a drifter/ is the hero of my book." But the narrator replies, confessing, "'I never read it... Not all the way through,'" but adding, "'Master, I was the freshest of all your readers.'" Confessing, he connects with and refreshes the past.

And that same freshness Walcott both asks and requires of his own readers, as he circles his island re-creation with his art. He sings the island into an epic, and the ocean sings its epic through him: "it drenched every survivor/ with blessing. It never altered its metre/ to suit the age, a wide page without metaphors./ Our last resort as much as yours, Omeros.... [A] quiet culture/ is branching from the white ribs of each ancestor" (59.1–2). As the fisherman "believed his work was prayer" (60.1), so the poet prays through his poem for respect and conservation in the face of growing tourism, modernization, and renewed if redirected exploitation. He sings, with the last line of the poem, of the fishermen still fishing, of the sea "still going on." The whole of the final chapter echoes the beginning of Classical epics: instead of beginning "I sing of the wrath of Achilles" or "I sing of arms and a man," Walcott concludes, "I sang of quiet Achille, Afolabe's son ... who had no passport, since the horizon needs none ... was nobody's waiter,/ whose end, when it comes, will be a death by water/ (which is not for this book...)" (64.1). "I sang our wide country, the Caribbean Sea./ Who hated shoes ... whom no man dared insult and who insulted no one ... but now the idyll dies.... So much left unspoken.... [L]et the deep hymn/ of the Caribbean continue my epilogue." With the end we find a beginning, an inversion, like a breaker that crashes down on the sand, to be drawn back into the deeps: epic as chorus, epic as riptide. The singing itself has passed, but island, waves, poem remain.

The whole of *Omeros* functions, I would like to suggest, as an inverted epiphany, an epic struggle disgorged, the author's battle with a past at once personal, artistic, and historical, with self and culture fragmented, with a love of place and a hatred of feeling displaced, swimming, yet also inevitably drowning in the torrent of artistic responsibility and the flood of dooming time. Any epic, Walcott seems to suggest, does little more than echo the liminality between the conscious and subconscious experience of a poet and a poet's time; *Omeros* sings as one hardly dare hope the great quest of the postcolonial Caribbean, the harmonies and discords, with barely a melody, the essential quest for continuity and meaning amidst the incumbency of loss. *Omeros* comprises, as Isabella Zoppi writes, "interwoven threads ... against the background of a collective memory"; it serves as the "odyssey of one individual and [in the epic tradition one may also say 'for'] his people," and it exhibits the "profound need to belong which makes the story of one man the epic History of Man"[6] — as epic always aims, I think, to do.

Omeros also further personalizes epic, postmodernizes it, in a story, often like Blake's, so maddeningly de-centered and vigorously variable that it floats among dream, reality, the instructive, and the ineffable. It does exactly what the English epic tradition needed someone to do. As it prepared to turn the calendar to the twenty-first century, *Omeros*, as did *Beowulf* once, turned the line of vision internationally, at once maintaining and broadening the tradition.

A Postscript on Tolkien and the Epic Novel, and a Conclusion

Grave danger confronts the awed reader who undertakes to become a scholar or critic of epic — a deep encounter with even one may take a lifetime's work — and yet the sheer magnitude of epic poetry as subject, its history and traditions, has its own inescapable magnetism. Whether or not one believes in a living epiphany, its literary appearance creates a grandeur unmatchable by any other trope. With respect to the critical tradition, so many specialists have laid claim to each one that the critic who faces them all together falls immediately into an abyss of traditional and modern readings that easily overwhelm; each poem claims a reading history both broad and daunting. The enormous, difficult, and often brilliant body of scholarship on any one of the great epic poems that I've included in this study, plus the proprietary feelings that accompany the poems and scholarship, make the process of crossing boundaries from one literary period to another intimidating at best. But sometimes useful thoughts, valuable approaches for reading, teaching, and further study come from projects that attempt too much — respect for the attempt, as well as love of the texts, may perhaps preserve the undoomed scholar, if his courage holds. And the focused study of epic poems, either in a college course or on one's own, makes continually fascinating reading, more so than an age dedicated to the sound bite may guess.

I suspect that epic poets have always believed that their genre outstrips all others, at least in magnitude and perhaps in the fullest embodiment of our striving for greatness — we may think that notion theoretically maudlin until we talk with any athlete who cares deeply for his or her sport, any scientist who approaches the most difficult problems, any physician who seeks a cure or even a treatment for the most harrowing diseases, any parent who would give his or her life for a child, any soldier who would give his or her life for a country or creed. Tragedy, necessarily foregrounding a fall (and until the Modern period as great a fall as possible), can surpass epic's depths, but not reach its heights. The novel can achieve a greater range of emotional variety and a more subtle expansion of character, but its native realism inhibits it from entering the loftiest realms of heroism and striving — they would seem in a novel inappropriately mythic and even silly, because the novel builds its foundations on irony.

Aristotle ranked tragedy above epic because it has greater concentration and therefore a greater likelihood of producing a catharsis, a cleansing of unhealthy emotion to allow the audience to return to life healthier and more rational, thus better able to live the Greek notion of a good life. But the epic's greater diffuseness and scope doesn't eliminate any possibility of catharsis; in fact, while epic tends not to end on the note of horror common to tragedy, its typical denouement in observation of what heroic action has won, where it has succeeded and where failed, may create a firmer, deeper, more lasting catharsis than tragedy. Because it doesn't depend on the horror of the moment, but on a sense of achievement, epic, particularly when it justifies the ways of gods to humans, may better than any other genre prepare us once again to meet life head on. It may cleanse fear, malaise, doubt about the virtue of trying; it may encourage, allow for the potential of hope, reconnect the hero to the community and the community to God — such results will answer any objections Plato expressed to including poets in his ideal Republic.

I feel confident that I may draw some useful general points from the line of vision that has guided the previous chapters. Epics tend to deal with questions that we all need to ask as individuals and as cultures. While historically they have paralleled the biologist's maxim that ontogeny recapitulates phylogeny — the course of an individual's concerns follows the course of epic concerns — they do not soar in the clouds: they retain considerable day-to-day applicability. Largely epic questions, like the central

A Postscript on Tolkien and the Epic Novel, and a Conclusion

tenets of Christian thought (to love God and love our neighbor), come down to simple but persistently demanding questions: how do I learn what God (or god) wants me to do? how do I learn and communicate something that people need to know now? how do I find the way to the "good life" or the "good death"? Those questions tend to appear age by age in a sensible order, though at any time we may, or even must, go back to old questions and old answers. The hard part requires looking ahead to the next one. That's why we have needed and continue to need Epic or something epic, so that we keep hunting for the new ones and struggling with the old ones that we've answered, having failed fully to apply those answers. From age to age our perceptions change, perhaps even the nature of our consciousness changes, but we still must deal with mortality, the individual's desire to learn, achieve, and excel, growing and more diverse populations and technologies, with more and more of us demanding to know more and more things while others of us, fearing what we've already found, simply want to return to a state of mind simpler and less fluid.

As fundamentalisms rise (see for example Karen Armstrong's book *The Battle for God*),[1] military firepower grows and spreads, and the world gets smaller but tighter around the waist as our taste for consumption rises, we need as much as ever a sense of or at least hope for epiphany: a way to get some assurance that life has meaning and value beyond consumption and power. The function of heroic acts may change, but their essence, motivation, and undergirdings remain the same: we need courage, independence of mind, a belief that virtue exists and that it matters, a willingness to deal with our past errors and our present limitations, a continuing commitment to learn more and promote human rights and equality in the present. For all its flaws, the epic tradition teaches us that and more. While some readers may begin associating that tradition with militarism, patriarchy, and oppression, it actually exhibits an enormous responsiveness, flexibility, and celebration of the spirit. Ideas such as duty, self-expression, and the willingness to grapple with and emerge affirming art and life still have value, and they always will.

I like to end courses in which we study epics by asking students, using our line of vision, what epic subjects and themes should or must come next?[2] Why should we believe, especially given the magnitude of the accomplishment in a poem such as Walcott's, that Epic will die as a genre?

Heroes, Gods and the Role of Epiphany

What concerns, quests, and questions emerge *today*, or will emerge in our future?

Some students wonder if epic must, if not die, peter out, subsumed at last entirely by the novel, at least in societies that have leveled (or claim to have) their class structures. I think a good deal of the epic impulse has indeed gone there. Many students think first of science fiction, with its "final frontiers," for its use of technology and it imaginative creation of new worlds, a direction humanity may one day need to take in fact to survive. Consideration also turns to fantasy literature — most students now interested in epic actually began their readings in fantasy — and suggestions turn then quickly to J.R.R. Tolkien. *The Lord of the Rings* and *The Silmarillion* represent creative achievements of a lifetime's effort by a scholar who loved and taught epic (for example, *Beowulf*) and the great medieval Romance epics (such as *Sir Gawain and the Green Knight*). While Tolkien intended *The Silmarillion* more as myth, to fill a cultural gap in England's literary history, *The Lord of the Rings* has many traditional epic qualities: a long narrative of a heroic quest to accomplish something essential to the characters involved and to their culture, mirroring something that the author's culture needs to confront (the cultural devastation and the almost unthinkable changes in the world wrought by the two world wars). Though he intersperses poetry in the story, Tolkien narrates largely in prose (though often a stylized prose that mimics varying registers of Old and Middle English to designate different levels of speakers and discourse situations). We must finally call *The Lord of the Rings* a novel, if a novel with epic elements and a strong dose of epic spirit — also because, while it engages the adventures of the great and mighty, it directs most of our attentions to the small and common — though thoroughly heroic — hobbits. But Tolkien doesn't spare the epiphanies: he uses many and powerful versions of them. The use of epic elements along with the enormous popularity of both the books and the films based on them suggest that Tolkien located something important in the epic line of vision, so I'd like to turn most of the remainder of this chapter to how, when, and why he takes an important step in the twentieth-century piece of the argument, a step that may point some likely directions following Walcott.

Tolkien's Middle-earth fantasy, though novel rather than epic in genre, meets *Beowulf* particularly and English epic generally at its pen-

A Postscript on Tolkien and the Epic Novel, and a Conclusion

chant for epiphany, typical of fantasy as of epic.[3] Fantasy has always sought boundary phenomena just as has science fiction, but through imagined worlds full of magic rather than through technology. Epiphany would in its traditional sense of human meeting God or gods appear to be missing from *The Lord of the Rings* (*LOTR*), but in a particular and peculiar form Tolkien borrows his method for them directly from the medieval poems he loved and knew so well. Given that epiphany implies a meeting with a being of a different order, either higher or lower on, one may say, the Great Chain of Being, we do find even in *LOTR* some fairly traditional examples: the wizards, minor deities of a sort, have regular interactions with other characters, and Sauron, of the same order of nature as the wizards, aims, to the degree that he can accomplish it, to control all earthly beings and end their hopes for any epiphanies greater than that. Fantasy moves as does Romance, on the wings of magic or special natural/supernatural powers. Epiphany stands in Tolkien as in epic at the gateway of a character's movement towards good or evil, and Tolkien's Hobbit saga makes no greater an exception than does the great Anglo-Saxon epic; in fact, I would like to propose that Tolkien borrows the kind of epiphanies we find in *Beowulf* as most appropriate for his own fictional world, where, for a writer of his concerns, specifically Christian or Germanic instances would not fit.

Epic, as I have argued throughout this book, has dealt with two major concerns: how we practice heroism and how we meet our gods. For instance, Gilgamesh must seek immortality, but, failing Utnapishtim's tests, accept mortality; Achilles and Hektor must meet in battle, the spoils to the victor; Odysseus must overcome all challenges and return to his kingship; Aeneas must submerge his personal desires and do his duty to gods and country: such deeds exhibit the heroism of the epics' respective ages of antiquity. Beowulf must show steadfast courage in combat against monsters: that is the heroism of the Germanic Age. But in *Beowulf*, unlike what we see in the epics of the ancient world, God or gods remain disturbingly silent: we hear that "god" moves in the world or that *wyrd* goes ever as it must, but the only supernatural beings we encounter are monsters: Grendel, Grendel's Mother, the dragon. Those meetings take place for us, according to Todorov's definition of *the fantastic*, in the realm of the fantastic: Anglo-Saxons believed, apparently, in literal monsters and dragons, but to modern readers, mostly because of those monsters, the world of *Beowulf* floats between what we accept as real and what we remit to fantasy. Through the terms *fantasy* and *the fantastic* and their application modern and contemporary critics more accustomed to the novel than the epic have found a palatable means to address epiphanies or boundary phenomena that epic poets didn't need: they felt epiphanal boundaries as always already present.

The Anglo-Saxon Maxims tell us such indisputable truths as "Beam sceal on eorðan/ leafum liþan," a tree must lay its leaves on the earth, "Fus sceal feran, fæge sweltan," a traveler must set forth, doomed to die (Krapp and Dobbie 157, translations mine), and "Draca sceal on hlæwe, frod, frætwum wlanc," a dragon must be in a barrow, old, proud of treasures.[4] What to us dwells on the fringe of sanity to the Anglo-Saxon lived in the world, if less than commonly, at least as naturally as trees and leaves.

Certainly the dragon even for the Anglo-Saxon is a magical being, in some cases a man who because of exceptional greed or savagery has become a dragon — rather like the vampires we keep telling ourselves we don't believe in but who continue to show up in our novels, movies, and fantasies. The magic of *Beowulf* and its world makes possible and even desirable extraordinary beings within the bounds of nature, beings such as Beowulf himself, whom the poet calls *aglæca*, the same word he or she uses for Grendel and the dragon, which must mean something like "big, powerful, extraordinary (but not unnatural) thing." Meetings of or with such creatures constitute in the poem both the means by which the hero establishes his heroic courage and the only epiphanies that that world offers. Minus its magic, Beowulf's is a world not so different from that of our own century, which has found its own particular monsters; with its magic, Beowulf's is essentially the same world as that of our fantasy.

Tolkien, one of the greatest *Beowulf* scholars, turned, I will argue, naturally in his epic-fantasy to Beowulfian epiphanies. Abjuring the person-meets-god epiphanies of ancient epics, the Christian or allegorical epiphanies of Renaissance epics and of many contemporary fantasies, and the psychological or social epiphanies of the Romantics and Victorians, Tolkien, despite his own commitment to Christianity, chose to have his heroes meet monsters and ghosts rather than God or gods because his pre–Christian Middle-earth — like the Middle-earth of his readers — shares with *Beowulf*'s the same heroic necessity: steadfast courage from heroes and common folk alike in the face of enemies natural or supernatural. Even help from semi-divine representatives of good, such as elves or wizards, doesn't absolve hobbits or people of their heroic responsibilities. There Tolkien's world also crosses over into our own, where ghostly epiphanies are more commonplace and pressing than divine, and where we share a hero's and a hobbit's desire (in lieu of a good meal) for the courage to complete our appointed — and sometimes, seemingly, impossible — tasks. And there also Tolkien's world — as Blake does, though with a different modus operandi and for different thematic purposes — crosses from pure fantasy into *the fantastic*: the immediacy of his epiphanies pulls the stories from our imagination into the world of our everyday fears, hopes, and needs, where we too must meet stealthy orcs and peace-consuming dragonfire with steadfast courage, yet a world where magic remains, as in *Beowulf*, an accepted and expected part of nature. As Peter Beagle says in his introductory blurb to the Ballantine editions, Tolkien's Middle-earth was not his own invention, but what "was there long before him," waiting for "a great enough magician to tap our most common nightmares, daydreams, and twilight fancies." It is a world into which we cross regularly, for as Tolkien himself said, "'I am a hobbit myself ... in all but size,'" and "'[H]obbits are just rustic English people, made small in size because it reflects the generally small reach of their imagination — not the small reach of their courage or latent power.'"[5] That comment applies normally to the rest of us as well, at least when our courage holds and when a magical writer gets hold of our imagination and shows us that we ourselves have the power to move the world toward evil or good.

Both epic poem and epic fantasy succeed because, as Eric Rabkin says, we "participate sympathetically in the ground rules of [the] narrative world," because we participate in their, to use the Tolkienian term, *subcreation*.[6] Rosemary Jackson argues that fantasy, a "free-floating form" (1), provides not something transcendental, but an escape into nostalgia, for "it is literature of desire, which seeks that which is experienced as absence and loss" (3). In both *Beowulf* and *The Lord of the Rings*, our subcreation is re-creation, an effort or desire to return to a time when character, author, and reader can participate in a clearer heroic than contemporary times allow, a time when we knew what to do and, in fact, had little choice but to do it. In the "Heroic Ages" of *Beowulf* and *The Lord of the Rings*, heroes, whether Nordic warriors or hobbits, always know what to do, what their situation demands of them, and they are not confusticated and bebothered by concerns of the Afterlife and how current deeds may affect the fate of their souls. They are able to act heroically without confusion, something that the age in which both pieces were written wouldn't have allowed their respective audiences to do, when heroism clashed at least potentially with religious and social dictates that commanded peaceful suffering in the face of aggression.

As T.A. Shippey has pointed out, Tolkien and other writers of his generation looked back to medieval models for their fantasy because contemporary thought provided no assurances about how best to deal with the twentieth-century "waste land"; because so many of their generation had fought in war and had known the potential of human atrocity, they saw that "the theme of human evil was not one which could be rendered adequately or confronted directly through the medium of realistic fiction alone" (221) because of the fog of contemporary politics and the difficulty in contemporary realism of not focusing the source of evil as "out there." The fantastic world allows for the connection between created and quotidian worlds, between the places that allow for a realistic shared burden of evil and a magical distancing from the finger pointing of politics. Following Professor Shippey's argument, I would add that what Tolkien borrows from the medieval world to address the problem of evil, he also borrows to create epiphanies in general (such as when hobbits or people meet elves or wraiths), those that involve special powers of good or evil alike, and that those epiphanies dot the landscape of Middle-earth as necessary and natural steps in the Hobbits' journeys.

Tolkien's operative notion of *subcreation* takes over when the landscape of the text moves from our world into the world of Faerie, where magic is still an intricate part of nature. We move likewise into the fantastic in both Tolkien's work and in *Beowulf* when the boundaries between worlds become blurred, when we accept the proffered world as grounds in which we can fight the battles of good and evil.

Tolkien asserts that

> fairy-stories as a whole have three faces: the Mystical towards the Supernatural; the Magical towards Nature; and the Mirror of scorn and pity towards

Man. The essential face of Faerie is the middle one, the Magical. But the degree to which the others appear (if at all) is variable and may be decided by the individual story-teller.[7]

When magic is part of nature, we have stepped across a boundary into Faerie; we may not have left mysticism, scorn and pity behind, but we have certainly moved to a place where we will have to confront both good and evil in ourselves and outside of ourselves, since wherever there is magic, there will be creatures who will use it for good and creatures who will use it for evil, and its effects will appear on a sufficiently grand scale that no one in the world, ultimately, can ignore it, as Hobbits find out with the Ring of Power. We also find that since the magic must finally touch us (as when Frodo must carry the ring in Bilbo's stead) and since its physical power will be more than we ourselves can generate in defense, our only hope rests in steadfast courage, in the hope that courage will allow us to sustain what we believe to be good long enough to disperse the magic, or to find a power sufficient to counter it, or until it destroys itself, or until we can find it within ourselves and eliminate it there either by an act of will, or, as in Frodo's case at the Crack of Doom, have it eliminated for us by good luck or fate.

With Bilbo and Frodo we do not have the power that we have with Beowulf: Beowulf has the strength of thirty men, the very strength of his opponent, Grendel, slightly more than that of Grendel's Mother, rather less than that of the fire-dragon. But humans do have something special about us, something more than meets the eye, as several characters remark about Hobbits in Tolkien's saga. What the Hobbits prove to have, though, is exactly what Beowulf has: sufficient resources to complete the task at hand. Beowulf defeats Grendel not because he has greater strength, but because he has greater courage: he simply hangs on as the monster tries to escape. He defeats Grendel's mother not because he has greater strength than she (though he does), but because he keeps his wits about him in battle and finds hanging above him a magic sword that he can use against her. He defeats the dragon, with Wiglaf's help, almost out of desperation, because he must do so or no one will, and he sacrifices his life in the process. No gods appear to help Beowulf, and he prays to none for help. As the hero himself has earlier observed, "Wyrd oft nereð/ unfægne eorl, þonne his ellen deah"(ll. 572–73), Fate oft preserves the undoomed man,

Heroes, Gods and the Role of Epiphany

if his courage holds. Nor does Beowulf meet a devil, other than symbolically, in the monsters: they do not literally threaten his soul, which according to Christian doctrine was already forfeit, he being a heathen, but rather his life, his fame, and later his kingdom. The monsters are a natural part of his world, and he meets them as a natural if extraordinary man, most extraordinary because his courage never flags, and most successful for the same reason. Beowulf's epiphanies came against creatures of magic — Grendel and Grendel's Mother, descendants of Cain and thus of murder, whose magic makes them impervious to all but magical weapons, and the scaled dragon that can spit fire and poison — and he uses not magic, but courage and attentiveness, even desperation, when necessary, to defeat them.

Bilbo and Frodo succeed similarly; they have no such strength as Beowulf's, but they have courage (Bilbo faces the dragon when the dwarves will not), they have a willingness to take up duties that fall to them (Frodo offers to carry the ring back to destroy it), and they have an uncanny luck (Gollum's appearance to bite the ring from Frodo's finger at the crucial, culminating moment of the quest). Like Beowulf they neither meet nor call upon any god (contrary to what one might expect of a Catholic writer), though Gandalf is a kind of demi-god, nor do they meet directly with a Satan, though Sauron, whom Frodo nearly meets, is obviously a Satan-figure. They do, though, meet plenty of extraordinary creatures, guides, monsters, and ghosts, everything from goblins to trolls to wraith-kings on the minus side and elves to forest-guardians to wizards on the plus side. In each case what characterizes the epiphany is that the Hobbit confronts a creature either able to use magic or a product of magic. The Hobbit always has less strength than the character who provides the epiphany, except in the remarkable instance of the Hobbit who possesses — but must not use — the ring. In such cases other beings who meet the Hobbit have an epiphany because of the magic associated with the ring. The parallel with *Beowulf* holds up on this point also: people who meet Beowulf do not meet a being of another order or with strength beyond human limits (though Beowulf defines the limit), except when Beowulf uses the magical sword to kill Grendel's Mother. Hobbits with or without magic pose no special threat to any other creatures until their lives are on the line; Beowulf poses a threat only to creatures who use magic to do evil or to those (like the Frankish hero Dæghrafn) who threaten his life or his king's.

A Postscript on Tolkien and the Epic Novel, and a Conclusion

The difference appears in the characters' separate notions of what finally constitutes *good* in the world. Beowulf seeks *lof* and *dom*, praise and glory, whereas the Hobbits seek a quiet and secure life with companionship and plenty of good meals. But Beowulf and the Hobbits are not creatures of a different order of being: neither desires to use magic or weapons at all. And both intend to do what they were clearly born to do. Beowulf wants to become a hero, and he does, by means of steadfast courage — no problem there.

The curious result is what becomes of the Hobbits: they are creatures who want no more than long, quiet, gentle lives, but when those lives are interrupted by evil from without, they have no choice but to exhibit that same steadfast courage as Beowulf's, not out of a desire for the heroic immortality of praise and fame, but to return once again to their Hobbit lives. The ends differ, except for the need to resist evil, which remains constant, but the means are the same, and the means call up for Tolkien, as they did for the *Beowulf* poet, the kind of epiphany necessary to their themes: the heroes must meet something within their worlds and beyond themselves, but not *unavailable* to themselves.

The Silmarillion, while we must probably term it *myth* rather than *epic*, has a long series of epiphanies, both superliminal and subliminal, as myth must nearly always have. Yet it exploits also the epic impulse. Germinating during Tolkien's time in France during World War I, but more than anything a function of his interest in philology, it deals with the problems of war, generational succession, and the difficulty flawed creatures with free will have in retaining our connection to the divine given our penchant for self-fixation. Tolkien needed a world in which beings would speak the languages he created, but that world might have turned into anything: it did turn into a battleground over the right to create and own treasures, the right to assert self even at the expense of others (or even so as to enslave others), and the need to strengthen one's connection to the earth and leadership roles even while struggling with the need for divine aid.

Having known war and having learned that evil arises from within as well as from without, and that one must *resist* it from within as well as from without, Tolkien went for his epiphanies to a hero, Beowulf, who fought magical monsters of chaos and greed and never gave in, but who may in the end have fallen to his own pride as well as to the fate of old age. Frodo nearly fails (and falls) similarly, prey to the ring and the pride of tyranny it offers, and only luck, or as the Germanic world might say, *wyrd*, preserves him. As Frodo returns briefly and reluctantly, changed, to his old life, we must be prepared, Tolkien suggests, to meet our own duties and quests with the same steadfast courage, knowing that even should we survive, we will have been immitigably changed, but perhaps we will have briefly staved off evil and preserved by our deeds at least a small corner of the world we loved. That victory, finally, is the goal of epiphanies in *Beowulf*, Tolkien, or anywhere, "real" or imagined. Their variability, affinity for the pleasures and pains of the quotidian, and expansiveness make them novels: while they use epiphanies, they lack the "boundary focus" common to epics. "The epic," Georg Lukács argues, gives form to a totality of life that is rounded from within; the novel seeks, by giving form, to uncover and construct the concealed totality of life"[8]: the goal of the novel better suits the appreciation of the readers of our time.

Tolkien's love of language, epic, and epic Romance undoubtedly influenced his choice of subject matter for his fiction, and if one leans toward calling Joyce's *Ulysses* epic rather than novel, one must do the same with *The Lord of the Rings*— though I feel relatively confident calling them both novels with epic foundations. Tolkien in his early works wrote mostly poetry, and he turned to fiction, I think, largely as a matter of expediency: most of the epic impulse after the Romantic Age went there to get its points to an audience more willing to read long, realistic prose works than long, heroic poems. Some readers resist seeing *Ulysses* as novel because of its exotic prose style (as well as its magnitude), and some resist seeing *The Lord of the Rings* as novel because of its occasional movement into high heroic style (as well as its magnitude).[9] Either way, both authors draw their drive for epiphany from the epic tradition.

Yet most of what once went into epic now goes into the novel, not an entirely bad result if more readers get from the novel what fewer once got from the epic. What urges us to consider the limits of our knowledge, wisdom, capacities, or imaginings does us good. When in *The Marriage of Heaven and Hell* Blake's narrator asserts that excess leads to wisdom or that we never know "enough" until we've reached "too much," he doesn't, I think, counsel overindulgence of the flesh; he promotes his (Romantic) notion of artistic striving, the artist as epic hero expanding the boundaries of what his or her art can produce. He makes the point (much like Tolkien's notion of artist as subcreator under God) again in the prefatory verses to *Milton*, "I will not cease from Mental Fight... Till we have built Jerusalem": true artists, to be true to themselves, their talent, and the God who made them, must[10] pursue their art to the limits of their energies and media, and perhaps beyond. One may write an epic novel as Joyce and Tolkien did, epic as adjective rather than noun, as mode rather than genre (so Frye might say), as impetus rather than product. Perhaps the epic impulse must, at least for a time, take the form of the novel to do what our time needs it to do, for the common soul to find epiphany available, rather than for us to relegate it only to the land of heroes.

Having followed me through Tolkien, you may wonder, going back to the earlier question of the future of epic poems, what other suggestions students have made, particularly if I press them to think about current and upcoming "epic questions."[11] Some address the needs of developing countries or of oppressed peoples. Maybe, if we may consider American epic as an offshoot of the English — as we did the Caribbean, with Walcott — the United States needs more than anything else the great American Indian epic. The outstanding balance against a government's attempted genocide, exclusive educational systems, and lack of full appreciation for insufficiently explored systems of heroism begs for payment, and an epic may do some cultural good where personal accounts lie beyond redress.

Can a poet create a great "environmental" epic without falling into sensationalism and the Hollywood-style melodrama of cataclysm stories? The green movement has not only passion, but also science on its side, and the future of our civilization may depend on our ability to tell a story that wins the hearts of the public to the cause of conservation, preservation, and protection. One vector of the epic impulse has certainly turned to the cinema, but cinematic epic must do more than fall into the trite patterns of disaster movies to give its points power beyond the expectations of casual popular entertainment. Plus with respect to cinema I must use *epic* adjectivally, not nominally: for this study I retain the definition of epic as a long, narrative poem aiming to encapsulate a heroic question or idea essential to a culture. Most cinema, aiming for box-office receipts rather than cultural statements, must fall short of the grandeur of epic in design and poetic execution, if not in budget, and even independent film would have to achieve an unprecedented level of poetic power to contend with the written genre. Yet perhaps epic, to survive, particularly with the novel having become the default popular, realistic genre, must find a way to move to cinema to reach an increasingly visually oriented culture, regardless of the subject epic writers want to attempt.

From a religious point of view, we may need epic to return to Milton, to a mind-set before Romanticism began to personalize and more fully secularize the epic. How does the post–Enlightenment Christian meet God? How does the post–Holocaust Jew regain confidence in a public life of spirituality? How will a post–911, post–Iraq War, post–Palestinian question (should that time come) Muslim embody the spiritual challenge of a peaceful yet passionate faith? Can epic say anything about peace among warring or at best mutually diffident religious groups? Has English society become too fully secular ever to return to religious epic (and has America become too addicted to televangelism to allow epic its proper grandeur, seriousness, and impecuniousness)? Must film inevitably turn Vida's *Christiad* into Mel Gibson's *The Passion*?

From a scientific point of view, can epic express the quest for a unified theory of nature and the cosmos or for cures for epidemic diseases or for responses to global warming? Could the discovery of the molecular structure of DNA, or Stephen Hawking's quest for the structure of the cosmos, for all their essential contribution to the modern world, ever have made a subject for poetry (beyond, of course, the concentrated poetry of mathematical formulae)?

From an athletic point of view — and one can hardly discount athletics, as they play a major part in our current popular culture and in our imagination — can epic narrate the quest to extend the limits of the physical body beyond accepted notion of human potential? The 1981 Oscar-winning British film *Chariots of Fire* showed public interest in not only current but also historical athletic battles, if the characters attract enough interest and the moral/philosophical questions have enough currency. Now "Human interest stories" often dominate Olympic Games coverage, but bound by sound-bite structure they inevitably give in to simplicity and melodrama. What if someone with a passion for sport and an understanding of its potential for social significance found a sufficiently compelling story and expanded it for all its fully human impact, say, Jesse Owens in 1932 Munich?

From an interpersonal point of view, can epic teach us tolerance and compassion, perhaps the most difficult goals for the personality but essential if we wish to assure international peace, prosperity, and cultural advancement while we yet preserve our history, traditions, and values? Western epic starts there, with Achilles bending over the white hairs of Priam, who kisses the hands of the monstrous boy-man who has killed his son and dragged his body mercilessly around the battlefield. Must epic return there, not in a final moment of personal reversal, but as the focus of an entire adventure: the life of Gandhi or Mother Theresa?

I think the answer must come from the Great Problem that next comes closest to bringing us together across political and national boundaries: globalization moves the big questions to the world-wide stage, at least for as long as English remains a lingua franca. Each age tends also to select its favorite "Deadly Sin" for literary focus; the ancient world, as Aristotle suggested and as a majority of writers responded, dealt thematically with pride more commonly than with any other sin. The Renaissance, with a rising middle class and international monied economy, began to shift thematic weight to greed, a problem we haven't begun to solve. Why, for instance, do so many persons in our world still suffer from hunger? Largely, I think, because somewhere in the distribution chain greed prohibits us from getting food (or the opportunity to raise it) to a great number of those who need it. Those who already have it continue to enjoy an excess. Passionate adherence to certain economic systems by governments and individuals in power stems more from a desire to control resources and wealth than from any natural necessity embedded in those systems, at least from what I have observed. Though a built-in human flaw, greed has brought us to the brink of disaster on so many fronts, from the aim to control oil to the unwillingness to admit and deal with global warming to the willingness to see pandemic diseases, as long as they remain distant from our doorstep, as someone else's problem. I suspect the next great epic must in some way start there, evolving a theme and story, whether it ends up more realistic, more fantastical, or more allegorical, to show us a way to deal with what may otherwise prove a terminal acquisitiveness. Following Walcott the line of vision points that way: what but greed caused and still causes colonialism?

Wherever epic turns, Walcott gives me hope that epic remains alive, if beneath cultural radar, spreading mycelially, waiting for its time, waiting for the next poet brave enough, audacious enough, committed and attentive enough to revive it and connect us to the God or god that we still need desperately to find. With Barrett Browning epic secularized, not so much in that she eliminates religion from epic concerns, but because she turns them so specifically and explicitly to an overriding social issue. Joyce turned epiphany into a sensual, even profane experience: the post–World War I world needed to come to grips with the fact that individual suffering has perhaps the most intense and persistent reality within the grasp of human experience, and poetry may and must treat it. In *Finnegans Wake* Northrop Frye found that "the whole of history itself is presented as a single gigantic ani-epiphany."[12] In Tolkien's fiction we move, if we're willing, into a fully imagined and fully detailed fictional world — another kind of artistic epiphany — that millions of readers (and now moviegoers) experience and willingly repeat because they love the world: often I've heard students, friends, colleagues say, "How I'd love to go to Middle-earth!" They mean Tolkien's Middle-earth rather than our own, because they enjoy being transported into a world that allows for the possibility of Elves, Hobbits, Ents, vast, living forests, creatures devoted enough to sacrifice themselves for good — even though that world also encompasses enormous potential for evil.

The power of literary epiphany replaces, at least temporarily, the lack of other epiphanies: we live in an age when we no longer believe in heroes better than we who will take up the quest for us, but we do count on art of all sorts to transport us beyond the humdrum. Many readers want the epic experience without the difficulty of epic reading. Each of us wants to find the liminal boundary and what lies beyond — we seldom recognize or feel willing to pay the cost that accompanies the journey. We live in a time of the lyric poem, of the quicker gratification of the brief encounter, but perhaps if dedication grows, epics will return in record numbers as more heroes seek their versions (and ours) of the great questions and then try them out for public view and judgment. Bad and good would come with that result: many more bad epics to sift; maybe a few great ones to add to a still necessary and always enlivening tradition.

Chapter Notes

Preface

1. Note, though, the fairly recent success of Seamus Heaney's rendering of *Beowulf*, as well as new popular translations of Homer and Dante and, if we may include mock-epic Romance, Cervantes.

2. M.M. Bakhtin, *The Dialogic Imagination: Four Essays*, ed. Michael Holquist, trans. Caryl Emerson and Michael Holquist (Austin: University of Texas Press, 1981), page 13. Epic's "absolute past," he adds, engages "*valorized* temporal categorizes" and comprises the "single source and beginning of everything good for all later times" (page 13). Thus epic remains comparatively free of irony, requires Matthew Arnold's "high seriousness," and sets a baseline that doesn't limit future action, but provides the grounding from which it may spring.

3. *Anatomy of Criticism: Four Essays* (1957; reprint, Princeton: Princeton University Press, 1971), page 120.

4. *Mimesis: The Representation of Reality in Western Literature*, trans. Willard R. Trask (Princeton: Princeton University Press, 1953), page 5.

5. *Epic and Romance: Essays on Medieval Literature* (1896; reprint, New York: Dover, 1957), page 28. A page later he adds, "The relation of epic poetry to its heroic age ... lies rather in the epic capacity for bringing together all manner of lively passages from the general experience of the age."

6. See *The Ritual Process: Structure and Anti-Structure* (Chicago: University of Chicago Press, 1969).

7. *The Epic Hero* (Baltimore: Johns Hopkins University Press, 2000), page 296.

8. Ibid., page 319.

9. Ibid., pages 322–23.

10. Epic as *genre* implies a long narrative poem with heroic and supernatural elements that follows a quest or question central to the culture that produces it. It typically has other secondary traits (largely following Homer), such as a decent into hell, catalogues of ships and warriors, and invocations of divine sources. E.M.W. Tillyard in *The English Epic and Its Background* (New York: Oxford University Press, 1966) suggests some other necessary and traits: stretching the human will; "high quality" and "high seriousness"; "breadth" and "inclusiveness"; control and organization; a sense of "powerful predetermination"; "sustained concentration"; support of civilization and faith in its beliefs; the creation of a "heroic impression"; a "choric" quality (the ability of the writer to speak an idea or "feeling" for a large number of persons from his or her time). See pages 5–13.

11. C.M. Bowra, *Heroic Poetry* (London and New York: Macmillan, 1964), page 537.

12. For instance, among Victorian poems I've chosen *Aurora Leigh* rather than Robert Browning's *The Ring and the Book* (published 1868–69). Massive (more than 21,000 lines) and eerily postmodern in its floating polyphony, Browning's poem in many ways exceeds rather than epitomizes its time. Mary Rose Sullivan calls it the "most monumental poem of the Victorian period," yet it exhibits not a stately stagnancy, but a lively variability of voices and

viewpoints (*Browning's Voices in the Ring and the Book: A Study of Method and Meaning* [Toronto: University of Toronto Press, 1969], pages ix, xi). I chose not to include it in this study because, while it has elements we may identify as epic, it hasn't the heroic quest with the goal of epiphany as its end. Moreover, as with Joyce, epiphany, if and when it appears, does so in small details and in the echoing of voices. It has, more than other epics, even Blake's and Milton's, a strongly personal reflexivity, as Browning himself ("R.B.") had "the ring" and "the book" and was metaphorizing the events of his "own recent life" (Adam Roberts, *Robert Browning Revisited* [New York: Twayne, 1996], pages 93–94). *The Ring and the Book* retains, too, a Romantic fascination for Mediterranean intrigue, and yet it embodies a Victorian balanced complexity, real-life issues of class, judgment, and empiricism. Yet as we move from book to book, and voice to voice, Browning unfolds a pre–Derridean exposition of how stories vary with the tellers' perspectives, predispositions, and biases. It lacks much of the traditional epic machinery, but it is a long, narrative poem that strains the boundaries of how we perceive, as G.K. Chesterton says, "endeavouring to depict the various strange ways in which a fact gets itself presented to the world" (in *Robert Browning* [London: Macmillan, 1925], page 160)—perhaps an "epic" concern in its own right. In fact, Chesterton calls *The Ring and the Book* "the great epic of the nineteenth century, because it is the great epic of the enormous importance of small things" (page 163). In that light we may consider it — if for a moment we again forget Blake — the *first* postmodern epic, more exemplary of what will come from our time, an age concerned with specific social questions, in the case of *Aurora Leigh*, the essential "woman question," which I find far more eminently Victorian and more epic rather than Robert Browning's more microscopic, novelistic focus. As Ker argues, the epic poet has no debt "to historical fact," but "cannot ... live without the ideas and sentiments of heroism" (*Epic and Romance*, page 26).

13. Frye writes of epiphany as the "point at which the undisplaced apocalyptic world and the cyclical world of nature come into alignment.... Its common settings are the mountain-top, the island, the tower, the lighthouse, and the ladder or staircase. Folk tales and mythologies are full of stories of an original connection between heaven or the sun and the earth" (page 203). I'll argue in later chapters that epiphanies may occur below as well as above, but Frye makes the essential point that, whether in epic or in novel, we look to boundaries for our revelations and to those revelations for our Truths.

14. As J.B. Hainsworth put it, an epic deals with "ideas that stood at the center of its audience's views of themselves and the world" (*The Idea of Epic* [Berkeley: University of California Press, 1991], page 150).

15. *Epic of the Dispossessed: Derek Walcott's Omeros* (Columbia: University of Missouri Press, 1997), page 9. C.M. Bowra wrote, "An epic poem is by common consent a narrative of some length and deals with events which have a certain grandeur and importance and come from a life of action." It tends to "enhance our belief in the worth of human achievement and in the dignity and nobility of man" (*From Vergil to Milton* [London: Macmillan, 1945], page 1). The epic at its best promotes dignity and encourages action.

Chapter 1

1. "Potlach and Charity: Notes on the Heroic in *Beowulf*," in *Anglo-Saxon Poetry: Essays in Appreciation for John C. McGalliard*, ed. Lewis Nicholson and Dolores W. Frese (Notre Dame: University of Notre Dame Press, 1975), page 382.

2. "Introduction," *The Bhagavad Gita* (New York: Oxford University Press, 1994), page viii.

3. "The Homeric bard is an inspired being," writes Penelope Murray, "blessed with the gift of divine knowledge; but he is also a craftsman, responsible for his own creations" *(Aspects of the Epic*, ed. Tom

Winnifrith, Penelope Murray, and K.W. Gransden [New York: St. Martin's, 1983], page 11). Nearly all of the later epic poets relied on the same notion of the divinely prompted architect, which has often lent credibility to the magnitude of their endeavors.

4. *The Iliad of Homer*, trans. Richard Lattimore (Chicago: University of Chicago Press, 1951), page 59.

5. In his *Preface to Paradise Lost* (Oxford: Oxford University Press, 1961), C.S. Lewis disputes the notion that the great theme or great subject provided the center of gravity of primary epic: "I believe we are now tempted to read the great subject into primary epic where it did not exist" (page 27), Lewis avers, citing *Beowulf* and the Homeric epics as examples. With respect to the *Iliad* Lewis certainly demolishes the notion that it centers on "east-west conflict"; he notes that Odysseus is king of a very small island and that the world would not "have been much altered if Odysseus had never got home at all" (page 28); as for *Beowulf*, he observes that the poem is English, the first scene set in Denmark, and the hero from Geatland — how can it have national significance? Noting the danger in differing from so great a scholar as Lewis, I would like to suggest that the great subjects and great questions arise not from issues of some early nationalism, but rather they appear as broader human issues when one views the epic impulse and epic subjects before the relief of time: the issues that emerge are *human* issues, showing our desire to use the battlefields of the imagination as the grounds for growth and understanding, both of ourselves and the nature of the world.

6. *The Odyssey of Homer*, trans. Richard Lattimore (Chicago: University of Chicago Press, 1965), page 27.

7. C.S. Lewis makes this point also in his *Preface*, using the *Odyssey* as his primary example. Ithaca is a small island and Odysseus no greatly important king, plus no history-changing event occurs. But the *Odyssey* asks one of the great questions, and the problem it presents comprises a significant piece in the great puzzle of epic history.

8. See *The Emerging Goddess: The Creative Process in Art, Science, and Other Fields* (Chicago: University of Chicago Press, 1979).

9. While I understand and appreciate the problems that anthropologists often have with Campbell's tendency to generalize and his occasional inexactness (or even inaccuracy) with details, I still believe his model applies profitably to many literary texts, particularly those of the older traditions. Erich Neumann suggests a similar pattern in *The Origin and History of Consciousness* (New York: Pantheon, 1949).

10. Paul Merchant, *The Epic* (London: Methuen, 1971).

11. Robert Longbaum, "The Epiphanic Mode in Wordsworth and Modern Literature," *New Literary History* 14 (1983): 350-52.

12. Irene H. Chayes, "Joyce's Epiphanies," in *Joyce's Portrait: Criticisms and Critiques*, ed. Thomas E. Connolly (New York: Appleton-Century-Crofts, 1962), page 206.

13. Longbaum, page 337.

14. Northrop Frye, *Anatomy of Criticism: Four Essays* (Princeton: Princeton University Press, 1957), page 61.

15. Ibid., page 121.

16. *James Joyce* (1959; rev. ed., Oxford: Oxford University Press, 1982), pages 83–84.

17. James Joyce, *Stephen Hero* (1944; reprint, New York: New Directions, 1959), page 211.

18. Ibid., *Stephen Hero*, page 213.

19. *A Portrait of the Artist as a Young Man* (1916; reprint, New York: Vintage, 1993), pages 205–6.

20. James Joyce, *Ulysses* (1922; reprint, New York: Vintage, 1986), page 573.

21. Ibid.

22. Ibid.

23. Ibid., page 577.

24. Joyce, *Portrait*, page 244.

25. Alf Hiltebeitel asserts that, as we reconstruct the religious contexts of our great epics, "[o]nly in India, then, are the epic poets not only fully aware of, but deeply involved in, a living mythology"

(*The Ritual of Battle: Krishna in the Mahabharata* [Ithaca and London: Cornell University Press, 1976], page 31). In reconstructing the social context of the *Mahabharata*, Hiltebeitel suggests a "dynastic struggle which brought to an end their 'heroic age' ... an epic crisis of what could justly be called 'eschatogical proportions'" (page 358). Such a time requires answers to epic questions and narratives to move the reader to understand and accept those answers. Hiltebeitel, following Stig Wikander and Georges Dumézil, firmly argues for the *Mahabharata* as part of the "Indo-European [epic] continuum," but he sees the background of the epic as more mythological than historical (page 18).

26. Johnson, page x.
27. Ibid., page xiii.
28. Ibid., page xiv. Ultimately, unlike Arjuna, Hamlet cannot act. Whereas Arjuna responds to Krishna's call to duty, Hamlet receives no revelation. Germanic law requires that he avenge his father's murder, while Christian law forbids him to do so. Intervention occurs for Hamlet not in an epiphany, but through the actions of his enemies. Claudius and Laertes provide the arena for Hamlet's revenge and force his hand, relieving him of responsibility. Arjuna accepts the responsibility to fight, relieved by Krishna of the cosmological consequences of battle.
29. With this wholly inadequate summary of an incredibly complex and sophisticated twenty-volume epic, I intend only to give some sense of the poetic context of the *Gita*'s narrative.
30. Hiltebeitel points out that the *Gita* displays not Krishna's first theophany in the *Mahabharata*, but his second, since Krishna has already revealed himself to Duryodhana (page 121).
31. Quotations from the *Gita* come from W.J. Johnson's Oxford University Press translation.
32. *The Bhagavad Gita*, trans. Franklin Edgerton (New York: Harper & Row, 1964), page 162.
33. Ibid., page 168.
34. Ibid., page viii.
35. Ibid., pages viii–ix.
36. Ibid., page ix.

Chapter 2

1. *The Iliad of Homer*, trans. Richard Lattimore (Chicago: University of Chicago Press, 1951), page 59.
2. Elias Lönnrot, *The Kalevala*, trans. Keith Bosley (New York: Oxford University Press, 1989), page xiii. The reader may also want to consult the recent translation by Eino Friberg, edited by George C. Schoolfield and illustrated by Björn Landström (Keuruu, Finland: Otava Publishing, 2004).
3. Ferdowsi, *The Legend of Seyavash*, trans. Dick Davis (London: Penguin, 1992), page ix.
4. Odysseus seems to see getting home as his duty, as fulfilling his promise to the other kings who courted Helen to help retrieve her constitutes a duty—one he tried to avoid. His journey home has, in a sense, duties as well: he must treat divine beings with respect, and trouble comes to him when he or his men don't. He hasn't the piety of Aeneas, but he has that necessary to complete the circle of his quest and regain his home.
5. *The Odyssey of Homer*, trans. Richard Lattimore (Chicago: University of Chicago Press, 1965), page 27.
6. Lines 1132–38. This quotation and other Vergil citations come from Allen Mandelbaum's verse translation, *The Aeneid of Virgil* (New York: Bantam, 1971).
7. "Introduction," *The Bhagavad Gita* (New York: Oxford University Press, 1994), page viii.
8. Johnson, page x.
9. Ibid., page xiv. Earlier I mentioned a thematic connection to *Hamlet*, and one may draw a similar line to the medieval romance *Sir Gawain and the Green Knight*. There the knight receives, though in disappointment rather than glory, a spiritual lesson. His epiphany with the enchanted knight teaches him the inescapability of human imperfection—a lesson Arjuna

learns too, but through an entirely different mood and tone. Gawain, too, faces a semingly irresolvable puzzle: how both to reveal the magic sash and not to reveal it.

10. *The Bhagavad Gita*, trans. Franklin Edgerton (New York: Harper & Row, 1964), page 162.

11. Ibid., page 168.

12. Johnson, page xi.

Chapter 3

1. W.T.H. Jackson calls the "conflict of hero and king" one of the most important of epic themes (*The Hero and the King: An Epic Theme* [New York: Columbia University Press, 1982], page 3). I see it more generally as a tension between individuality and loyalty (or duty).

2. Lukács asserts that the "epic hero is, strictly speaking, never an individual," since the "epic theme is not a personal destiny but the destiny of a community." "The novel," he adds later, "is the form of mature virility; its song of comfort rings out of the dawning recognition that traces or lost meaning are to be found everywhere" (Georg Lukács, *The Theory of the Novel: A Historico-philosophical Essay on the Forms of Great Epic Literature* [1920; reprint, trans. Anna Bostock, Cambridge, MA: MIT Press, 1971], pages 66, 123). I agree that heroes in the ancient epics, up to the modern world, have distinctly less fully realized individuality than do the protagonists of our best novels, but I don't think anyone would have a hard time distinguishing Achilles from Odysseus or Hektor—and certainly not Adam from Satan or the Son. That problems come down to what the epic poets sought versus what novelists seek: the way to the boundary rather than the expression of everyday—or anyone's—life. I wouldn't agree that the ancient epic heroes lacked virility in any sense—though I don't think Lukács does, either—but I would agree that the novel typically gives us a truer sense of what heroic action means to the normal person, the human being not bent on seeking epiphany or boundary phenomena. Novel protagonists come more fully to life, while epic heroes give greater impulse to our dreams.

3. C.S. Lewis, *Preface to Paradise Lost* (New York: Oxford University Press, 1961), from an earlier university lecture series.

4. For more on this subject see particularly M.H. Abrams' *The Mirror and the Lamp: Romantic Theory and the Critical Tradition* (New York: Oxford University Press, 1953, page 195).

5. Dean Miller notes that the "romantic recovery of the powerful individual ... sets us both a serious and a specifically modern problem, of directed force and passionate individuality versus the grand patterns of history," and that tension continues into our time (*The Epic Hero*, page 20). But to some extent, greater or lesser, that problem has always troubled epic, as it must with anyone who stands out as "hero."

6. Chapter 5, page 28.

7. Chapter 28, page 150.

8. Chapter 58, page 291.

Chapter 4

1. One of the great debates of *Beowulf* criticism, whether we should call the poem Christian or pagan, has found reasonable resolution in the assertion that we may call it both and neither: it includes both Judeo-Christian and traditional Germanic elements and symbols, but it refers specifically to neither Christ nor pagan deities. The poet has interwoven both worlds artfully and almost inseparably. L.E. Nicholson's volume *An Anthology of Beowulf Criticism* still offers a good place to start on this issue; see especially the chapter by F.A. Blackburn on "The Christian Coloring of *Beowulf*," pages 1–21; see also Larry D. Benson's "The Pagan Coloring of *Beowulf*," in *Old English Poetry: Fifteen Essays*, ed. Robert P. Creed (Providence: Brown University Press, 1967), pages 193–213.

2. Fred Robinson, *Beowulf and the Appositive Style* (Knoxville: University of Tennessee Press, 1985); Mary Parker, *Beowulf*

and Christianity (New York: Peter Lang, 1987).

3. I have done the translations here, but for interested readers others abound, including Seamus Heaney's recent best-selling rendering and E.T. Donaldson's prose version, which formerly had great popularity in anthologies. My own complete translation, *Beowulf in Faithful Verse*, is available from Whitston Publishing.

4. A recent interesting but truncated Canadian-produced film version, *Beowulf and Grendel*, revises the story and its purpose considerably. Grendel, a troll, attacks the Danes because they murdered his father. Beowulf comes to fight him, but finds himself helpless against subsequent attacks; he does, however, come to understand and appreciate the "monster's" anger and revenge. This recreation of the epic features an entirely different idea than the original, presenting the problem as a sort of racism: a theme common to much of contemporary art and cultural criticism important in itself, but one the reader should avoid confusing with the mythic/heroic world of the epic poem.

5. See his "*Beowulf:* The Monsters and the Critics," available in several books, but most readily in *An Anthology of Beowulf Criticism*, ed. L.E. Nicholson (Notre Dame: University of Notre Dame Press, 1963), pages 51–103. It remains one of the most helpful studies of the poem.

6. For instance, Fafnir in *Volsungasaga* became a dragon after killing his father to acquire a vast, cursed hoard of treasure.

7. See for instance Ursula Dronke, "*Beowulf* and Ragnarök," *Saga-Book of the Viking Society* 17 (1969): 302–25. For a more expansive view on the implications of the monsters see Zacharias Thundy's *Millennium: Apocalypse, Antichrist, and Old English Monsters c. 1000* (South Bend, IN: Cross Cultural Publications, 1998), and my *Beasts of Time: Apocalyptic Beowulf* (New York: Peter Lang, 1994).

Chapter 5

1. For an excellent study of the use and implications of magic in medieval Romance, see especially Mickey Sweeney's *Magic in Medieval Romance from Chretien de Troyes to Geoffrey Chaucer* (Dublin: Four Courts Press, 2000). An essential element of Romance, magic would seemingly create a problem for Christian storytellers, but they incorporate it normally without difficulty, more often as a part of nature and human experience than as an artificial evil or artifice of the Devil, to avoid at all costs.

2. In the lull between *Beowulf* and Spenser we find plenty of Romances, but little significant truly epic poetry in England; however, Epic and Romance Epic remained active genres on the Continent, including some of the great poems of Western culture: the twelfth-century French *Chanson de Roland*, early thirteenth-century Spanish *Poema de Mio Cid* and German *Nibelungenlied*, and the early fourteenth-century *Commedia* of Dante. The sixteenth century saw a relative flurry of activity (with an increasing interest in Romance) with the Italian *Orlando Furioso* of Ariosto and Tasso's *Gerusalemme Liberata* (as well as Marco Girolamo Vida's *Christiad* [1535]), plus the Portuguese *Lusiads* of Luis de Camões (1572). Each of course deserves its own study, had we not turned our attentions toward the epic in England.

3. *Spiritus Mundi: Essays on Literature, Myth, and Society* (Bloomington: Indiana University Press, 1976), pages 123, 124.

4. Ibid., pages 135, 137.

5. Ibid., page 125.

6. In *Magic in the Middle Ages* (Cambridge: Cambridge University Press, 1989), Richard Kieckhefer shows that magic in medieval Romances differ from that in Norse sagas in that while sagas focus power "mainly in words," in Romance it "resides more in objects" (e.g., swords, rings, the Holy Grail; page 106). While that point remains true as late as Malory, Chaucer has already begun to parody it (in the "Squire's Tale") as does the *Gawain*-poet. Spenser,

though he harkens to medieval models, takes a greater interest in the interaction of person and place: insufficiently virtuous characters arriving at liminal boundaries find passage unavailable until someone rescues them or until they gain the virtues necessary to cross over and achieve their quests. Frye in *Anatomy of Criticism* discusses a "distinction of levels" that create "analogous forms of the point of epiphany": they range from the sexual to the apocalyptic depending on the virtue that typifies the knight, the kind and purpose of the quest, and the stage of the journey. All the knights face varying challenges ([Princeton: Princeton University Press, 1957], page 205.)

7. *Occult Philosophy or Magic*, ed. Willis F. Whitehead (New York: Samuel Weiser, 1971), page 201.

8. Agrippa, page 197.

9. Ibid., pages 203–4.

10. Ibid., page 206.

11. Ibid., page 123.

12. Ibid., page 123.

13. Ibid., page 208.

14. Ibid., pages 209, 212–13.

15. Ibid., page 139.

16. See Dorothy Waley Singer, *Giordano Bruno: His Life and Thought, Universe and Worlds* (New York: Greenwood, 1968), page 148.

17. See, for example, Frances A. Yates, *Giordano Bruno and the Hermetic Tradition* (Chicago: University of Chicago Press, 1964), and D.P. Walker, *Spiritual and Demonic Magic from Ficino to Campanella* (London: University of London, Warburg Institute, 1958).

18. Yates, page 133.

19. Ibid., pages 92–93.

20. Marcel Mauss, *A General Theory of Magic* (1950; reprint, trans. Robert Brain, Boston: Routledge and Kegan Paul, 1972), pages 54–55.

21. Ibid., page 56.

22. Ibid., pages 57–58.

23. Ibid., page 130.

24. Ibid., page 80.

25. For text see *The Works of Christopher Marlowe*, ed. C.F. Tucker Brooke (Oxford: Clarendon Press, 1910), page 153.

26. Several scholars reflect on this point, but see especially Kathleen Williams, "Milton, Greatest Spenserian," in *Milton and the Line of Vision*, ed. Joseph Wittreich (Madison: University of Wisconsin Press, 1975), pages 25–55.

27. *Inescapable Romance: Studies in the Poetics of a Mode* (Princeton: Princeton University Press, 1979), pages 57, 59.

28. Parker, page 79. Compare especially Michael Murrin, *The Allegorical Epic* (Chicago: University of Chicago Press, 1980).

29. David Bevington, *Medieval Drama* (Boston: Houghton-Mifflin, 1975).

30. Kenneth Gross, *Spenserian Poetics: Idolatry, Iconoclasm, and Magic* (Ithaca: Cornell University Press, 1985), page 16.

31. Ibid., pages 36 and 24.

32. See ibid., page 169.

33. Ibid., pages 195, 191.

34. Murrin, pages 143, 145.

35. Micheal Murrin, *Veil of Allegory* (Chicago: University of Chicago Press, 1969), page 64.

36. Ibid., page 70.

37. Ibid., page 66.

38. Ibid., page 72.

39. Ibid., page 73.

40. Douglas Brooks-Davies, *The Mercurian Monarch: Magical Politics from Spenser to Pope* (Manchester: Manchester University Press, 1983), page 1.

41. Ibid., page 3.

42. J.E. Cirlot, *A Dictionary of Symbols*, 2nd ed., trans. Jack Sage (New York: Philosophical Library, 1971), page 112.

43. Spenser quotations come from the Oxford University Press edition (London) of 1912, edited by J.C. Smith and E. De Selincourt.

44. George Luck, *Arcana Mundi: Magic and the Occult in the Greek and Roman Worlds* (Baltimore: Johns Hopkins University Press, 1985), page 10.

45. See ibid., page 11.

46. See Gross.

47. Luck, page 5.

Chapter 6

1. Robert Longbaum, "The Epipha-

Notes — Chapter 6

nic Mode in Wordsworth and Modern Literature," *New Literary History* 14 (1983): 341.

2. Frye, *Anatomy of Criticism*, page 320.

3. Of course for many readers danger lies in seeing Satan as hero; as Stanley Fish put it, "Satan's initial attractiveness owes as much to a traditional idea of what is heroic as it does to our weakness before the rhetorical lure" (*Surprised by Sin: The Reader in Paradise Lost* [New York: St. Martin's, 1967], pages 48–49). Perhaps, too, contemporary readers find the vigor and ambiguity of Satan's rhetoric more appealing than, as Fish describes it, God's rhetoric of clarity. Milton shows both the difficulty and necessity of reconstructing epiphany, and he seeks an ultimate clarity in how to get there. The "functional dissonance between Milton's kind of epic hero and the hero of the epic tradition" creates the "unique epicness of *Paradise Lost*," argues Ralph Condee (*Structure in Milton's Poetry: From the Foundation to the Pinnacles* [University Park: Penn State University Press, 1974], page 20): Milton needed such a contrast to move not only beyond Classical models but also past Spenser, whose blend of the Classical and medieval must have loomed large in his imagination.

4. In *The Reason of Church Government* Milton had addressed both the notion of the epic poet as inspired by God and the laudability of poets who could offer something "doctrinal and exemplary to a nation" (page 237). For a lengthy discussion of such issues see John Spencer Hill, *John Milton: Poet, Priest, and Prophet: A Study of Divine Vocation in Milton's Poetry and Prose* (London: Macmillan, 1979).

5. Longbaum, pages 350–52.

6. Irene H. Chayes, "Joyce's Epiphanies," in *Joyce's Portrait: Criticisms and Critiques*, ed. Thomas E. Connolly (New York: Appleton-Century-Crofts, 1962), page 206.

7. Longbaum, page 337.

8. Frye, page 61.

9. Frye, page 121.

10. "'A Poet Amongst Poets': Milton and the Tradition of Prophecy," in *Milton and the Line of Vision*, ed. J. Wittreich (Madison: University of Wisconsin Press, 1975), page 110.

11. William Kerrigan, *The Prophetic Milton* (Charlottesville: University of Virginia Press, 1974), pages 12–13.

12. Nora Chadwick, *Poetry and Prophecy* (Cambridge: Cambridge University Press, 1942).

13. Wittreich, page 102.

14. R.A. Shoaf's "lexicon of duality" identifies and employs several "master puns," one of which, on pair/repair, focuses the reader's attention on Milton's continuing desire in *PL* to restore lost connections, human to human or human to God, even Satan to God. See *Milton, Poet of Duality: A Study of Semiosis in the Poetry and the Prose* (New Haven: Yale University Press, 1985).

15. One may well consider Adam's first waking to consciousness an epiphany as well.

16. *Paradise Lost* quotations come from 1901 Clarendon Press edition edited by Henry Bradley.

17. Adam seeing himself in a dream, Eve seeing herself in the water, Satan begetting Sin and Death may constitute epiphanies in the more modern sense of the word. They don't involve cross-liminal perceptions, but they do create increases in the perceiver's consciousness of self or other.

18. Possession of the snake by Satan also constitutes a kind of epiphany, sub-liminal or super-liminal depending on where one sees Satan on the Great Chain of Being (or off it) after his fall.

19. H.J.C. Grierson, *Milton and Wordsworth: Poets and Prophets* (London: Chatto & Windus, 1960), page 9.

20. Ibid., page 17.

21. Wittreich, "A Poet Amongst Poets," page 99.

22. John Steadman, *Epic and Tragic Structure in Paradise Lost* (Chicago: University of Chicago Press, 1976), page 125.

23. Steadman, page 126.

24. Wittreich, "'All Angelic Natures Joined in One': Epic Convention and Prophetic Interiority in the Council Scenes in *Paradise Lost*," *Milton Studies* 17 (1983): 44.

25. Wittreich, "All Angelic Natures," page 45.
26. Ibid.

Chapter 7

1. Appropriately, both in print and in the accompanying visual plate, Milton's spirit descends like a falling star and strikes Blake in the tarsus, the large bone in the heel. St. Paul was on his way from Tarsus to Damascus when he was struck from his horse and inspired by God to spread the Gospel. At the exact point of inspiration Blake keeps touch with both the stars and the earth, his way of suggesting that his work has both spiritual power and earthly (social) practicality.

2. In some ways Blake more than anyone else is the precursor of much of modern fantasy. As does J.R.R. Tolkien in *The Silmarillion*, he creates not only a world, but a cosmology, and he encourages other artists, as they feel moved, to do the same. *Fantasy* literature implies first and foremost a created world; it may have similarities to our own, but it differs enough to allow juxtapositions impossible for us and to permit far greater freedom in the construction of adventure, quest, character, and, as with Spenser, magic.

3. Northrop Frye suggests in *Fearful Symmetry* that Blake intended the engraved poems "to form an exclusive and definitive canon," and because he left *The Four Zoas* in manuscript, we may guess *Milton* and *Jerusalem* as the more dependable embodiments of his personal mythology (page 6). But *The Four Zoas* does probably most clearly lay out the character of the other prophetic books. The Zoas or creatures represent aspects of the Universal Man, Albion, when he becomes sick and his psyche fragments. The four figures themselves — Urthona, imagination; Urizen, reason; Tharmas, instinct or drive; Luvah, love or passion — devolve into fallen forms and even split themselves, and Albion only recovers when they stop vying for supremacy and contribute according to their proper nature to Albion's health. This mythic figuration has a strong allegorical vector, and we can read it much after the traditional medieval fourfold exegetical method, derived from biblical criticism: the epic has its literal story, but that story also applies to the individual in his or her moral life (or, for Blake, artistic life), to the state or nation in balancing governance, and to spiritual hope for eternity (Albion represents humanity in our perfect, unfallen state, connected with God and redeemed).

4. David Riede, *Oracles and Hierophanies: Constructions of Romantic Authority* (Ithaca: Cornell University Press, 1991), page 36.

5. Ibid., page 70.

6. An earlier version of this discussion appeared in article form in the *Journal of the Fantastic in the Arts*, 1998, 9.3.

7. Riede, page 35.

8. Erdman argues that the "political relevance of *Milton* is indicated by the fact that Blake sees Milton's relation to the English Revolution as similar to that of Paine, Voltaire, and Rousseau to the American and French Revolutions. The anxious emphasis on matters of timing is political. And ... Milton is charged with the same political mistake as Paine, Voltaire, Rousseau — and Blake himself...— that of trusting too much to analytics and not enough to spontaneous movement." See *Blake: Prophet against Empire*, 3rd ed. (Princeton: Princeton University Press, 1977), page 422. With Blake prophecy, like epic, moves internally for its source and its particular mode of mythic expression.

9. Harold Bloom, "States of Being: *The Four Zoas*," in *Blake: A Collection of Critical Essays*, ed. Northrop Frye (Englewood Cliffs, NJ: Prentice Hall, 1966), page 107.

10. Victoria Myers, "The Dialogues as Interpretive Focus in Blake's The Four Zoas," *Philological Quarterly* 56 (Spring 1977): 227.

11. Myers, page 234.

12. Bloom, page 108.

13. "Urizen and the Comedy of Automatism in Blake's The Four Zoas," *Philological Quarterly* 56 (spring 1977): 204.

14. Bloom, pages 109–110.
15. Myers, page 235.
16. Ibid., page 238.
17. I've drawn the Blake quotations from the 1943 Nonesuch Press edition of his works, edited by Geoffrey Keynes.
18. Samuel Taylor Coleridge, *Biographia Literaria*, Vol. 1, ed. John Shawcross (London: Oxford University Press, 1962), page 202.
19. Jacques Lacan, *The Language of the Self: The Function of Language in Psycho-Analysis*, trans. Anthony Wiklin (New York: Delta, 1968), page 57.
20. Ronald L. Grimes, *The Divine Imagination: William Blake's Major Prophetic Visions* (Metuchen, NJ: Scarecrow Press and American Theological Library Association, 1972), pages 4–5.
21. Harold Bloom, *Blake's Apocalypse: A Study in Poetic Argument* (Garden City, NY: Doubleday, 1963), page 283.
22. Erdman, page 423.
23. Ibid.
24. Ibid., page 427.
25. Ibid., page 431.
26. Riede, page 35.
27. Ibid., page 45.
28. Ibid., page 44.
29. Riede, Page 73.
30. *The New Apocalypse: The Radical Christian Vision of William Blake* (East Lansing: Michigan State University Press, 1967), page 110.

Chapter 8

1. For an interesting discussion of *The Prelude*'s predecessors, see Abbie Finley Potts, *Wordsworth's Prelude: A Study in a Literary Form* (Ithaca: Cornell University Press, 1953). She notes connections to the pastoral tradition, but adds that while in form the poem bares little resemblance to Homeric or Vergilian epic, it "deals with the professional career of a hero," though the "warrior has made way for the poet" (page 26). For studies of *The Prelude* see Stephen Gill, *Wordsworth: The Prelude* (Cambridge: Cambridge University Press, 1991), and Frank D. McConnell, *The Confessional Imagination: A Reading of Wordsworth's Prelude* (Baltimore: Johns Hopkins University Press, 1974). For biographies of Wordsworth see *A Preface to Wordsworth* by John Arthur Purkis (New York: Longman, 1986), Stephen Gill's *Wordsworth: A Life* (New York: Oxford University Press, 1989), and George Lyman Nesbitt's *Wordsworth: The Biographical Background of His Poetry* (New York: Pegasus, 1970).

2. Romantic literary authority rests, according to David Riede, in "valorization of the imagination and ultimately in the Romantic conceptualization of self," but both Wordsworth and Blake "attempted to proclaim their prophetic power by either augmenting or combating the authority of Milton, the last prophetic voice in the English tradition" (*Oracles and Hierophants: Construction of Romantic Authority* [Ithaca: Cornell University Press, 1991], page 9). The Romantics, while accepting the ancient connection between epic and prophecy, to some extent democratize both; we may see, Riede adds later, "the sacralizing by later writers not only of their own imaginations but also of the imaginations of others" (page 32). Yet poetic authority shows not only the everting of the private self, but also "the influences of the public road ... in response to, even in defense against ... threatening elements in society" (page 101) — epic, as previous chapters have discussed, aims at social as well as personal comment and criticism. Though, Hartman notes, *The Prelude* "traces imagination to its sources in childhood, it is the French Revolution which emerges as the focus of the poet's own spirit" (*Unremarkable*, page xv) — public or social experience as much as private inspiration urge expression, clarification, and inculcation of his most important ideas. For more on Wordsworth and prophesy see especially H.J.C. Grierson, *Milton and Wordsworth: Poets and Prophets* (London: Chatto & Windus, 1960). For more on Wordsworth and epiphany see Robert Longbaum, "The Epiphanic Mode in Wordsworth and Modern Literature," *New Literary History* 14 (1983): 335–58.

While some scholars prefer to call *The Prelude* poetic autobiography rather than epic, the larger number of critics who have argued the point place it as I do within the epic tradition. "*The Prelude*," Lindenberger shows, "remains epic by Wordsworth's broad definition" (*On Wordsworth's Prelude* [Princeton, Princeton University Press, 1963], page 14), though the poet claimed it only as "ante-chapel" to his more vastly conceived *The Recluse*. After a fairly substantial introduction in which she discusses "What Is It?" and "What Is It Like?" Abbie Potts concludes much later in her book that "we can scarcely deny to *The Prelude* its place among English epics" (*Wordsworth's Prelude: A Study of Its Literary Form* [Ithaca: Cornell University Press, 1953], page 337). She sees as the "main discovery" of the poem "the Poet's recognition that he himself and every other human being is by nature a poet, and intellectual lover, however long or woefully the fulfilment of his destiny may be delayed" (page 381) — the "'fructifying,' 'vivifying,' 'renovating virtue'" (page 382) that we gain through the spots of time fulfill the needs of the age.

3. Unless I note otherwise quotations come from the 1850 text as it appears in the 1911 *Complete Poetical Works of William Wordsworth* edited by John Morley. For this chapter readers may want to see the Norton Critical Edition of *The Prelude* since it includes the 1799, 1805, and 1850 versions and because it is perhaps the most readily available to teachers, students, and general readers.

4. In *The Unremarkable Wordsworth* Geoffrey Hartman duly warns, "In our honorific or sophomoric moods, we like to think that poets are prophets. At least that certain great poets have something of the audacity and intensity — the strong speech — of Old Testament prophets who claimed that the word of God came to them" (*The Unremarkable Wordsworth* [Minneapolis: University of Minnesota Press, 1987], page 163). Yet he adds points later about the typical "ambivalent sympathy shown by the prophet for the powerful and terrible thing he envisions" (page 165), which allows that the poet may be "speaking out" with a sense that the words come not merely self-generated, and about how the powerful prophetic quality of the "language of the old belief," which comprises a "mighty scheme not of truth but of troth — of trusting the old language, its pathos, its animism, its fallacious figures" which connects poets and prophets (page 179). Whether we accept as either possible or metaphorical the poet as prophet or dismiss the notion as self-aggrandizing ruse, we may identify the use of traditional rhetoric of prophecy as a means to communicate ideas that the source finds important — just as we may recognize as epic a poem that omits some of the Homeric and Vergilian conventions.

5. "[F]using not only time and place but also stasis and continuity," Harman explains, the "fixity or fixation" of such occurrences "points to an apocalyptic consciousness of self" that "is temporalized, reintegrated in the stream of life" (Geoffrey Hartman, *Wordsworth's Poetry*, page 212); the spot serves repeatedly, reflexively, prophylactically.

Chapter 9

1. As Philip C. Rule puts it ("The Gendered Imagination in Religion and Literature," in *Seeing Into the Life of Things: Essays on Literature and the Religious Experience*, ed. John L. Mahoney [New York: Fordham University Press, 1988], page 66), "One of Browning's tenets is that poetry should deal with the present, not the past, precisely because contemporary society needs what poets do best — mediation between the worlds of spirit and matter" (i.e., epiphany).

2. Aurora prays periodically and passionately through the epic, as in Book 7: Alas, long-suffering and most patient God,/ Thou needst be surelier God to bear with us/ Than even to have made us! ... I walk these waves,/ Resisting!— breathe me upward, thou in me/ Aspiring" (1027–36) — the prayer begs an epiphany. Quotations come from the 1911 Oxford University Press edition of *The Poetical Works of Elizabeth Barrett Browning*, with line numbers checked in the 1993/1998 edition.

Notes — Chapter 9

3. Some of the most useful criticism of *Aurora Leigh* appears in the introductions to various editions. See particularly those of Cora Kaplan (London: The Women's Press, 1989), Kerry McSweeney (Oxford: Oxford University Press, 1993), and Gardner B. Taplin (Chicago: Academy Chicago, 1979).

4. Meg Tasker contrasts Cora Kaplan's claim of the radical attitude and influence of *Aurora Leigh* with Deirdre David's observation that Browning held conservative political and sexual views; Tasker suggests that finally the poem "affirms the possibility of fulfilled love ... without necessitating the renunciation of art" (*"Aurora Leigh*: Elizabeth Barrett Browning's Novel Approach to the Woman Poet," in *Tradition and the Poetics of Self in Nineteenth-Century Women's Poetry*, ed. Barbara Gorlick [New York: Rodopi, 2002], pages 23, 39). Christine Sutphin adds, "In spite of the fact that Barrett Browning was not always sympathetic to women's rights ... the ending of Aurora's story is a remarkably liberating one" ("Revising Old Scripts: The Fusion of Independence and Intimacy in *Aurora Leigh*," *Browning Institute Studies* 15 [1987]: 43). For biographies with useful critical matter on the poem see especially Simon Avery and Rebecca Stott's *Elizabeth Barrett Browning* (London and New York: Pearson, 2003), Dorothy Hewlett's *Elizabeth Barrett Browning: A Life* (New York: Knopf, 1952), and Angela Leighton's *Elizabeth Barrett Browning* (Bloomington: Indiana University Press).

5. See Joseph Campbell, *The Hero with a Thousand Faces* (New York: MJF Books, 1949).

6. Ibid., pages ix–x and following.

7. Maureen Murdock, *The Heroine's Journey* (Boston: Shambhala, 1990), page 2.

8. Murdock, page 5. For additional interesting and useful mythic background, see Pamela Berger, *The Goddess Obscured: Transformation of the Grain Protectress from Goddess to Saint* (Boston: Beacon, 1985). As her title suggests, Berger describes the process of the evolution of a symbol, and that evolution turns a goddess figure into a human with a story, a story that reflects a new "paradigm of faith" necessary when "alienation from" an old model occurs (page 146). The new story requires both interpretation and reconstruction, but the primary figure remains as a means to epiphany, simply re-enculturated.

9. Upon Romney's repeating his proposal by letter, Aurora responds, "Then let me grow/ Within my wayside hedge, and pass your way!" (Book II, pages 850–51).

10. Marjorie Stone notes that the poet has "turned to gender inversion as a rhetorical strategy" partly in response to less conscious use of similar concerns in earlier works ("Genre Subversion and Gender Subversion: *The Princess* and *Aurora Leigh*," *Victorian Poetry* 25.2 [summer 1987]: 103). We may say that by placing Aurora in the superior position, Romney experiences a super-liminal epiphany upon his reintroduction to Aurora and especially in her accepting him as husband and love.

11. While McSweeney calls the poem a "self-confident bravura performance" (page xx), there remained, as Taplin explains, "no place in English society for an accomplished [sic], intellectual unmarried woman" (page xiii); thus, given social circumstance the narrator gains some credibility with Barrett Browning's audience through the use of a male muse. For related discussions see Dorothy Mermin, *Elizabeth Barrett Browning: The Origin of a New Poetry* (Chicago: University of Chicago Press, 1989), and her "Genre and Gender in Aurora Leigh," *Victorian Newsletter* 69 (1986): 7–11. See also Alison Case's "Gender and Narration in *Aurora Leigh*," *Victorian Poetry* 29 (1991): 17–32; Barbara Charlesworth Gelpi, "Aurora Leigh: The Vocation of the Woman Poet," *Victorian Poetry* 19 (1981): 35–48; Marjorie Stone, "Genre Subversion and Gender Inversion: *The Princess* and *Aurora Leigh*," *Victorian Poetry* 25 (1987): 101–27; and Meg Tasker, "*Aurora Leigh*: Elizabeth Barrett Browning's Novel Approach to the Woman Poet," in *Tradition and the Poetics of Self in Nineteenth-Century Women's Poetry*, ed. Barbara Gorlick (New York: Rodopi, 2002), pages 23–41.

12. Note the interesting image-fulfillment

and image-reversal that highlight this point, just before the end of the poem. Aurora (dawn, light), Romney says, has come to rule the night and day (Book IX, page 832); then Aurora says, "I flung closer to his breast,/ As sword that, after battle, flings to sheath" (pages 833–34). Aurora takes the traditional male symbol and Romney the female, a liberating epiphany for Aurora certainly but in this case perhaps for Romney as well.

Chapter 10

1. *Milton and the Line of Vision*, ed. Joseph Wittreich (Madison: University of Wisconsin Press, 1975).

2. Epiphany in Walcott again flirts with the traditional meaning, a meeting with a being of a different order by means of one's crossing some liminal boundary, but in *Omeros* it occurs interpersonally, across time and space, intertextually, inter-racially, inter-colonially, and between persons and the sea (Walcott's symbol of both movement and constancy). For instance, as Charlotte McClure aptly asserts, "*Omeros* is [both] a late twentieth-century fulfillment of Homer's promise to Helen of Troy in the *Iliad* that her story would never die" and a fulfillment of Walcott's "artistic goal of giving the people of his island realm an identity expressed in their own words rather than the words from European and African predecessors" ("Helen of the 'West Indies': History or Poetry of a Caribbean Realm," *Studies in the Literary Imagination* 26.2 [1993]: 7). He gives them an epic that they may call their own and that also invokes English and European as well as African traditions.

3. In "Walcott, Homer, and the 'Black Atlantic'" (*Research in African Literatures* 33.1 [2002]: 27–44), Isidore Okpewho concludes that *Omeros* "represents [Walcott's] hopes for a universe self-sufficient and at peace with itself; a unified society in which the varied cultural identities ... find a welcome home however they may have been brought there by the vagaries of history; most of all, a society in which the dispossessed elements are finally restored to their due place as the true energies driving Caribbean society. That pride of place basically privileges the Black factor in the Caribbean" (page 39). While Walcott uses the epic to attack imperialism, he also approves, Okpewho suggests, of compassionate resolution. McClure adds the importance of the poetic effort to name the Caribbean "Helen," that is, to draw out the character, beauty, and essence of place (page 9). Jahan Ramazani identifies in much of Third World Anglophone literature what he calls a "hybrid muse," a mix of English with African, Indian, and Caribbean sensibilities (page 1). Walcott also expresses an affinity for Irish writers, "especially in their conflicted response to the cultural inheritances of the British Empire — its literature, religion, and language" — in *Omeros* "Walcott is still puzzling out what it means to love the English language yet hate English imperialism" (page 49). I see Walcott's work not as not as colonized by the English epic tradition, but as having picked up the strand of epic history to refashion it with his own personal and cultural poetic imperatives. See *The Hybrid Muse: Postcolonial Poetry in English* (Chicago: University of Chicago Press, 2001).

4. Permission to quote from Walcott has graciously been granted by Farrar, Straus and Giroux.

5. In "*Omeros*, Derek Wallcott [sic] and the Contemporary Epic Poem" (*Callaloo* 22.2 [1999]: 509–28), Isabella Maria Zoppi calls the poem "a case of searching for a new dimension of the epic, which preserves the whole mythic stratification of the original transferred into a modern world by this Caribbean poet" (page 512); even the name *Omeros* creates levels both timeless and contemporary, "poetic inspiration, the sea as source of life, and the whole skeleton of the earth itself— primordial referents common to all civilizations, whether Atlantic or Mediterranean, which are the woof on which the warp of the poem is to be woven" (page 511). Walcott joins, revises, re-weaves the tradition — as each new epic writer seeks to do.

6. Ibid., page 509.

A Postscript on Tolkien

1. Karen Armstrong, *The Battle for God*, (New York: Ballantine, 2001).

2. Tillyard once asserted that to "conjecture what will be the fate of epic in the near future would be an act of quite uncommon stupidity" (*The English Epic and Its Background* [New York: Oxford University Press, 1966], page 531), yet he suggests at least the likelihood that epics will continue to appear. I accept the warning, but I find pedagogical value in asking the question, both in helping students to reconsider the motivations and products of past poets and encouraging them to retain an interest in the genre in the present — we need not limit our poetic experience to the ubiquitous lyric — and also perhaps to plant the idea that poets may valuably attempt the epic, however daunting it seems.

3. An earlier version of this discussion appeared in article form in the *Journal of the Fantastic in the Arts*, 2002, 12.4.

4. Dobbie, page 56.

5 Carpenter, page 197.

6. Rabkin, page 4; Tolkien, page 9.

7. "On Fairy Stories," in *The Tolkien Reader* (New York: Ballantine, 1966), page 52.

8. George Lukács, *The Theory of the Novel: A Historico–philosophical Essay on the Forms of Great Epic Literature* (1920; reprint, trans. Anna Bostok, Cambridge, MA: MIT Press, 1971), page 60. "The novel," he adds later, "is the necessary epic form of our time" (page 146). Yet we see from such work as Walcott's that the epic, though periodically apparently moribund, manages to rise again.

9. As Shippey argues in *J.R.R. Tolkien: The Author of the Century* (London: HarperCollins, 2000), Tolkien shifts style to exhibit changes in register, from the common chat of Hobbits to the elevated Common Speech of the Elves to the formal speechmaking of kings.

10. I wish I had here the Old English word *sceal*, which combines the meanings of shall, will, must: I shall do it, I will do it (i.e., desire to do it and pursue it with an iron will), and I must do it (God or gods bid me, my own nature drives me, the necessity of my place in life compels results or collapse in the attempt).

11. We see, of course, through an American perspective and therefore tend to ask questions more typical of American culture, though many would pertain to contemporary Britain as well. We may also argue about the degree to which Americans as English speakers may extend or participate in the English epic tradition. Americans have produced epic poems, but few have gained as great and lasting attention as their English counterparts. While critics may expand the definition of epic for the sake of inclusiveness, those best fitting the tradition include, I think, Joel Barlow's *The Columbiad: A Poem* (1809), Longfellow's *Song of Hiawatha* (1855), Stephen Vincent Benét's *John Brown's Body* (1928), William Carlos Williams' *Paterson* (1963), and Frederick Turner's *The New World: An Epic Poem* (1985). While Turner is British-born, and one could make a case for my including an analysis of his extremely interesting epic in this volume both by author and as another extension (as with Walcott) of colonialism, I find not only the subject matter but also the referentiality thoroughly American: set in the Ohio Valley in a fragmented 24th-century America, the plot follows a hero who leads a confederation of small republics in defense against an invading Appalachian fundamentalist army. This interesting poem offers hope that American as well as English epic poetry has far from died out.

12. *Anatomy of Criticism*, page 61. For me *Finnegans Wake* even further than *Ulysses* blurs the distinction between internal and external. One of its many difficulties comes from the constant state of "dream" confusion resulting from such a blur. But we may equally call that confusion a constant epiphany: do I as reader, as person, always know how much of my experience comes from internal and how much from external stimulus (a big part also of the Postmodernist dilemma)?

Bibliography

Abrams, M.H. *The Mirror and the Lamp: Romantic Theory and the Critical Tradition*. New York: Oxford University Press, 1953.

Agrippa, Henry Cornelius. *Occult Philosophy or Magic*. Ed. Willis F. Whitehead. New York: Samuel Weiser, 1971.

Altizer, Thomas J.J. *The New Apocalypse: The Radical Christian Vision of William Blake*. East Lansing: Michigan State University Press, 1967.

Auerbach, Erich. *Mimesis: The Representation of Reality in Western Literature*. Trans. Willard R. Trask. Princeton: Princeton University Press, 1953.

Avery, Simon, and Rebecca Stott. *Elizabeth Barrett Browning*. London and New York: Pearson, 2003.

Bakhtin, M.M. *The Dialogic Imagination: Four Essays*. Ed. Michael Holquist. Trans. Caryl Emerson and Michael Holquist. Austin: University of Texas Press, 1981.

Barrett Browning, Elizabeth. *Aurora Leigh*. 1856. Ed. Kerry McSweeney. Oxford: Oxford University Press, 1993.

———. *Aurora Leigh, With Other Poems*. Ed. Cora Kaplan. London: The Women's Press, 1989.

———. *Aurora Leigh*. Ed. Gardner B. Taplin. Chicago: Academy Chicago, 1979.

———. *The Complete Poetical Works of Elizabeth Barrett Browning*. London: Oxford University Press, 1911.

Beagle, Peter S. Introductory Note. In *The Hobbit: Or, There and Back Again*, by J.R.R. Tolkien. New York: Ballantine, 1973.

Benson, Larry D. "The Pagan Coloring of *Beowulf*." In *Old English Poetry: Fifteen Essays*, ed. Robert P. Creed. Providence: Brown University Press, 1967. 193–213.

Beowulf, With the Finnesburg Fragment. Ed. C.L. Wrenn. Rev. W.F. Bolton. London: Harrap, 1973.

Bevington, David, ed. *Medieval Drama*. Boston: Houghton-Mifflin, 1975.

Bidney, Martin. "Urizen and the Comedy of Automatism in Blake's *The Four Zoas*." *Philological Quarterly* 56 (Spring 1977): 204–219.

Blackburn, F.A. "The Christian Coloring of *Beowulf*." In *An Anthology of Beowulf Criticism*, ed. L.E. Nicholson. Notre Dame: University of Notre Dame Press, 1963. 1–21.

Blake, William. *Poetry and Prose of William Blake*. Ed. Geoffrey Keynes. London: Nonesuch Press, 1943.

Bloom, Harold. *Blake's Apocalypse: A Study in Poetic Argument*. Garden City, NY: Doubleday, 1963.

———. "States of Being: *The Four Zoas*." In *Blake: A Collection of Critical Essays*, ed. Northrop Frye. Englewood Cliffs, NJ: Prentice Hall, 1966. 104–118.

Bowra, C. M. *From Vergil to Milton*. London: Macmillan, 1945.

———. *Heroic Poetry*. London and New York: Macmillan, 1964.

Brooks-Davies, Douglas. *The Mercurian Monarch: Magical Politics from Spenser to Pope*. Manchester: Manchester University Press, 1983.

Campbell, Joseph. *The Hero with a Thousand Faces*. New York: MJF Books, 1949.

Bibliography

Carpenter, Humphrey. *Tolkien: A Biography*. New York: Ballantine, 1977.

Chadwick, Nora. *Poetry and Prophecy*. Cambridge: Cambridge University Press, 1942.

Chayes, Irene H. "Joyce's Epiphanies." In *Joyce's Portrait: Criticisms and Critiques*, ed. Thomas E. Connolly. New York: Appleton-Century-Crofts, 1962. 206–220.

Chesterton, G.K. *Robert Browning*. London: Macmillan, 1925.

Cirlot, J.E. *A Dictionary of Symbols*. 2nd ed. Trans. Jack Sage. New York: Philosophical Library, 1971.

Coleridge, Samuel Taylor. *Biographia Literaria*. Vol. 1. Ed. J. Shawcross. London: Oxford University Press, 1962.

Condee, Ralph Waterbury. *Structure in Milton's Poetry: From the Foundation to the Pinnacles*. University Park: Penn State University Press, 1974.

David, Deirdre. *Intellectual Women and Victorian Patriarchy*. Ithaca: Cornell University Press, 1987.

Dobbie, Elliott van Kirk, ed. *The Anglo-Saxon Minor Poems*. Anglo-Saxon Poetic Records 6. New York: Columbia University Press; London: Routledge and Kegan Paul, 1942.

Donahue, Charles. "Potlach and Charity: Notes on the Heroic in *Beowulf*." In *Anglo-Saxon Poetry: Essays in Appreciation for John C. McGalliard*, ed. Lewis Nicholson and Dolores W. Frese. Notre Dame: University of Notre Dame Press, 1975. 23–40.

Dronke, Ursula. "*Beowulf* and Ragnarök." *Saga-Book of the Viking Society* 17 (1969): 302–325.

Edgerton, Franklin, trans. *The Bhagavad Gita*. New York: Harper & Row, 1964.

Erdman, David. *Blake: Prophet against Empire*. 3rd ed. Princeton: Princeton University Press, 1977.

Ferdowsi. *The Legend of Seyavash*. Trans. Dick Davis. London: Penguin, 1992.

Fish, Stanley Eugene. *Surprised by Sin: The Reader in Paradise Lost*. London: Macmillan; New York: St. Martin's, 1967.

Frye, Northrop. *Anatomy of Criticism: Four Essays*. Princeton: Princeton University Press, 1957.

———. *Fearful Symmetry: A Study of William Blake*. 1947. Princeton: Princeton University Press, 1969.

———. *Spiritus Mundi: Essays on Literature, Myth, and Society*. Bloomington and London: Indiana University Press, 1976.

Gill, Stephen. *Wordsworth: A Life*. New York: Oxford University Press, 1989.

———. *Wordsworth: The Prelude*. Cambridge: Cambridge University Press, 1991.

Grierson, H.J.C. *Milton and Wordsworth: Poets and Prophets*. London: Chatto & Windus, 1960.

Grimes, Ronald L. *The Divine Imagination: William Blake's Major Prophetic Visions*. ATLA Monograph Series 1. Metuchen, NJ: Scarecrow Press and American Theological Library Association, 1972.

Gross, Kenneth. *Spenserian Poetics: Idolatry, Iconoclasm, and Magic*. Ithaca: Cornell University Press, 1985.

Hainsworth, J.B. *The Idea of Epic*. Berkeley: University of California Press, 1991.

Hamner, Robert. *Epic of the Dispossesed: Derek Walcott's Omeros*. Columbia: University of Missouri Press, 1997.

Hartman, Geoffrey. *The Unremarkable Wordsworth*. Theory and History of Literature 34. Minneapolis: University of Minnesota Press, 1987.

———. *Wordsworth's Poetry: 1787–1814*. New Haven: Yale University Press, 1964.

Hermetica: The Ancient Greek and Latin Writings Which Contain Religious or Philosophic Teachings Ascribed to Hermes Trismegistus. 4 vols. Ed. Walter Scott. Oxford: Clarendon, 1924.

Hewlett, Dorothy. *Elizabeth Barrett Browning: A Life*. New York: Knopf, 1952.

Hiltebeitel, Alf. *The Ritual of Battle: Krishna in the Mahabharata*. Ithaca: Cornell University Press, 1976.

The Iliad of Homer. Trans. Richard Lattimore. Chicago: University of Chicago Press, 1951.

Jackson, Rosemary. *Fantasy: The Literature of Subversion*. London and New York: Methuen, 1981.

Jackson, W.T.H. *The Hero and the King: An Epic Theme*. New York: Columbia University Press, 1982.

Johnson, W.J. "Introduction." In *The Bhagavad Gita*, trans. W.J. Johnson. New York: Oxford University Press, 1994.

Joyce, James. *A Portrait of the Artist as a Young Man*. 1916. New York: Vintage, 1993.

———. *Stephen Hero*. 1944. New York: New Directions, 1959.

———. *Ulysses*. 1922. New York: Vintage, 1986.

Ker, W.P. *Epic and Romance: Essays on Medieval Literature*. 1896. New York: Dover, 1957.

Kerrigan, William. *The Prophetic Milton*. Charlottesville: University of Virginia Press, 1974.

Kieckhefer, Richard. *Magic in the Middle Ages*. Cambridge: Cambridge University Press, 1989.

Krapp, George Philip, and Elliott van Kirk Dobbie, eds. *The Exeter Book*. Anglo-Saxon Poetic Records 3. New York: Columbia University Press; London: Routledge and Kegan Paul, 1936.

Lacan, Jacques. *The Language of the Self: The Function of Language in Psycho-Analysis*. Trans. Anthony Wiklen. New York: Delta, 1968.

Leighton, Angela. *Elizabeth Barrett Browning*. Bloomington: Indiana University Press, 1986.

Lindenberger, Herbert. *On Wordsworth's Prelude*. Princeton: Princeton University Press, 1963.

Longbaum, Robert. "The Epiphanic Mode in Wordsworth and Modern Literature." *New Literary History* 14 (1983): 335–358.

Lönnrot, Elias. *The Kalevala*. Trans. Keith Bosley. New York: Oxford University Press, 1989.

Luck, George. *Arcana Mundi: Magic and the Occult in the Greek and Roman Worlds*. Baltimore: Johns Hopkins University Press, 1985.

Lukács, Georg. *The Theory of the Novel: A Historico-philosophical Essay on the Forms of Great Epic Literature*. 1920. Trans. Anna Bostock, Cambridge, MA: MIT Press, 1971.

Marlowe, Christopher. *Doctor Faustus*. In *The Works of Christopher Marlowe*, ed. C.F. Tucker Brooke. Oxford: Clarendon, 1910. 139–194.

Mauss, Marcel. *A General Theory of Magic*. 1950. Trans. Robert Brain. Boston: Routledge and Kegan Paul, 1972.

McClure, Charlotte S. "Helen of the 'West Indies': History or Poetry of a Caribbean Realm." *Studies in the Literary Imagination* 26.2 (1993): 7–20.

McConnell, Frank D. *The Confessional Imagination: A Reading of Wordsworth's Prelude*. Baltimore: Johns Hopkins University Press, 1974.

Merchant, Paul. *The Epic*. London: Methuen, 1971.

Miller, Dean A. *The Epic Hero*. Baltimore: Johns Hopkins University Press, 2000.

Milton, John. *English Poems by John Milton*. Vols. 1, 2. Ed. Henry Bradley. Oxford: Clarendon, 1901.

Murdock, Maureen. *The Heroine's Journey*. Boston: Shambhala, 1990.

Murray, Penelope. *Aspects of the Epic*. Ed. Tom Winnifrith, Penelope Murray, and K.W. Gransden. New York: St. Martin's, 1983. 1–15.

Murrin, Michael. *The Allegorical Epic*. Chicago: University of Chicago Press, 1980.

———. *The Veil of Allegory*. Chicago: University of Chicago Press, 1969.

Myers, Victoria. "The Dialogues as Interpretive Focus in Blake's *The Four Zoas*." *Philological Quarterly* 56 (Spring 1977): 221–238.

Nesbitt, George Lyman. *Wordsworth: The Biographical Background of His Poetry*. New York: Pegasus, 1970.

Neumann, Erich. *The Origin and History of Consciousness*. New York: Pantheon, 1949.

Nicholson, L.E., ed. *An Anthology of Beowulf Criticism*. Notre Dame: University of Notre Dame Press, 1963.

The Odyssey of Homer. Trans. Richard Lattimore. Chicago: University of Chicago Press, 1965.

Okpewho, Isidore. "Walcott, Homer, and the 'Black Atlantic.'" *Research in African Literatures* 33.1 (2002): 27–44.

Bibliography

Paracelsus. *Selected Writings*. Ed. Jolande Jacobi. Trans. Norbert Guterman. Bolingen Series 28. New York: Pantheon, 1958.

Parker, Mary. *Beowulf and Christianity*. New York: Peter Lang, 1987.

Parker, Patricia. *Inescapable Romance: Studies in the Poetics of a Mode*. Princeton: Princeton University Press, 1979.

Potts, Abbie Findlay. *Wordsworth's Prelude: A Study of Its Literary Form*. Ithaca: Cornell University Press, 1953.

Rabkin, Eric S. *The Fantastic in Literature*. Princeton: Princeton University Press, 1976.

Ramazani, Jahan. *The Hybrid Muse: Postcolonial Poetry in English*. Chicago: University of Chicago Press, 2001.

Riede, David G. *Oracles and Hierophants: Constructions of Romantic Authority*. Ithaca: Cornell University Press, 1991.

Risden, Edward L. *Beasts of Time: Apocalyptic Beowulf*. New York: Peter Lang, 1994.

Roberts, Adam. *Robert Browning Revisited*. New York: Twayne, 1996.

Robinson, Fred. *Beowulf and the Appositive Style*. Knoxville: University of Tennessee Press, 1985.

Rothenberg, Albert. *The Emerging Goddess: The Creative Process in Art, Science, and Other Fields*. Chicago: University of Chicago Press, 1979.

Rule, Philip C. "The Gendered Imagination in Religion and Literature." In *Seeing into the Life of Things: Essays on Literature and the Religious Experience*, ed. John L. Mahoney. New York: Fordham University Press, 1988. 59–72.

Ryken, Leland. *The Apocalyptic Vision in Paradise Lost*. Ithaca and London: Cornell University Press, 1970.

Shippey, T.A. "Tolkien as Post-War Writer." *Proceedings of The Tolkien Phenomenon*. Ed. K.J. Battarbee. Turku: Anglicana Turkuensia, 1992. 217–236.

Shoaf, R.A. *Milton, Poet of Duality: A Study of Semiosis in the Poetry and the Prose*. New Haven: Yale University Press, 1985.

Singer, Dorothea Waley. *Giordano Bruno: His Life and Thought. With Annotated Translation of His Work* On the Infinite Universe and Worlds. New York: Greenwood Press, 1968.

Spenser, Edmund. *The Poetical Works of Edmund Spenser*. Ed. J.C. Smith and E. De Selincourt. London: Oxford University Press, 1912.

Steadman, John M. *Epic and Tragic Structure in Paradise Lost*. Chicago: University of Chicago Press, 1976.

Stone, Marjorie. "Genre Subversion and Gender Subversion: *The Princess* and *Aurora Leigh*." *Victorian Poetry* 25.2 (summer 1987): 101–127.

Sutphin, Christine. "Revising Old Scripts: The Fusion of Independence and Intimacy in *Aurora Leigh*." *Browning Institute Studies* 15 (1987): 43–54.

Sweeney, Mickey. *Magic in Medieval Romance from Chretien de Troyes to Geoffrey Chaucer*. Dublin: Four Courts Press, 2000.

Tasker, Meg. "*Aurora Leigh*: Elizabeth Barrett Browning's Novel Approach to the Woman Poet." In *Tradition and the Poetics of Self in Nineteenth-Century Women's Poetry*, ed. Barbara Gorlick. New York: Rodopi, 2002. 23–41.

Thundy, Zacharias. *Millennium: Apocalypse, Antichrist, and Old English Monsters c. 1000*. South Bend, IN: Cross Cultural Publications, 1998.

Tillyard, E.M.W. *The English Epic and Its Background*. New York: Oxford University Press, 1966.

Todorov, Tzvetan. *The Fantastic: A Structural Approach to a Literary Genre*. Trans. Richard Howard. Ithaca: Cornell University Press, 1975.

Tolkien, J.R.R. "*Beowulf*: The Monsters and the Critics." In *An Anthology of Beowulf Criticism*, ed. L.E. Nicholson. Notre Dame: University of Notre Dame Press, 1963. 51–103.

———. "On Fairy-Stories." In *The Tolkien Reader*. New York: Ballantine, 1966. 33–99.

Turner, Victor. *The Ritual Process: Structure and Anti-Structure*. Chicago: University of Chicago Press, 1969.

Vergil. *The Aeneid of Virgil*. Trans. Allen Mandelbaum. New York: Bantam, 1971.

Walcott, Derek. *Omeros*. New York: The Noonday Press, Farrar, Straus & Giroux, 1990.

Walker, D.P. *Spiritual and Demonic Magic from Ficino to Campanella*. London: University of London, Warburg Institute, 1958.

Williams, Kathleen. "Milton, Greatest Spenserian." In *Milton and the Line of Vision*, ed. Joseph Anthony Wittreich, Jr. Madison: University of Wisconsin Press, 1975. 25–55.

Wittreich, Joseph. "'All Angelic Natures Joined in One': Epic Convention and Prophetic Interiority in the Council Scenes in Paradise Lost." *Milton Studies* 17 (1983): 43–74.

———, ed. *Milton and the Line of Vision*. Madison: University of Wisconsin Press, 1975.

———. "'A Poet amongst Poets': Milton and the Tradition of Prophecy." In *Milton and the Line of Vision*, ed. J. Wittreich. Madison: University of Wisconsin Press, 1975. 97–142.

Wordsworth, William. *The Complete Poetical Works of William Wordsworth*. Ed. and Intro. John Morley. New York: Thomas Y. Crowell, 1911. 267–377.

———. *The Prelude: 1799, 1805, 1850: Authoritative Texts, Context and Reception, Recent Critical Essays*. Ed. Jonathan Wordsworth, M. H. Abrams, and Stephen Gill. New York: Norton, 1979.

Yates, Frances A. *Giordano Bruno and the Hermetic Tradition*. Chicago: University of Chicago Press, 1964.

Zoppi, Isabella Maria. "*Omeros*, Walcott and the Contemporary Epic Poem." *Callaloo* 22.2 (1999): 509–528.

Index

Abrams, M.H. 185, 195
Achilles 3, 10, 13–15, 40–41, 49–51, 60, 62, 70, 73, 96, 106, 169, 185
Aeneas 3, 5, 16–17, 41–43, 54, 60, 62, 169, 184
Aeneid 5, 16–17, 38, 41–43, 73
Agamemnon 14, 40
Agrippa, Henry C. 77–78, 187, 195
allegory 57, 76, 82–83, 85, 88, 91, 170, 189
Altizer, Thomas 116, 195
Anchises 17
apocalypse 4, 21, 72, 81, 94, 106, 111, 112, 114, 155, 184, 187, 191
Ariosto, Ludovico 84, 186
Aristotle 2, 51
Arjuna 9–10, 29–34, 43–44, 50, 74, 96, 184
Armstrong, Karen 167
Arnold, Matthew 11, 181
Arthur (King) 5, 20, 55, 84, 87–88, 91
Athena 50, 70, 73
Auerbach, Erich 2, 195
Aurora Leigh 6, 24, 59–61, 143–156, 182, 191–193, 195
Avery, Simon 192, 195

Bakhtin, M.M. 1, 181, 195
Barrett Browning, Elizabeth 5, 6, 11, 24, 39, 48, 59–60, 63, 141, 142–156, 157, 180, 191–193, 195
Beagle, Peter 171, 195
Beasts of Time: Apocalyptic Beowulf 186, 198
Benét, Stephen Vincent 28, 194
Benson, Larry 185, 195
Beowulf 2, 3, 5, 6, 9, 10, 18–20, 45–46, 54, 60, 62, 63, 64–74, 106, 128, 157, 168–176, 181, 183, 195

Beowulf and Grendel 186
Beowulf in Faithful Verse 186
Berger, Pamela 192
Bevington, David 82, 195
Bhagavad Gita 9, 10, 28–36, 38, 43, 44–45, 50, 64, 182, 184, 185
Bidney, Martin 112, 195
Blackburn, F.A. 185, 195
Blake, William 6, 23–24, 39, 48, 56, 62, 108, 109–117, 119, 121, 122, 124, 130, 142, 157, 164, 171, 176–177, 182, 189–190, 195
Bloom, Harold 114, 189, 195
Bosley, Keith 37
Bowra, C.M. 4, 6, 182, 195
Brahman 10
Brooks-Davies, Douglas 84, 195
Browning, Robert 36, 181–182
Bruno, Giordano 79
Byron, Lord 118

Campbell, Joseph 19, 24, 64, 143–144, 183, 195
Carpenter, Humphrey 193, 196
catharsis 166
Chadwick, Nora 95, 196
Chanson de Roland 19, 186
Chariots of Fire 178
Chaucer, Geoffrey 109, 186
Chayes, Irene 188, 196
Chesterton, G.K. 182, 196
Christianity 11, 19, 20–22, 53, 55–57, 64–66, 72–74, 76, 85–87, 91–92, 93–107, 116, 142, 157, 167, 170, 174
Cirlot, J.E. 84, 187, 196
claritas 26
Coleridge, Samuel T. 114, 131, 135, 140, 190, 196

201

Index

colonialism 48, 61, 158ff., 194
comedy 5
Condee, Ralph 188, 196
Consuelo 147
copia 3
Corinne 147

Dante (Alighieri) 2, 10, 20, 34–35, 47, 64, 109, 181, 186
David, Deirdre 192, 196
Davis, Dick 37, 46
Dido 17, 42–43, 54, 60, 70
Dobbie, Eliott van Kirk 194, 196
Doctor Faustus 75, 81–82
Donahue, Charles 9, 37, 196
Donaldson, E.T. 186
dragon 5, 21, 45–46, 54, 67–68, 70–72, 85, 169–171, 173, 186
Dronke, Ursula 186, 196
duty 6, 20, 31–35, 37–48, 54

Edgerton, Franklin 32, 44, 196
Eliot, T.S. 94
Elizabeth I (Queen) 84, 86
Ellman, Richard 26
Erdman, David 115, 189–190, 196
Evander (King) 17
Everyman 76

Faerie Queene 6, 21, 47, 57, 73, 76–92, 113
fate 67, 173
Ferdowsi 184, 196
Ficino, Marsilio 79
Finnegans Wake 180, 194
Fish, Stanley 188
Four Zoas 110–115, 189
Freud, Sigmund 6
Frye, Northrop 2, 77, 93, 96, 180, 182, 183, 187, 188, 189, 194, 196

Gardner, John 5
Gelpi, Barbara 192
Genesis 55, 73
Geoffrey of Monmouth 2
Gilgamesh 3, 11–14, 28, 38, 39, 49, 62, 65, 74, 96, 106, 113, 169
Gill, Stephen 190, 196
Godfrey de Bouillon 20
Goethe, Johann 57, 124
Grail 20, 47, 67, 186

Great Chain of Being 65, 169, 188
Grierson, H.J.C. 188, 190, 196
Grimes, Ronald 190, 196
Gross, Kenneth 83, 187, 196

Hainsworth, J.B. 182, 196
Hamner, Robert 7, 196
Hartman, Geoffrey 190, 191, 196
Heaney, Seamus 11, 181, 186
Hektor (Hector) 3, 14, 41–42, 49, 51, 70, 73, 96, 106, 169, 185
Hermes Trismegistus 79
Hermetica 196
heroism 1, 9, 10–11, 15–20, 25, 43, 45, 47, 51, 62, 66, 68, 93–94, 146, 166, 168–170, 172, 188
Hewlett, Dorothy 192, 196
Hill, John Spencer 188
Hiltebeitel, Alf 183–184, 196
Homer 2, 9, 10, 13, 18, 29, 37, 44, 45, 64–67, 73, 84, 110, 129, 158, 159, 162, 163, 181, 183, 190

Iliad 10, 13–17, 183–184, 193, 196
Immortality Ode 24
incantation 75, 77ff.
individualism 35, 49–63

Jackson, Rosemary 171, 196
Jackson, W.T.H. 185, 196
Jane Eyre 147, 151
Jesus (Christ or Son of God) 22, 78, 93, 97, 102–104, 106, 107, 114, 185
John Brown's Body 28, 194
Johnson, W.J. 9, 32, 43, 184, 185, 197
Jonson, Ben 82
Joyce, James 18, 24–28, 93, 94, 122, 157, 162, 176, 180, 182, 183, 197

Kalevala 28, 106, 184
Kalevipoeg 28
Kaplan, Cora 192
Keats, John 24, 58, 118, 121, 158
Ker, W.P. 3, 182, 197
Kerrigan, William 95, 188, 197
Kieckhefer, Richard 186, 197
Krapp, George 170, 197

Lacan, Jacques 114, 190, 197
Leighton, Angela 192, 197
Lewis, C.S. 55, 183

Index

liminality 4, 6, 83–84, 87, 91, 96, 140, 152, 155, 164, 180, 185, 187
Lindenberger, Herbert 191, 197
Longbaum, Robert 26, 183, 187, 188, 190, 197
Lönnrot, Elias 184, 197
Lord of the Rings 52, 168–169, 171–177
Los 23, 58, 110, 113
Luck, George 91, 187, 197
Lukács, Georg 176, 185, 197
Lusiads 86, 186
Lyrical Ballads 130

Macbeth 5
magic 75ff., 170–174
Mahabharata 9, 10, 20, 29, 30, 43–44, 65, 74, 184
Malory, Thomas 20, 186
Marlowe, Christopher 75, 81–82, 197
Mauss, Marcel 20, 197
McClure, Charlotte 193, 197
McConnell, Frank 190, 197
McSweeney, Kerry 192
Merchant, Paul 25, 197
Mermin, Dorothy 192
Michelangelo 5
Miller, Dean 3, 185, 197
Milton 6, 109–110, 114–117
Milton, John 2–4, 6, 11, 21–24, 34, 47, 54–57, 65, 86, 92, 93–108, 110, 117, 119, 128–129, 134, 157, 182, 188, 190, 197
monomyth 24, 143, 146
Monty Python and the Holy Grail 68
Murdock, Maureen 143–145, 192, 197
Murray, Penelope 182
Murrin, Michael 83, 187, 197
muse 21–23, 84, 96, 103, 104, 147, 154, 162, 193
Myers, Victoria 189, 197

Nesbitt, George 190, 197
Neumann, Erich 3, 183, 197
Nibelungenlied 29, 186
Nicholson, L.E. 29, 186
novel 5, 6, 165ff.

Odysseus 3, 15–17, 41, 43, 46, 50, 169, 183–185
Odyssey 5, 10, 15–16, 41, 50, 113, 183–184, 197
Oedipus 5, 14–17

Okpewho, 193, 197
Omeros 6, 7, 39, 60–62, 157–164, 182, 193
Othello 5
Ovid 51
Owens, Jesse 179

Paracelsus 78–79, 198
Paradise Lost 6, 21–23, 47, 54–57, 63, 86, 93–108, 110, 119, 122, 128, 188
Paradise Regained 22, 110, 155
Parker, Mary 18, 65, 185, 198
Parker, Patricia 82, 187, 198
Paterson 28
Paul (Saint) 23, 189
Penelope 5, 16, 41, 50
Plato 2, 166
Poema de Mio Cid 186
Pope, Alexander 58
Portrait of the Artist as a Young Man 26, 28, 65, 183
Potts, Abbie 190–191, 198
The Prelude 6, 23–24, 58, 119–141, 190–191
Priam 50, 60
prophecy 87, 91, 94–97ff., 107, 109–116, 135–138, 140, 150, 189, 191
Purkis, John 190

Rabkin, Eric 171, 194, 198
Ragnarök 73
Ramazani, Jahan 193, 198
renunciation 32
Riede, David 110, 115, 189, 190, 198
Risden, E.L. 186, 198
Roberts, Adam 182, 198
Robinson, Fred 18, 65, 185, 198
Romanticism 23, 58, 117, 118ff, 176, 178, 190
Rome 2, 10, 16–17, 42–43, 54, 56
Rothenberg, Albert 19, 198
Rule, Philip 191, 198
Ryken, Leland 95, 198

Satan 22, 54–57, 96ff., 112, 117, 124, 174, 185, 188
Seyavash 46–47
Shah-Nameh 29, 37, 38, 46–47
Shakespeare, William 11, 75
Shelley, Percy 118
Shippey, T.A. 172, 194, 198
Shoaf, R.A. 188, 198

Sibyl 17
Sidney, Philip 31–32, 107
Silmarillion 28, 168, 175, 189
Singer, Dorothea 187, 198
Sir Gawain and the Green Knight (or *Gawain*-poet) 2, 53, 168, 186
Spenser, Edmund 2, 6, 11, 20, 47, 55, 57, 63, 65, 66, 73, 74, 76–92, 96, 106, 107, 123, 128, 133, 157, 186, 188, 189, 198
spots of time 122ff., 191
Statius 51
Steadman, John 106, 188, 198
Stephen Hero 26, 183
Stone, Marjorie 192, 198
Stott, Rebecca 192, 195
Sullivan, Mary Rose 181
Sutphin, Christine 192, 198
Sweeney, Mickey 186, 198

Taplin, Gardner 192
Tasker, Meg 192, 198
Tasso, Torquato 20, 84, 86, 107, 186
Thor 72
Thundy, Zacharias 186, 198
Tillyard, E.M.W. 181, 194, 198
Tintern Abbey 24, 123–124
Todorov, Tzvetan 169, 198
Tolkien, J.R.R. 5, 28, 52–53, 58, 66, 70, 132, 165, 168–177, 180, 189, 194, 198
tragedy 2
Troy 2, 13–15, 17, 41–42, 49–51, 54, 63

Turner, Frederick 194
Turner, Victor 3, 198
Turnus 17, 42, 73

Ulysses 27–28, 65, 176, 194

vates 10
Vergil 2, 9, 10, 16–18, 41–42, 45, 54, 56, 65–67, 73, 84, 110, 184, 190, 199
Vida, Marco Girolamo 178, 186
Visio Sancti Pauli 19, 65
Volsungasaga 29, 186

Walcott, Derek 2, 6, 7, 39, 48, 60–63, 157–164, 167, 180, 193, 194, 199
Walker, D.P. 187, 199
Williams, Kathleen 187, 199
Williams, William Carlos 28, 194
Wittreich, Joseph 95–96, 107, 109, 157, 187, 193, 199
Wordsworth, William 6, 11, 23–24, 39, 48, 58–59, 63, 117, 118–141, 142, 148, 157, 182, 190–191, 199
Wulfstan 66
Wuthering Heights 147
wyrd 70, 169, 173, 176

Yates, Frances 187, 199
yoga 32, 45

Zoppi, Isabella 164, 193, 199

www.ingramcontent.com/pod-product-compliance
Lightning Source LLC
Chambersburg PA
CBHW032059300426
44116CB00007B/807